Postwar Trends in Japan

Postwar Trends
in Japan

Studies in Commemoration of Rev. Aloysius Miller, S.J.

Edited by

Shunichi Takayanagi

and

Kimitada Miwa

UNIVERSITY OF TOKYO PRESS

© University of Tokyo Press, 1975
UTP   3021-27094-5149
ISBN 0-86008-129-X
Printed in Japan

Contents

Preface   vii

Introduction   ix

Contributors' Sketches   xxi

Shusaku Endo: The Second Period   Francis Mathy   3

A Note on Trilateral Crisis Diplomacy:
   The Irritants in the Japan-U.S.-E.C.
   Relations   Kinhide Mushakoji 15

Japanese Public Opinion and
   Sino-Japanese Relations, 1969–1972   Kan Ori   37

Evolving Japanese Policy Toward Inward
   Foreign Direct Investment in the
   Postwar Period   Yusaku Furuhashi   61

Christology and Postwar Theologians
   in Japan   Shunichi Takayanagi 119

An Interpretation of *The Ruined Map*
   by Kōbō Abe   Kinya Tsuruta   169

Student Movements in 1960 and 1969:
   Continuity and Change   Kazuko Tsurumi   195

In the Shadow of Leaves and
   Mishima's Death   Kimitada Miwa   229

The Canons of Journalism and
   Trends in Japanese Dailies   Yasuhiro Kawanaka   251

v

Preface

Father Al Miller's death in 1971 at the age of sixty put an end to a long, distinguished career of service to God, the Society of Jesus, Sophia University, and the youth of Japan he loved so much. Arriving on the Sophia campus in 1947 with but a meager knowledge of Japanese—which, because of the ever-accelerating pace of his activities at the university was never to increase—he plunged himself immediately into two major projects: the establishment of the International Division, where foreigners and Japanese might pursue a full college program in the English language, and the modernization of the university's financial administration. For many years the dean of the division he had established, in the last years of his life he served as dean of the division's graduate school, and he was for twelve years the treasurer of the university corporation.

But if these were his official assignments at Sophia, there was another work still closer to his heart, a work that has been quite as fruitful: encouraging the young students who came within his sphere of influence to go as far as their talents would carry them. In the bleak immediate postwar years, when discouragement was rife, Father Miller's warm heart and discerning eye saw through to his students' potentialities, and in slow and easy English he gave the encouragement that they needed to realize what was in them. Frequently this encouragement was not only verbal but took a more practical turn as he arranged scholarships and sought other financial means to enable talented students to study abroad.

This volume of essays was conceived and brought to fruition by one of these former students, Professor Miwa Kimitada of the Institute of International Relations of Sophia University. Professor Miwa, reflecting upon the meaning that Father Miller's dedicated life had for the men whom he had sent abroad for further studies and who are now active in Japan as professors and scholars, solicited manuscripts from them and from Father Miller's associates at Sophia. Professor Takayanagi of the Department of English Literature assumed the practical task of organizing and bringing the assembled manuscripts to their final stage.

Except for short visits to his native America, Father Miller was active at Sophia from 1947 to 1971, a period that coincides with the history of postwar Japan. He was, therefore, an observer of almost all the exciting incidents and currents of the period. Now that this era is rapidly becoming a matter of history, it seems a fitting tribute to him to record and analyze at least a few of its aspects. Though Father Miller was never a scholar—he was never given the time to be—he was one of a group of dedicated men, scholars, teachers, and administrators, who carried Sophia through the momentous period treated in these essays. Since the Jesuit manner is "ordinary," he would undoubtedly have preferred to remain anonymous, unnoticed after his death. But he contributed significantly to the formation of the minds of many scholars who worked together in the postwar academic community of Sophia. Thus, it is fitting that he be commemorated for the great intellectual and spiritual influence that he exerted upon this community.

In conclusion, I would like to express my deep gratitude to Professors Takayanagi and Miwa for their devoted efforts in bringing this volume to publication and thereby giving added assurance that their teacher and mentor—and my Jesuit colleague and friend—Father Al Miller, will not soon be forgotten.

Joseph Pittau
Institute of International Relations
Sophia, University

Introduction[1]

All the articles assembled here were written by spring, 1972, though in the course of editing some elements were introduced to update them. With the beginning of the 1970s, Japan entered into a new era, the postwar period becoming a thing of the past. The generations that were not there at that fateful moment of surrender on August 15, 1945—"*sensō o shiranai sedai*" (generations with no wartime experience), as a popular folk song has it—are steadily outnumbering and becoming more influential than those who have wartime and postwar experiences. In many ways it is evident that Japan's postwar period is over. There is the obvious fact of her growth as an economic superpower, but this status is not always pleasant to the Japanese. Japan now has begun to be envied, feared and even hated. Her new superpower status ironically isolates her from the rest of the world, when better relations in the international community are imperative for her survival. Japan is now at a critical point and must steer with care on the international waters into a new age.

No one could describe the postwar period in a comprehensive manner. All we intend in this book is to present a few attempts to interpret it as manifested in certain trends. There may be several approaches to characterizing the postwar period. Here we take up the theme of continuity and discontinuity between the pre-war and postwar periods.[2]

The Pacific War came to its end in an abrupt manner. The atomic bombs, exploded over Hiroshima on August 6, 1945, and over Nagasaki on August 9, 1945, made the unwilling war leaders accept the terms of the Potsdam Declaration. Although this use of nuclear weapons was the first in the history of mankind and was a most cruel means of massacre—killing hundreds of thousands of noncombatants in an instant and leaving thousands of hospitalized people with no hope of social rehabilitation—it preserved Japan as a unified nation. But the military use of nuclear fission over Japan prepared the way for her spiritual division. The war had been rapidly deteriorating toward catastrophe with the Soviet participation between August 6 and 9. The atomic bombs in a sense helped Japan to seize a chance to surrender and preserve her national unity without being partitioned. She could face a new period as one nation, unlike divided Germany.

Seen in the context of international politics, the atomic bombs were exploded over Japan against the U.S.S.R. The postwar period was set in the international environment of the Cold War. The U.S.A. and the U.S.S.R. avoided a direct confrontation, but the Cold War became a fighting war carried out by proxy on the Korean Peninsula. This basic division in international politics was soon to be reflected in postwar Japan's internal division. It is almost symbolic that the May Day riot, the first open anti-American demonstration, occurred in 1952, a few days before the termination of the unilateral occupation by American forces upon the coming into effect of the San Francisco Peace Treaty. This unfortuante incident would never have occurred had Japan been divided into two occupation areas. The anti-American and pro-Russian Japanese would have had only to move to the Russian Occupied area, while the anti-Russian and pro-American would have had only to flee to "liberty."

The San Francisco Peace Treaty, arranged to make inevitable the Russian walkout, is another reflection of the Cold War. The treaty guaranteed Japan's reappearance on the international political scene as a unified nation, but de facto, in one camp despite her avowed intention of malice towards none. Against the outside Japan maintained her national unity, but this in turn has had internal repercussions. It has had the effect of deepening her division within. Though Japan has acted on the international scene as a unified nation, there has existed a polarization of public opinion. The monthly magazine *Sekai* ran a series of articles against the peace treaty by famous intellectuals and has become the organ of anti-government, leftist-pacifist intellectuals. Although the Liberal Democrats always won despite their permanent unpopularity among intellectuals, the leftist anti-American sentiment always has to be taken into consideration. This undertone has occasionally burst into violent demonstrations of power, when combined with some popular uneasiness and resentment over a nation-wide (as opposed to a foreign) issue. If the government was inflexible (e.g., as in the case of Kishi), it was to face a crisis. If it was flexible, this undertone would help in negotiations with the U.S.A., for the Japanese government could always remind its counterpart at the bargaining table of the existence of this sentiment and deplore optional scarcity. It seems also that there has existed a duplicity of foreign policies, official and unofficial: the one committed Japan to the free world, and the other maintained Japan's place in the other half of the world. The former was supported by the bureaucratic machinery and the Liberal Democratic Party, while the other was advocated by the combination of the Socialist Party and leftist intellectuals, who constituted a permanent opposition. These two radically opposite sets of foreign policies have worked from a long range of view for the benefit of Japan as a whole. With the postwar period about to end, the two foreign policies tend to be unified, e.g., in the case of reopening relations with Mainland China.

Despite bitter division within, Japan could throughout maintain her unified national identity. It may be due to the extreme homogeneity of the Japanese, called *Nihonism*. Even with the radical changes of social values, institutions and culture, several institutions were available to enable postwar Japan to preserve her unity as a nation. Most important among these is the emperor system. With the new constitution it was decided to keep the emperor as the symbol of national unity, and there has arisen a strong group consciousness to make this new constitution the norm for the establishment of the new Japan. This consciousness was already fairly universal. It is maintained with some justification that Japan did not surrender unconditionally but rather under the conditions specified in the Potsdam Declaration, which bound the victor nations as well as Japan. There had been an understanding between the Allies and Japan as to the maintenance of the emperor system. One can perceive this in the emperor's edict to accept the Potsdam Declaration to end the war in order to preserve the national unity. Moreover, retention of the emperor system even after the war's end was taken for granted by the generations who had received prewar education.

It was on September 27, 1945, less than one month after Gen. Douglas MacArthur's historic arrival at Atsugi, that the emperor made a visit to the Allied commander. Events following reminded the Japanese that the continuity of their national unity was to be vouchsafed by partial negation of prewar tradition. The emperor himself made his famous declaration to deny his own "divinity" on January 1, 1946. This declaration was quietly accepted by the people, who had seen in newspapers a photograph of the emperor standing with General MacArthur in khakis. The new constitution promulgated two years later made the emperor the symbol of national unity. It was, however, one year before the promulgation that the Chief Prosecutor for the Far East War Criminal Court, Kenan, declared that the emperor was not to be included in the war criminal list. Thus the Japanese were to start rebuilding their national fabric with the new constitution under the same emperor who had signed the imperial declaration of war against the Allied Powers. National energy mobilized for the war effort under the old imperial constitution was now directed almost intact toward "peace"—a slogan which is a nationalism without face, without articulation.

Partial negation of prewar tradition as the principle of gradual reformism has functioned as it was expected. It was beneficial for the occupation forces to secure the structure for their indirect control, and thus they could with minimal cost and maximal efficiency execute their occupation policies. The Japanese on the other hand could put into effect national transformation at minimal sacrifice, maintaining a more or less stabilized social structure after the disaster of defeat. Despite the reality of occupation, the Japanese could certainly be saved from the loss of national identity because of the continuation of the institution of the emperor.

The occupation policies had three "D's " as their fundamental goals: demilitarization, decentralization and democratization. Decentralization was to be carried out in order to foster local autonomy as the basis for democracy by abolishing the evils of centralized government as well as to revive the principle of free competition in the business world by stripping the *zaibatsu* of their power. Foremost among reforms for democratization was the new system of education. It was concerned not only with the system but also with the content of education and the broader aim of liberation of thought. As enlightened counsel, however, Gen. MacArthur gave Christian missionaries preferential treatment. As a matter of fact, they were the first nonmilitary persons who were allowed into Japan, and could reactivate their missionary work all over Japan under the protection and with the help of the General Headquarters. As part of this general development, Mrs. Elizabeth Gray Vining arrived in Tokyo from Philadelphia as tutor to the crown prince. She left interesting observations on the new constitution, which was in a sense the heart of the Allied occupation policies. First of all she noted that it had not been promulgated under the pressure of the occupation forces but expressed some misgivings that it is too perfect (like the Weimar Constitution) and feared that the same misfortune might befall the new constitution and the Japanese. She writes: "I have no doubt that in future times it will be repealed or allowed to fall into disuse, but I think that there will be some residue which will be irreducible and out of which new and more solid and characteristic structures will rise."[3] Mrs. Vining asked the crown prince if he thought that the new constitution was written first in English and then translated into Japanese. She tells us that the answer was different from what she had expected. The crown prince answered that he did not think that it was a translation, though written in a curious style mixing *bungo* ("literary language") and *kōgo* ("colloquial language"): "Written language is more beautiful and the Constitution should be written in beautiful language." "The Meiji Constitution," he said, "was all in written Japanese; it had beauty and people respected it."

This unexpected answer was in a way what she wanted to hear from the crown prince. (It is reported from memory.) Mrs. Vining, however, valued the importance of aesthetic sense in Japanese social life as highly as Christian Weltanschauung and moral sense. The former she came to learn from her contact with the crown prince and the imperial family with her perceptive eyes. This observation was made possible by her humanism and understanding and by the crown prince's personality.

The crown prince's place in the course of democratization is symbolic of the partial negation of the emperor system after World War II. His 1959 marriage with a daughter of a commoner (a rare event in the history of the imperial family) was to bring closer the future emperor and the nation and was in a way to strengthen political stability. The eventual political effect of this spectacular event, however, can nowadays be said to be slightly doubtful. In the sixteen years since the marriage pageantry, relations between the imperial family and the nation have become increasingly more intimate, but this is only one aspect of the story. In the past the imperial family had possessed a transcendental quality over all the classes of the population. Now, however, it can be said to have become the status symbol of the class from which the crown princess came. In the past there was an element of national identity every member of the nation could share, because the imperial family was a class apart, and it has now become the core of identity that, commoners as they are, the new affluent class possesses. The assassination attempt by an adolescent from the countryside, as the coach of the crown prince and princess passed, underlined the fact. There was at least one person who thought that the crown prince at the height of his popularity was transferred to a realm that he could no longer touch—transformed into the symbol of a class. Two years later, in February, a boy entered the residence of the president of the Chūō Kōron publishing company and injured some members of the household. He wanted to condemn and hold responsible the president for a novel that appeared in *Chūō Kōron* on a revolution in which the crown prince and princess are beheaded by the mob. The first was an act by an extreme egalitarian, who wanted to go beyond the reforms based on the prinicple of partial negation of tradition, while the second was a reaction by an imperialist, who could not tolerate even a fictional description of a revolution that toppled the ancien régime.

One can never discuss in a simplistic manner the intellectual formation of these almost psychopathetic adolescents, but material offered through postwar compulsory education would give us some indications. Above all, the presentation of modern Japanese history in schools cannot but be said to be a distortion of historical facts by omissions. There is practically no readiness to evaluate modern Japanese history in a positive way. History textbooks are full of a negative spirit describing the wrongdoings of the militarists and capitalists. Originally this was promoted by the occupation policy of demilitarization, but it has been inherited in the postoccupation era. The Russo-Japanese War is now interpreted not as a war of national mobilization and liberation but solely as a war of invasion carried out by the imperialist elements. Taro Wakamori's *Dictionary of Japanese History* contains no geneology of the imperial family, though it meticulously gathers those of the Fujiwaras, the Heike and the Genji, as well as those of warlord families in the Sengoku period.

If what is still left by the principle of partial negation is to be denied its proper place in the postwar historical presentation, it is only natural to provoke rightist reaction. If what is denied by the principle is about to be restored, it is only natural for the generations educated after the war to push back at least to the demarcation line of partial negation such a "reactionary tendency." This intellectual situation brings us back to the fundamental problems already at hand at the moment of decision to preserve the emperor system through the principle of partial negation. By experiencing atomic bombing, the Japanese became ready to put peace as an absolute premise. In this sense they made a discovery of a value beyond nationalism and ideological conflict. Nevertheless, the Cold War division was brought to the forum of opinion-forming intellectual life, though Japan luckily did not face partition.

Literary phenomena in postwar Japan reflect this intellectual climate. Yukio Mishima not only refused to subscribe to the general feeling of utter pacifism, which in an illusory way posits a world of denationalized universal love, but also regarded it as a crisis that the Japanese have lost a sense for international politics and a national identity. He concluded in his own way that this crisis had been brought about through the shattering by postwar reforms of traditional culture centering around the emperor cult; for him the gradual reforms based on the principle of partial negation must in their logical consequences lead to total negation, and were not to be tolerated. Mishima had already started his literary career during the war and been recognized by Yasunari Kawabata. Kōbō Abe was two years older than Mishima, but his recognition came in 1951 when he was awarded the famous Akutagawa Prize for the year. Free from the traditional cultural milieu and refusal to accept the postwar situation—unlike Mishima— because he had been brought up in Manchuria, he has not been put in the difficult position of negating the emperor system totally, although he came very close to Marxism at one time. Fundamentally he refuses to subscribe to totalitarianism in any form. Abe always creates an avant-garde atmosphere and has become a fad in the literary world. Established already in 1935, and disrupted between 1944 and 1949, the Akutagawa Prize has become a literary institution setting the tone for the postwar literary world and largely reflecting the intellectual situation created by postwar reforms and events. Shusaku Endo, winner of the Akutagawa Prize for 1955 with his novel *White Man*, has brought to the literary world a unique international theme of Christianity versus adaptation or its failure, universal love versus racial differences in thinking. It is to be noted that Shintarō Ishihara won the prize for the latter half of the same year with his *Season of the Sun*, in which he depicted the aimless life of the youngsters, the inanity of their rebellion and love. His novel is in a sense a description of the manners of youth, which gave rise to the expression *taiyō-zoku,* "sun tribe." It was Mishima who praised this novel highly. Both Mishima and Ishihara were versatile. Ishihara recently turned to politics and belongs to a new rightist club of the Liberal Democratic Party called *Seiran-kai*. Resort to purposeless physical prowess is now turned into his conduct for the establishment of order.

Writers who received postwar education started gradually to make literary debuts and winning Akutagawa prizes by describing war or postwar experiences, for example, Ken Kaikō and Kenzaburō Ōe. Kaikō later became active in the anti-Vietnam War campaign, while Oe concentrated on anti-Okinawa military base activities through his political writings. Morio Kita's Akutagawa Prize novel, *Yoru to Kiri no Sumi de* (At the Corner of Night and Mist), describes the mental torture of the physicians who had to execute the physically unfit in southern Germany under the Nazi regime. He seems to possess a definite audience for his satirical fantasy. Fantasy on a grand scale was used by Koichiro Uno, whose Akutagawa novel was *Geishin* (Whale God), but later he appeared to write only comedies of manners. The sense of emptiness and frustration became increasingly the theme of postwar Akutagawa Prize writers. Sho Shibata described in his *Saredo Wareraga Hibi* (But Our Days) the frustration of student activists after the Russian anti-Stalin phase.

The Akutagawa Prize is no absolute guarantee for a place in the sun in the Japanese literary world, though it is a measure of the winner's accomplishments. It reflects also the intellectual climate of the year. The postwar literary world is essentially a narrow world of literary tradesmen, though the profession of novelist has become economically lucrative and socially respected, due to the growth of the reading public as the result of the postwar extension of compulsory educaion and increasing affluence. But its exclusiveness does not mean that it has not been concerned with the problems of society at large. Literary men have been genuinely or perhaps too seriously interested in social and political issues. In their high seriousness, however, they show their inability to come to grips with reality. Their rather formalist contact with contemporary issues that would not be issues at all in a year or so was unfortunate.

Perhaps this is due to the particular geographical and cultural position of Japan in the world. Geographically isolated, the Japanese constitute a group with a special mentality. It determines their conduct, individually or as a nation, at home and abroad, culturally, economically and politically. In the case of cultural assimilation and internal politics versus international issues, they react either too naively or too jingoistically. Extremely worried about the world around them and morbidly introspective—in fact soliciting criticism by foreigners—they manifest tactlessness abroad in their pattern of conduct. The polarities of nationalism and internationalism exist in the Japanese mentality. Thus there is a curious combination of rabidly leftist socialism with anti-foreignism. Smooth-looking suave representatives of international business concerns act abroad as a group. Diplomatic issues are often distorted and too hotly overplayed, making it impossible to maintain a balanced position. The combination of cleverness and naiveté presents the Japanese abroad as an inscrutable race. Japan after all faced in the postwar period some major social violence and unrest, e.g., the 1960 anti-Security Treaty riot and student unrest several years ago. On the surface, from reading newspapers and intellectual journals, one might have had the impression that social revolution was imminent. Student demonstrations and leftist writing played a major role, but essentially they are not the ones who can make a revolution. The political establishment has always managed to steer itself through in relative calm. The political establishment composed of elite university graduates has had practically no intellectual voice to be heard, and has remained inarticulate and anonymous. Internationally Japan is an economic magnate without a moral voice. The most vocal voice in the intellectual world sounds highly emotional if translated into English.

If this demonstrates the isolation of Japanese intellectuals from the trends of the rest of the world, it does not mean that they shut their eyes. In their eagerness to follow contemporary trends, they tend to swallow easily catch phrases and set formulations. There have been many controversial issues in postwar literary intellectual circles. It was almost ten years ago that the issue on the meaning of postwar literature was hotly debated, involving many novelists and critics. It was in a large sense a continuation of Marxism versus humanism, social sciences versus aestheticism, but the controversy indicates, at least in the literary world, the end of the postwar period. This occurred almost simultaneously with efforts to rediscover the original Japanese way of thinking, with the boom of history and folklore, recently in the form of interest in the charismatic figure of Yanagita Kunio. Leftist intellectuals and student activists have been deeply disappointed with the countries where Marxism is actually practiced. Thus, ironically, Yanagita Kunio the traditionalist is avidly read by Marxist students who are eager to find an indigenous basis for Marxism and in a sense seek for the synthesis of Marxism and humanism.

This search for indigenous elements is shared with a small but influential group of Christian thinkers, though it can hardly be said that they have caused a sensation in the postwar intellectual world. Perhaps Yoshizō Kitamori came close to doing so with his popular *Theology of the Pain of God*. Well versed in contemporary biblical scholarship and systematic theology and competent in their researches as they are, they try to integrate indigenous ideas in their thought. Endo's *Shikai no Hotori* and *Life of Jesus* as well as Kunio Ogawa's *Aru Seisho*, which are all contemporary best sellers, show their close contact with Christian theologians.

All indications of the end of the postwar period in Japan stemmed ultimately from a consciousness that Japan now has reached the status of a national power. This is true even among the leftist intellectuals, though they dislike the superpower economic status. With this, they yearn for a new extended horizon in order to cope with multiple problems arising from being an economic superpower. The Japanese as a whole are now looking for a principle other than that of partial negation, which has so far been effective but at the same time has caused a division within the postwar mind. Japan's new position is by no means comfortable to the world or to the Japanese themselves. Its economic structure is highly vulnerable as was shown in the recent oil crisis. Its behavior still too much based on the structure of dependence appears egoistic and uncanny to other nations. Almost three decades after World War II, the discovery of fossil soldiers like Yokoi and Onoda makes the Japanese unintelligible even to the Japanese themselves, reminding them of their psychology curiously common with the small group of young men who made commando attacks at Tel Aviv and Amsterdam with the upsidedown *joi* (anti-alien) spirit.

---

1. A large part of this introduction was first drafted by Kimitada Miwa in Japanese. The rest was written by Shunichi Takayanagi in the course of the translation made by him.
2. Inoue Kiyoshi, *Sengo Nihon Shi*, History of Post-War Japan, 1966, p. 111.
3. Vining, Elizabeth Gray, *Windows for the Crown Prince*, Philadelphia and New York, 1952, p. 266.
4. *Op. Cit.*, p. 267.
5. Usui Yoshimi (ed.), *Sengo Bungaku Ronso*, vol. II, Post-War Literary Controversies, Tokyo, 1972, pp. 559ff.

Contributors' Sketches

FRANCIS MATHY was born in Red River, Wisconsin, U.S.A., in 1925. He entered the Society of Jesus in 1947 and was ordained in 1958. He began teaching at Sophia University in 1953 and is now a professor of English and American literature. He received his Ph.D. in comparative literature from the University of Michigan. His doctoral dissertation was a study of a Japanese writer of the Meiji period, Tōkoku Kitamura. He is the translator of one of Shūsaku Endō's novels, *Wonderful Fool*, and one of his plays, *The Golden Country*. He has also translated into English Sōseki Natsume's novel *Mon*. Recently, his full-length study of the Japanese writer Naoya Shiga was published in the Twayne World Authors Series.

SHUNICHI TAKAYANAGI was born in Niigata, Japan, in 1932. At Sophia University, he studied English literature before going to the United States in 1954, where he studied both English and American literature, and in 1958 obtained a Ph.D. in English literature at Fordham University. He entered the Society of Jesus in 1960, and studied theology in St. Georgen, Frankfurt am Main, Germany, from 1966 to 1970. (This school sent three theological *periti* [experts] to the Vatican II.) He stayed a short while in München and Münster and was ordained in Frankfurt in 1969. He writes extensively on English literature, history of ideas, and theology, mainly in Japanese, but occasionally in English and German. His reviews have appeared in *Catholic Biblical Quarterly* and *Monumenta Nipponica*. He has published two books in Japanese, one of which is *Theology for Modern Man: Christological Sketch* (Tokyo: Shinkyō Shuppan, 1974). Currently he is professor of English literature at Sophia University.

YASUHIRO KAWANAKA was born in Tokyo in 1930. He was one of the first students of journalism at Sophia University. He continued his studies at Seattle University and earned his B.S. (S.S.) in 1951 when he graduated magna cum laude. At Marquette University he earned his M.A. in journalism in 1953. In 1964–1966 he was an International Development Fellow of East-West Center engaged in advanced studies at the Department of Communications, University of Illinois. He has been on the Faculty of the Department of Journalism, Sophia University, since 1953, and has been its chairman since 1957. He initiated a graduate program there, and it was the first Catholic institution to offer the doctorate degree in Communications. His professional activities extend from serving as chairman of the Research Council, Japan Society of Journalism and Mass Communications, to working as Consulta, Pontifical Commission for Social Communications. He is the author of *Modern Communications* (Tokyo: Veritas Publishing Co., 1961), *The Freedom and Responsibility of the Press* (Tokyo: Nanso Sha, 1970), and a contributor to professional journals.

KINYA TSURUTA was born in Tokyo in 1932. After studying English literature at Sophia University, he went to the United States for further studies in 1956. He has a Ph.D. in comparative literature from the University of Washington (1967). He taught at the University of Washington, Washington University in St. Louis, University of Toronto, and is currently professor of Japanese literature at the University of British Columbia. He has published two books and over sixty articles on modern Japanese literature in English and Japanese.

KAN ORI was born in Osaka, Japan, in 1933. Educated in England and the United States, he obtained his Ph.D. at Indiana University (1961). Since 1965, he has been with Sophia University, being appointed professor of political science in 1970, and, since

1969, has been a member of the Institute of International Relations for Advanced Studies on Peace and Development in Asia. He has been a visiting professor, among other places, at Minnesota, Indiana (as a senior Fulbright lecturer), and the University of Malaya (holding the endowed chair of Japanese History). He has also given special lectures on Japanese politics at Bergen, Loyola (Chicago), Marquette, Miami (Ohio), Notre Dame, Oslo, and Universidad Nacional Autonoma de Mexico. He is the co-author of *Anti-Japanese Land Law Controversy in California* (1971) and *Political Parties, Elites, and Conflict Resolution in Japanese Politics: Explorations in Comparative Analysis* (forthcoming) and other works in English as well as in Japanese.

KINHIDE MUSHAKOJI has been the director of Sophia University Institute of International Relations for Advanced Studies on Peace and Development in Asia since its inauguration in 1968. Born in Belgium in 1929, he studied International Politics at Gakushūin University, Tokyo, the University of Paris, and Princeton University. Before coming to Sophia, he taught at Gakushūin, and was a visiting professor at Northwestern University in 1965 and a senior specialist at the University of Hawaii's East-West Center in 1968. His professional activities are very expansive and truly global in character. For example, in the year 1971–1972, he served as a consultant on the Committee on Society, Development, and Peace in Geneva, Switzerland. He is the author of many books and articles and a contributor to many professional journals. Among his works are *Introduction to Peace Research* (Tokyo: Kōdan Sha, 1969), and *Behavioral Science and International Politics* (Tokyo: Tokyo Daigaku Shuppan Kyoku, 1972).

YUSAKU FURUHASHI, born in Shizuoka prefecture (Japan) in 1931, is the author of many publications, including *Social Issues of Marketing in American Economy* (Columbus, Ohio: Grid Publishing Co., 1971). After studying at Sophia for several years, he went to the United States for further studies. His degrees are B.S., Seattle University, 1956; M.B.A., University of Washington, 1958; and Ph.D., University of Illinois, 1961. Since 1961, he has been on the faculty of the Department of Marketing, the University of Notre Dame, and is currently acting dean of its College of Business Administration. His professional activities include serving as a consultant for both American and Japanese business firms.

KAZUKO TSURUMI, the author of *Social Change and the Individual: Japan Before and After Defeat in World War II* (Princeton, N.J.: Princeton University Press, 1970) and many other books and articles, was born in Tokyo, in 1918. She studied at Tsuda College, Tokyo, and earned a M.A. from Vassar College and a Ph.D. in sociology from Princeton University. She taught at the University of British Columbia and Seikei University, Tokyo, and since 1968 she has been a professor and staff member of the Institute of International Relations of Sophia University. In the year 1973-1974, she was visiting professor at the University of Toronto. Recently she has been interested in constructing a theory of indigenous development in modern Japan based upon Kunio Yanagita's works, which is partly presented already in *Adventure of Ideas: Toward a New Paradigm of Social Change* (Tokyo: Chikuma Shobō, 1974), which she coedited and coauthored.

KIMITADA MIWA was born in Matsumoto City, Japan, in 1929. While studying at Sophia, he was awarded an Edmund Walsh Scholarship to study at Georgetown University, where he earned his B.S. (S.S.) in 1955 and M.A. in 1957. His Ph.D. in history (1967) is from Princeton University. He has been on the faculty of Sophia University since 1957 and is currently professor and staff member of its Institute of International Relations. In 1969-1970, he was visiting professor at El Colegio de Mexico for half a year. He has published *Yōsuke Matsuoka: Man and Diplomacy* (Tokyo: Chūō Kōron Sha, 1971), *Images and Structure of U.S.-Japanese Relations* (Tokyo: Nansō Sha, 1974), and several other books and articles. An English article, "The Rejection of Localism: An Origin of Ultranationalism in Japan," which appeared in *Japan Interpreter* (Spring 1974), IX, no. 1, is a part of his recent book, *A Study of Localism: Subnationalism, Ultranationalism and Transnationalism* (Tokyo: Nansō Sha, 1975), and is reflective of where his recent interests lie.

Postwar Trends in Japan

Francis Mathy

Shusaku Endo
The Second Period

Since the writing of his prize-winning novel *Silence* in 1966, a steady stream of novels and plays, short story and essay collections has continued to flow from Shusaku Endo's pen, making him one of the most prolific as well as one of the most popular of Japanese writers. (During recent years there has almost always been at least one of his books, at times two and even three, on the weekly best seller lists.) While many of these works have been in that genre of light entertainment that most Japanese writers resort to in order to secure their living as they toil away at their "serious literature" (*junbungaku*), a number of the books of this period have taken up and further developed themes that were first sounded in the earlier writing. The reader who has followed Endo to the publication of *Silence* in 1966 may be interested in knowing what direction his writing has taken in the years that have followed.

Endo himself gives a valuable hint to the nature of this development in a recent statement in the magazine *Bungakkai* (Feb., 1974).

It was just seven years ago that I published *Silence*, putting an end to my first period of literary activity. Being after all a Japanese, I took as my constant theme during this early period Christianity and the Japanese, Japan and the West. This was natural enough for one like myself who, though Japanese, had been brought up a Christian. In *Silence* I took up the problem of what Christianity meant to a Japanese and speculated on how deeply it was possible for the Christian faith to sink its roots into the Japanese people. Since then I have been trying to reflect upon the way I as a Japanese encounter Christ. Approaching him as a Japanese, do I not in fact encounter

3

a Christ that is also Japanese? It is with this possibility in mind that I have written my last two books, *Shikai no hotori* (On the Shore of the Dead Sea) and *Iesu no Shogai* (The Life of Jesus). In these two works I have tried to give some kind of form to thoughts and feelings that have been growing to ripeness within me in the course of many years.

In an earlier essay on Endo* I tried to point out the manner in which he goes about opposing the "Japanese *boko* world without a God" to the "Western *deko* world that has known the existence of God." The central focus of the essay was upon the two novels, *Silence* and *And you, Too*, one dramatizing the disastrous encounter of a Westerner with the all-assimilating Mother culture of Japan, and the other the equally disastrous encounter of a Japanese with the tradition-laden, goal-directed Father culture of the West.

Endo's first period was largely devoted to this work of opposition. In the years that have followed, the stress has been rather on harmonization and reconciliation. The problem Endo has raised in this later period can be put in terms of Inoue's words to the fallen Father Ferreira at the end of *The Golden Country*: how can the flame of Christianity rescue the denizens of the Japanese mudswamp from their comfortable moral apathy?

Before showing how this reconciliation is attempted, it may be well to say a word about Endo's metaphor of the mudswamp, a figure that runs through almost all of his work. Basically, the metaphor signifies the Japanese insensitivity to sin that Endo referred to in one of his essays. The student Chiba in *The Yellow Man* states that the Japanese have nothing so "profound or exaggerated" as the Westerner's consciousness of sin; that all they experience is a deep fatigue, "weariness murky as the color of my skin, dank, heavily submerged." Most of Endo's characters have this fatigue and lack both the energy and the will to deal effectively with moral issues.

At one level the mudswamp is simply the safe, uneventful life without purpose, such as appears in the following description of a father in the short story *"Rokka-kan no ryokō"* (A Six-day Journey): "My father always said that the greatest happiness a man could hope for was that of an uneventful life. Man is happiest when

*"Endo Shusaku: White Man, Yellow Man," *Comparative Literature*, Vol. XIX, No. 1 (Winter, 1967), pp. 58–74.

nothing happens to him. . . . All Father ever wanted was a humdrum, uneventful life." This is also the life that the father in *Taidaima ronin* (In Preparation for College) wants for his son and daughter. But the son wants something more. "Doesn't there have to be more to life," he asks himself, "than just this? Something more vigorous, more intense? Something that sets a man on fire like a flame?"

The inhabitants of the mudswamp will, under sufficient provocation, become quite predatory in order not to lose their comfortable warmth. In *Umi to dokuyaku* (The Sea and Poison), for example, the doctors and nurses that take part in the vivisection experiments on living American prisoners of war do so out of no other motive than to hold on to their "ordinary little parcel of happiness." The narrator of the story who ferrets out the details of the grisly event several years later is a company employee who also feels that "the greatest happiness for man is to live an ordinary humdrum life in which nothing happens." Endo implies that the only real difference between the narrator and the killers is one of circumstance. Had the narrator been placed in the situation of the latter, he too would undoubtedly have cooperated with the killers. Every species of human vice is found represented in Endo's mudswamp, from petty jealousy and neglect of duty to shameful exploitation and murder.

While mindful of the great harm his mudswamp characters do to themselves and others, Endo does not stand over them and deliver judgement. On the frontispiece of the Shueisha volume of Endo's works he has written in his own hand: "When one becomes a novelist, he finds it no longer possible to pass judgement on others." The fact is that Endo is all too aware of the mudswamp in himself; he is as much in need of salvation as they are, so that he can look upon them with eyes of sympathy and concern. In the short story "*Haha naru mono*" (Mother and Things Maternal), one of Endo's finest pieces of writing, the central character states:

I began to feel myself drawn to the descendants of the fallen Christians. I came to find a reflection of myself in them. All their days these fallen Christians were condemned to live a double life, presenting a false face to the world and never exposing their true loyalties. I too have a secret that I have never revealed to anyone and probably never will so long as I live.

In this story we see that Endo, unable to discover within himself the strength to put up the struggle against the mudswamp that Western Christianity seems to him to demand, finds in the history of the hidden Christians of Kyushu another possible way to salvation. The Christians who stepped on the *fumi-e* were not strong enough to persevere in the profession of their faith. Yet even after their act of apostasy they were unable to forget their God. They banded together in hidden villages and continued to practise Christianity secretly. Each year they went through the ritual of stepping on the *fumi-e*, as was demanded of them, and then returned to their villages and scourged themselves in penance for their betrayal. In their conscience-stricken misery they turned to Mary, the mother of Christ, and fervently implored her intercession. In this way their Christianity became transformed gradually into a religion with Mother at the center rather than Father. The narrator of "Mother and Things Maternal" sums it up as follows:

> The missionaries long ago brought to this country the teaching of a Father God. But in the course of time, after the missionaries had been drive out and the churches destroyed, . . . this teaching came to be replaced by what is most essential in Japanese religion, devotion to Mother.

This does not mean, however, that Christianity was thereby vanquished, as both Ferreira and Inoue seemed to imply in *Silence*. In one of his latest essays, "*Chichi no shūkyo, haha no shūkyo*" (Father Religion, Mother Religion), Endo points out that whatever may be said about the religion of the Old Testament, Christ introduced into the New Testament "a maternal element, so that Christianity is also a religion of Mother. Many of the characters appearing in the New Testament could be called 'fallen' or at least belong to that same general category." Christ in his tender, unqualified love for men is more mother than father. Endo is always conscious of the fact that the weakest and most vicious of his swamp dwellers are ever looked upon by the loving eyes of Christ; Christ will not desert them, even while they are committing their crimes. This is the meaning of the voice that urges Father Ferreira to go ahead and step on the *fumi-e*: Christ forgives him in his weakness.

It is the maternal love of Christ that makes it possible for even a Japanese to be a Christian, that rescues the Japanese from the mudswamp. But how does this take place? In a series of novels Endo presents characters that are Christ figures and shows how their great love effects change in the other characters, giving them the power to take at least the first step out of the swamp. Then finally in his most recent novel Endo makes Christ himself the central character, bringing the work of this second period to its logical conclusion.

The first of these novels, *Obaka san* (Wonderful Fool), is earlier than *Silence* but received very little attention at the time of publication. This is perhaps because it was a humorous novel, written, presumably, only for entertainment—far less serious in tone than Endo's so-called "pure literature." But it is not the least of Endo's accomplishments that he is able to present his principal themes in a light and comic vein as well as in a more serious one.

Wonderful Fool is the story of a huge, ugly, horse-faced Frenchman, Gaston Bonaparte, who suddenly descends upon an average Japanese family and totally disrupts their humdrum life. Takamori, the son, is a typical Japanese office worker: he has no object in life and is inexorably bound to his uneventful narrow circle of work and play. His sister, Tomo-e, is a pragmatic career woman —an "economic animal" that assesses everything in terms of profit and loss. Gaston, in his complete simplicity and utter disregard for appearance and convention, appears to them to be a fool.

Gaston, however, has one great compensating virtue: an overpowering, totally self-sacrificing love for people, especially the poor and afflicted. His love and trust force all who come into contact with him to face up to themselves and challenge them to change. Takamori, until now the typical swamp dweller, comes to realize that Gaston is somehow connected with the best part of himself, and begins for the first time to take note of the poverty and misery about him. Even Tomo-e has her moment of insight:

A man with a simple love for others, trusting everyone, who, no matter how often he is deceived or betrayed continues to keep his flame of trust and love from going out—such a man is bound to seem a fool, in the world of today. But he is no ordinary fool. He is a wonderful fool.

The greatest change is effected in the professional killer Endo, who has hardened himself to all human emotion and is out to avenge himself on his brother's murderers. (It must be significant that Endo gives his own name to the seemingly most irredeemable of the swamp dwellers.) At the last minute, influenced by Gaston, he does not carry out his revenge.

What Endo does in this novel is suggest a way out of the mud-swamp. That way is love: self-sacrificing, trusting, gentle love. In short, the love of a Christ. The denizens of the swamp must first be loved without measure and then they become themselves capable of love—and of action. Symbolic also is the fact that the climactic scene takes place in an actual swamp into which Gaston and the killer Endo fall and but narrowly escape.

In subsequent novels Endo pursued the same theme and showed the effect of other "fools" upon the people about them. There is Mitchan in *Watashi ga suteta onna* (The Woman I Betrayed); the Baron, escaped from an insane asylum but more sane than the swamp dwellers, in *Ichi ni san* (One, Two, Three); Hechima-kun in the novel of the same name, a Japanese version of Gaston, the wonderful fool; Brother Ussan in the play *"Bara no yakata"* (The House of the Roses). Through their love these characters are also able to lift their fellowmen out of the swamp and help them to realize their better selves.

Always the love of these characters is an analogue of the love of God for men. What Endo is saying is that only the love of God, flowing through the love of those who are close to him, can free a man from the mudswamp and give him the freedom to act and realize his best self. Toda in *The Sea and Poison* says: "There is nothing a man can do to free himself from those forces—shall we call them Fate?—that carry him along. We would have to give the name of God to anything that could set him free from them." In *The Woman I Betrayed* one of the characters explains why Mitchan—and Gaston, Brother Ussan, and others—are so close to God and can mirror his love on earth:

"I reflected that God must have a very special love for people like Mit-chan. I don't know if you believe in God or not, but the God in whom we believe wants us to become like little children . . . in the sense that we are to rejoice simply when good fortune comes our way and weep simply in our sorrow. And we are to love with a simple, uncalculating love."

Obsessed as he is with the figure of Christ, it was inevitable that Endo should eventually hazard a novel with Christ himself as one of the main characters. This has been on his mind since the completion of *Silence.* Seven years of brooding upon the figure of Christ and trying to puzzle out what Christ must have meant to his contemporaries and what he means to people today—what he means to Endo himself—went into the writing of *On the Shore of the Dead Sea* and its companion, *The Life of Jesus.*

Part of the novel was first published in various magazines under the title of *People of the Crowd.* This consisted of a series of sketches dramatizing Christ's encounter with people of his own time and place: disillusioned followers, the high priest Annas, Pontius Pilate, the Roman centurion. The figure of Christ that emerges from these sketches is that of the Suffering Servant passage in Isaiah 53: a Christ "without beauty, without majesty . . . despised and rejected by men, a man of sorrow and familiar with suffering . . . pierced through for our faults, crushed for our sins." But his is a "punishment that brings us peace, and through his wounds we are healed." (Jerusalem Bible) At first men flock to him because they think he has the power to heal their afflictions and that he is the Messiah that will liberate them from Roman rule. But the only miracle that Endo's Christ will work is that of his own resurrection. He either can not or will not work any other.

If he is not a miracle worker, the Christ of *On the Shore of the Dead Sea* and of *The Life of Jesus* is a lover who loves without measure. All men are the objects of his love, but especially the "poor of Jahveh" mentioned in the Beatitudes of Matthew 5. No man ever loved as this man.

The swamp dwellers of the Palestinian mudswamp, however, can not be satisfied with mere love. When it becomes clear that their Messiah is powerless to help them *now,* they abandon him. Even his apostles betray him. (Endo assimilates the apostles, all without exception, to the characters of Kichijiro of *Silence* and Kasuke of *The Golden Country.*) But Christ continues to love even in his abandonment. However weak and sinful they may be, he loves them to the end. When Pilate is about to sentence him to death, he tells him that he, Pilate, will never be able to forget him, because he will never forget Pilate, and then adds: "I never forget anyone whose path I have ever crossed. . . . That's the kind of person I am."

The second story recounted in *On The Shore of the Dead Sea,* in alternate chapters, is that of a middle-aged Japanese novelist, similar in all respects to Endo, who travels to Israel in search of the answer to the question Jesus once put to Peter: "What think ye of Christ?" Among the historic monuments of the Holy Land he hopes to encounter Christ and solve once and for all the puzzle of what Christ is to him. But so overlaid with falsifying myth are these monuments that the search is at first unfruitful. The novelist then branches out in a completely different direction and comes at last to the resolution he has been seeking.

The key to this resolution is the character of Rat, a foreigner the novelist had known in his university days. Rat, to the novelist's mind, was the most ignoble of men: self-centered, cowardly, physically and mentally unattractive—in short, a man without a single redeeming human trait. In Rat it is obvious that the novelist sees a reflection of himself. The novelist discovers that Rat after returning to his native Poland was seized by the Nazis and sent to a concentration camp where he was eventually executed. He discovers too that Rat remained unchanged to the very end: no act of generosity or human affection illuminated his final hours. But the novelist learns something else: he learns that at the very end, just as Rat, still whimpering, faced his executioner, Christ demonstrated his unchanging love for this most despicable of men in a singularly striking manner. This fact gives the novelist hope and confidence that he too, sinful and wretched man that he is, is ever loved by Christ and will never be abandoned by him. The novel ends with the following passage, which provides a suitable climax to the principal theme that has obsessed Endo through the years:

> Despite the many long years that had intervened, Toda [the novelist's friend from university days who is now living in Jerusalem, a one-time Christian like himself] and I are still hung up on Christ. 'And know that I am with you always; yes, even to the end of time.' (Mt. 28, 20)

"He really won't let us alone, will he?"

Toda made no reply . . . . What was it that brought me to Israel? I am no longer sure. Was it Jesus? Or was it Rat? I am certain of just one thing. You have been standing in the shadow of Rat. It is even possible that in the same way as you attached yourself to Rat, you attach yourself also to me and to all other men. You may even have insinuated yourself into the lives of the characters of the old manuscripts locked away in my desk drawers. Into the life of the toothless, prevaricating thirteenth apostle I wrote about. Into the lives of all the other weaklings in my novels. You have been present in all the people I have created and through them you have been trying to get an ever firmer hold upon me. Even when I was doing my best to cast you off, you would not let go of my life.

The above lines should be read in conjunction with a passage in a recent essay, "*Watakushi no bungaku*" (My Writing). There Endo affirms that as he writes he is conscious of the eyes of Christ fixed in love upon his characters. He goes on to say:

The more conscious I am of that gaze as I write my story, the better, I think, the story comes off. When I lose consciousness of those eyes, it seems to me that my story becomes just another psychological tale as far as characterization is concerned. Such a tale can grasp only the psychology of the characters. But behind that psychology, in the inner heart of each character, there lies hidden another dimension. It is that dimension that the eyes of Christ penetrate to.

However much a reader may admire Endo's intentions in *On the Shore of the Dead Sea* and discover in the novel the resolution to the themes that have occupied Endo through so many years, it can not be denied that considered as literature the novel is a greatly flawed work that does not quite come off. There is too much talk and not enough action, and the gimmick Endo uses to bring the novel to its climax is as contrived a *deus ex machina* as can be found in any literature. Fortunately, Endo does a much finer job of resolution in his play "*The Japanese of the Menam River*" (*Menamgawa no Nihonjin*), written immediately after the novel. (This reader also considers the play "*The Golden Country*," immediately after *Silence*, a finer piece of work than the novel. Perhaps Endo is in need of the discipline that stage presentation exacts from him.)

"*The Japanese of the Menam River*" contrasts the careers of two of the most exotic of Japanese historical figures, Yamada Nagamasa and Pedro Kibe, whose paths crossed for the brief period of two years, 1627 to 1629, in the Japanese village on the Menam River near Ayudhaya, the ancient capital of Siam.

Yamada Nagamasa was the third elected head of the Japanese community on the Menam River, which numbered some fifteen hundred people, among them about four hundred Christians who had escaped to Siam from the persecution raging in their native country. A brave and capable samurai, Yamada and his four hundred soldiers were a powerful component of the Siamese Imperial Guard. Yamada was a skilled diplomat as well, and as a reward for his military and diplomatic services to the Siamese throne, he was raised to the highest rank of Siamese nobility. However, after the death of the king he served, he became embroiled in the politics of succession and was killed by the court doctor, who on the pretense of treating a wound incurred in defending Siam against an enemy invader annointed him with poison.

Pedro Kibe was a young Japanese Christian who traveled alone halfway round the world to Rome in order to study for the priesthood—from Macao to India, through Persia and Palestine, along an overland route to Rome. Ordained in 1620 and accepted into the Jesuit Order, he set out at once upon his return journey, despite the fact that persecution was raging more fiercely than ever. Boarding a ship bound for India, he sailed around the southern coast of Africa to Goa and from there to Manila and Macao. In Macao he was unable to find a ship that would take him to Japan, so he set out once again for the Japanese settlement in Siam, where he hoped to have better luck. His ship was attacked by Dutch pirates, but Kibe managed to escape and after two weeks of plowing through jungle reached Malacca. There he fought a severe bout with Malaria and almost died. He finally reached Ayudhaya in July of 1627. There he spent two years looking for a ship that would give him passage to Japan, but since no ship captain would take this risk, he finally gave up and sailed to the Philippines instead. Then from the island of Lubang he set out for Japan in a termite-eaten old ship, which got him as far as the southernmost islands of that country before it was shattered by a typhoon. Japanese fishermen rescued him, and he set foot on his native soil at last, sixteen years after he had begun his odyssey. For some three years he succeeded in eluding the Bureau of Persecution, working first in Nagasaki and then in Sendai. Captured finally in 1639, he suffered the torture of the pit, but unlike Ferreira and Roderigo he not only refused to give up his faith but was so successful in persuading his companions in the pit to persevere in theirs that he was taken down and put to death by the sword.

Yamada and Kibe are effectively contrasted in the play: their encounter is highly dramatic. In Act I, Scene iii, for example, there takes place the following dialogue:

Yamada: . . . Somewhere in this vast country I want to build a kingdom of my own. How about you, Kibe?

Kibe: Like you, I no longer think of Japan as my country. I have no other country now but the Kingdom of God.

Yamada: Kingdom of God? The world of the dead . . . is that your country?

Kibe: No. God's kingdom is not just of the next world. His kingdom is being built up within the dark recesses of every person's heart.

Yamada: In the dark recesses of the heart? You mean in mine, too?

Kibe: Yes.

Yamada: Nonsense. You won't find any such foolish illusion in my heart. Instead, I am using my hands to pile brick upon brick until I succeed in establishing the glory of this Japanese settlement. And that's all that is in my heart.

Kibe: That is not all. Every person has an inner heart that he does not expose to others.

Two valiant and totally dedicated men struggle for the establishment of two very different kinds of kingdoms. But Kibe is right: Yamada does have an inner heart that he refuses to reveal to others, and this inner heart is finally the cause for the defeat of his grandiose plans and assimilates him at the end to the kingdom that Kibe speaks of. Yamada's tender compassion for the young princess is, in Endo's figure, the lotus that rises beautifully out of the mudswamp of his heart, and it is this compassion that is his undoing. Or rather, his salvation.

Kibe is the latest in the long line of Endo's "holy fools." Weak and vulnerable in appearance, he is inwardly strong and undefeatable. He too has the all-encompassing love of Christ for others. To the renegade Christian, Kasuke (apparently the very Kasuke that betrayed Ferreira in *The Golden Country*), Kibe states his reason for returning to Japan as follows:

> Listen carefully, Kasuke. God is still with you and the others who are heart-broken over your betrayal. If all the defected Christians in Japan are in such despair as you . . . . That is all the more reason for my wanting to return to Japan. I must let them know that God does not exist for punishing and judging. I must go and tell them that God has a deep understanding of how they suffer as a result of their weakness.

Later in the play Kibe tells Yamada that "God reveals himself through the life of every human being—yes, even your life and Mokichi's and Kasuke's."

Despite Yamada's attempts to dissuade him from leaving the safety of Siam, Kibe sets out for Japan and certain death. After his smiling departure Yamada reflects:

> "I don't know why I am so concerned about him. He's nothing but a fool. Still, now that he is gone I find it impossible to forget him. He is so weak that one would never guess that samurai blood ran in his veins. Besides, he was still suffering from fever. His is a completely different way of life from mine. And yet, I almost feel as if he were my brother."

The play ends with Yamada's betrayal and death (on stage) and Kibe's martyrdom (recounted according to the report of an eyewitness). Each in his own way, it is implied, has discovered the kingdom of God.

This play gives what seems to be a final answer to the questions Endo raised in *Silence* and *The Golden Country*. God is not and never was silent. In his infinite love he raises from the mudswamp of each human heart a beautiful lotus flower. He is the Saviour even of the Japanese.

With these last three works, *On the Shore of the Dead Sea*, *The Life of Jesus*, and *The Japanese of the Menam River*, Endo seems to have reached a conclusion. All his works to this point arrange themselves into an integral whole. What will he do next? Will he start repeating himself or will he launch forth in a new direction? The next seven years of this middle-aged writer will be interesting to observe.

Kinhide Mushakoji

A Note on Trilateral Crisis Diplomacy*
The Irritants in the Japan-U.S.-E.C. Relations

1. Introduction

One of the most conspicuous trends in contemporary international relations is the growing trend toward interdependence, especially among the highly industrialized countries. This tendency, which forces them to cooperate more closely for their common benefit as well as for the common good of the planet, is nonethelesss divisive in that it intensifies competition among the parties that are willing to cooperate only under certain conditions consonant with their national or regional interests Hence, sources of friction among the industrialized countries are increasing, especially between Japan, the United States and the European countries. This short essay tries to describe different aspects of the issues faced by the three parties in the conduct of trilateral crisis diplomatic exchanges.[1]

In contrast to the past twenty-five years, the three parties cannot rely on the formal ties linking them, either in terms of the North Atlantic Alliance or of the Japan-U.S. Mutual Security Treaty, in solving their differences. The danger of nuclear war having receded, the centrifugal forces of economic competition now prevail over the centripetal influence of security interests. Within this overall context crisis diplomacy over economic issues

*This article is based on a paper called "A Note on Trilateral Crises," prepared for the Political Task Force of the Trilateral Commission (1973). The author expresses his gratitude for the comments and remarks made by the members of this organization, which enabled him to improve his original draft.

has become so important for the industrialized countries that it is impossible to leave low politics in the shadow and pay attention only to the grandiose feats of high politics.[2]

This short note addresses itself to this burning problem, taking as its frame of reference Japan, the United States, and the European countries. The trilateral relations among them now constitute a typical case of a crisis diplomatic setting. Leaving the task of studying the concrete contents of all the trilateral issues to the specialists in each area, we will focus on the structure of this setting. If crisis diplomacy consisted merely of finding reasonable solutions to each problem, it would be relatively easy to settle disputes among the three parties. The fact of the matter is that specific issues are combined and mixed together by various objective and subjective circumstances, so that diplomatic crisis management requires before anything else the disentanglement of all the bits and pieces of the various causes of irritation that exist among the three parties, and hence, a study of how these factors are intertwined within the crisis structure is very necessary. Our aim here is merely to draw a sketch of this structure as a starting point for a more careful study, which cannot be made by the author alone but requires joint efforts, multiregional and multidisciplinary, to determine how the political, economic, social, and psychological factors in each of the three units work in the trilateral crisis diplomatic setting.

In this article, we will first draw a rough sketch of how these factors are interrelated. We will first enumerate the issues that confront the three parties. We will then turn to the asymmetry built into the trilateral relations, since the difference of the mutual role images caused by this very asymmetry makes it difficult for the three parties to arrive at a common understanding about the issues under negotiation. The third topic to be discussed will be the obstacles the trilateral negotiators have to face; some due to the very nature of the national, international, or transnational economic-political structures, others to the way negotiators communicate with each other. A final section will be devoted to the implications of an improvement of trilateral relations on the international system as a whole.

2. The Issues

It is possible to identify, broadly, three categories of issues that involve either two or all three of the trilateral parties, i.e., economic, political and military.

Among the economic issues, the monetary, trade, investment, energy resources, technological issues, and development aid problems are of particular importance.

Monetary issues involve all three parties.[3] Although the monetary conflict is, objectively, to be solved in the long run only through the creation of a new and more stable system, it is subjectively a conflict of the three parties who attribute the crisis to different causes. Europeans and Japanese tend to point out the American responsibility in the weakening of the dollar, and the Americans and Europeans point out the overly strong position of the yen.

Mainly trade issues are exacerbating U.S.-Japanese relations and E.C.-Japanese relations.[4] The increase of Japanese products in U.S. and, to a lesser degree, in European markets is a cause of alarm for the other two parties. This issue is linked to the monetary problem because it creates a trade imbalance to the benefit of Japan. The two parties not only perceive its economic development as a threat to their own economic well-being, but also criticize its economic behavior as unfair and unruly.

Investment issues oppose the U.S. and the E.C. countries, and they exist between Japan on the one side and the U.S. as well as the E.C. countries on the other.[5] The former opposition is often referred to as the *American Challenge*. The latter involves the various barriers and restrictions put by Japan on foreign investments. Objectively, these issues are closely related to the recent development of multinational corporations. Psychologically, the economic and technological gaps between the U.S., the E.C. countries and Japan are mutually irritating to the three parties.

Energy resources issues are not yet openly irritating trilateral relations.[6] However, a gradual depletion of oil resources combined with the increasingly strong position of the Organization of Petroleum Exporting Countries will create a situation where the distribution of energy resources among the three industrialized parts of the world is a serious source of conflict. It seems that, at least for the time being, no psychological irritation comparable to the monetary, trade and investment issues exists in this field. The conflict should be coped with before such embitterment begins to complicate the situation.

Technological issues are intricately linked to others, both economic and military.[7] Psychologically, there is a strong feeling in the E.C. countries as well as in Japan about the need to bridge the technological gap; there is, for example, a private Italian proposal for a technological Marshall Plan in which the U.S. is expected to transmit without remuneration its technical knowhow. On the other hand, the U.S. perceives the flow of its technology toward the E.C. countries and Japan as part of its business relations and demands a fair price for the knowhow it has developed through its research development investments.

Aid policy issues also exist among the three parties.[8] The global nature of the aid provided by the United States, the aid links existing very often between the European nations and their ex-colonies, and the short term economic merits sought by the Japanese aid make the policy of the three partners often mutually dissonant. The reduction of American aid is not well received by the other parties. The U.S. expects on its side, that Japan, for example, should shoulder part of the burden in a way not exactly acceptable to the latter. Japan should support the Saigon Government or provide semimilitary aid to Southeast Asian countries, a demand delicate to comply with because of a highly negative public reaction. European links with African countries are, on the other side, often considered as a means to maintain this continent as a European "territory".

On the political level, the dissimilarity in the foci of attention of the three regions is a source of conflict. The United States sees its foreign relations in a global perspective that includes the North Atlantic and the Asian-Pacific regions together with all the other parts of the world, while Europe is primarily interested in the first and the Japanese in the latter region. In its global perspectives, the United States very naturally seeks to create a tripolar balance of power with the Soviet Union and the People's Republic of China. This tripolar diplomatic action is conducted outside the trilateral context. This has created in the past some conflicts with Japan (the Nixon shock), as well as with certain European countries (notably the French resentment about having the United States and the Soviet Union negotiate the destiny of Europe without its participation).

On the United States side, there is a growing need for the participation of the two regions' countries to its tripolar policy efforts. The New Atlantic Charter proposal represents this expectation, which is seen by some of its partners as an attempt to regain an American global leadership over the other regions, keeping them in a more or less subordinate position.[9] The necessity the United States had in its tripolar diplomacy to put an emphasis first on Asia—since the early seventies—and next on Europe—in 1973, the "Year of the Europeans"—caused alternately a concern in Europe and then in Japan, where it was felt that each region was given by the U.S. a peripheral position in its global political activities. It is noteworthy that on the polititcal level, in contrast to the economic, the major issues involve either the United States and Europe, or the former and Japan, leaving the European-Japanese side of the triangle relatively free of important conflicts.

On the military level, there are nuclear and ACD (Arms Control and Disarmament) issues, collective security issues, maritime issues and arms trade issues. As to the nuclear and ACD issues, the French nuclear policy and that country's refusal to participate in the other nuclear countries' ACD agreements constitute a major problem. Although not vitally negative toward the United States nuclear and ACD efforts, the French nuclear tests are objects of public and private protest in Japan. Another dissonant note among the three parties' nuclear and ACD cooperation is the non-ratification of the Nonproliferation Treaty by Japan, which has delayed this move after having signed the treaty, explaining the lack of enthusiasm by the disadvantage it would face in terms of the inspection procedures.

As to collective security issues, there is between the United States and Europe the problem of the former's troop withdrawal under U.S. congressional pressure.[10] On the other hand, the quasi-hegemonic structure of NATO is not satisfactory to the latter, and France notably keeps her distance from certain organizational aspects of NATO. Between the United States and Japan, the

Mutual Security Treaty is a cause of some concern.[11] The former fears that the internal situtaion in the latter, in case of emergency, would not permit it to make free use of the bases. In the latter there is an increasing opinion supporting either the revision, the phasing out, or a simple abolition of the treaty. On the other hand, a drastic reduction of the U.S. presence in East Asia is feared by some Japanese because of the destabilizing effect it would have and the increased pressure it would build for a Japanese military role in Asia. The lack of enthusisam in this country to cooperate with the American security efforts in the Asian-Pacific region is strongly criticized by the United States, which sees in it a free ride profitting from the U.S. military burden. A Japanese concession on the economic level is expected in return.

Maritime issues are not pressing for the moment, but the increasingly active moves of the U.S.S.R. on the seas causes a U.S. need for European and Japanese participation in surveillance efforts in different oceans.[12] A few American ballons d'essai test ing the possibility of Japanese willingness to participate in the surveillance of the Pacific and Indian oceans were rejected.

3. Trilateral Asymmetry and Image Gaps

All the trilateral issues mentioned above could be much more easily handled if the three parties involved accepted the same definition of the problems. Even if their basic interests were different, it would be possible to find a cooperative solution to each issue, since by the very fact of their interdependence the three parties play non zero-sum game where all lose together if the diplomatic crises are not solved soon enough.[13]

One crucial factor that obstructs the way to such a rational approach is the very fact that the three partners perceive their mutual roles in an asymmetrical way, so that the issues are put in quite different contexts among them.[14]

On the economic level, for example, there are three quite dissimilar economies: the U.S. receding but yet dominant economy, the European integrating economy and the Japanese growing economy. From an American point of view, it is an unquestionable fact that the dollar is the key of the trilateral economic system, and it is natural that the other two parties should cooperate to stabilize its position. The danger of a closed integration of the European community and the threat coming from a too aggressive Japanese expansion are both detrimental to the dominant economy in crises. Viewed from the European side, integration is of prime importance not only to Europe but to the reorganization of a stable economic order among the free industrialized countries. For it and for Japan, it is not necessarily true that the reassertion of a dominant U.S. economic role would be stabilizing. For Europe as well as for the United States, the rapid growth of the Japanese economy, with increases in its share in the world market, constitutes a destabilizing force that should be coped with and paced down. This, on the Japanese side, is considered as unfair discrimination against a late-coming partner.[15]

On the political and military levels, the one global and the two regional sides of the triangle do not share exactly the same perspectives. They agree only to say that others should respect their own views. The United States expects Europe and Japan to assume their responsibilities in meeting together the global challenges it feels it faces for the three partners in the tripolar entanglements.[16] The Europeans and the Japanese do not necessarily agree to this approach, which seems to link trilateral relations to tripolar politics under the hegemonic guidance of the United States. Europe and Japan are each interested in developing contacts—more or less independently from their relations with the United States—with the Soviet Union and with China. For many Europeans, their regional security requires a good Atlantic partnership, but it does not imply a subordination of its affairs to a U.S.-U.S.S.R. bipolar equilibrium. For many Japanese, even without denying the reason for the existence of a U.S.-Japanese security partnership, the stability of the Asian-Pacific region cannot be achieved without improved relations with the People's Republic of China and the U.S.S.R. Because of the high vulnerability of its economy and of the delicate geographic location close to the two opposed superpowers, China and the Soviet Union, as well as internal political conditions, Japan is extremely reluctant to assume an active military role on the side of the United States.

Besides the way the three parties define their relations with the tripolar superpowers, there is also a less conspicuous but yet important dissimilarity arising from the relations of the three industrialized actors with the Third World. The United States has a traditional interest in Latin America, Europe in Africa and Japan in Asia. The American isolationism so often mentioned as a threat to good trilateral relations is represented as a return to traditional policy centered on the Western Hemisphere. The special economic ties of the European Community with African countries, symbolized by the Yaunde Agreement, give to some observers in the other two parts of the trilateral system the impression that Eurafrica may develop into a closed market detrimental to the trilateral free economic relations. The rapid economic expansion of Japan in Asia is the cause of a mixed feeling of fear and expectation not only in the region but in the United States, where people welcome a certain kind of burden-sharing by Japan but not a too independent policy that may be competitive with its own military, political, or economic efforts in this region.

It is important to notice how the above-mentioned asymmetrical aspects create noncomplementary mutual images among the three parties. For the sake of simplicity, as well as of comparability, we will summarize the essential differences that exist among those images in Table 1. Each row represents the images of the party whose name appears in the left column. On the diagonal are found the self-images of the three parties. The essential points that build into the economic, political, and military image asymmetrical role expectations are mentioned in a telegraphic style.

Table 1. Self-images and Role Images of the United States, E.C., and Japan

U.S.	E.C.	J.	Extra-Trilateral World Priorities
(E): Global responsibility of $. Deficit due to U.S. con-	(E): Danger of closed regionalism. Euro $, monetary	(E): Too much restriction on own market and too much	

Table 1 (cont).

U. S.	tribution to Free World security and development. (P): Tripolar balance priority and U.S. leadership role in Free World (M): U.S. nuclear guarantee plus Free World countries contribution	imbalance. (P): North Atlantic co-indispensable for Free World. (M): Increased security responsibility needed as well as co-operation with U.S. nuclear and ACD policy.	agressiveness in U.S. market. (P): Should play a political role in accordance with economic power in cooperation with U.S. (M): Insufficient sharing of security burden in Asia.	(E): Latin America. (P). U.S.S.R. & P.R.C. (M): U.S.S.R.
E. C.	(E): Dominant economy. Economic and technological gaps. (P): N. Atlantic hegemony questioned. (M): Nuclear bipolar balance. U.S. presence in Europe necessary for E.C.	(E): E.C. integration stabilizing factor for world economy. (P): East-West European affairs key role in the world. (M). European regional security.	(E):Same as the U.S. (P): Economic diplomacy with no relevant role in high politics. (M): No interest	(E):Africa. (P): Eastern European countries. (M): Same as above
J A P A N	(E): Same as Europe, plus fear of protectionistic reactions. (P): Special U.S.-Japanese relations. (M): Pressure on Japan for burden-sharing unreasonable.	(E): Profit from integration, danger or closed market. (P): Europe-centered. Not enough interest in Asia. (M): Indifferent.	(E): Late-comer deserving special treatment. Not yet strong enough. (P): Necessity to cope with extreme dependence on foreign countries. (M): Limited to self-defense.	(E): Asia. P.R.C. & U.S.S.R. (P): P.R.C. & U.S.S.R. (M): —

In the rightmost column, the priorities in the interests and attention of the three parties outside of the trilateral partnership are mentioned.

The asymmetrical role images of the trilateral actors must be changed, and symmetrical expectations should be created among them. This requires a creative approach by the three parties who should reformulate their roles in an entirely new context.[16] Naturally, such a process cannot be achieved in a few years. Yet, if we want to stabilize trilateral relations for the coming generations, we should start now to think about the various measures we should take in order to initiate this process of redefinition, on the cultural exchange level, on the educational policy level, and so on. Needless to say, trilateral role complementarity should not be achieved by making the three parties a closed club of the rich countries. The roles of the three parties must be determined not only among themselves but also in relation to the superpowers in the tripolar system, and even more importantly to the three Third World regions. This point will be dealt with more extensively in section 5 of this article.

4. Structural Complications and Discommunication

Once conflicts arise caused by the above asymmetrical factors, the following structural factors intervene and complicate their solution. First, there is the intraregional pluralism, which works within the three parties.[17] For that matter, the European Community has more difficulties overcoming its internal diversity, since it has to deal with the different member countries' governments. Among other things, independent French initiatives and positions regarding military (nuclear and NATO related) as well as political and economic matters are a dissonant factor in transatlantic relations.[18] In the United States and in Japan, internal pluralism on the nongovernmental level is a problem. The growing influence of the opposition both in the United States and in Japan as well as the proliferation of interest groups complicate trilateral relations on all levels. Bureaucratic infighting among different sections of the governments is an aggravating factor.[19]

On the economic level, there are also new transnational actors who exercise a powerful influence on trilateral relations, i.e., the multinational corporations. As the chief artisans of the American challenge or as manipulators of the Eurodollar, the multinational corporations of American origin tend to play an independent role often difficult to control. The problems are not less difficult with the European and the now emerging Japanese multinational corporations.

With such a plurality of interested parties, intraregional, national and transnational, it is difficult to arrive at a commonly acceptable definition of the preferable options to be chosen by the three parties.

This is why we should not conclude too hastily that the three parties can find a solution acceptable to all parties. It is not self-evident that global perspectives are more relevant than regional ones by all so that some groups should bear the cost for the sake of all others.

In a setting as intricate as the above-described trilateral context, it is highly unrealistic to hope for a final solution of all trilateral conflicts and contentions. What we must seek is a set of rules and mechanisms that allow the three parties to adjust their mutual positions as new issues appear, so as to avoid that the piling up of irritants makes their interrelationship unmanageable. Those rules should primarily apply to trilateral communications for the following reason: over and above the psychological difficulties created by the image gaps and the structural obstacles on the national, international and transnational levels, discommunication comes to aggravate trilateral relations when no proper measures are taken to cope with the various complicating factors arising during the trilateral consultation and negotiation process and the internal communication process in each country.

The consultation process among the three partners is normally healthy as long as it concerns periodical exchanges of views on well-studied issues.[20] Consultation about newly emerged issues or newly adopted policies constitute a more delicate case for the three parties. Such new issues or policies may either involve one party's extratrilateral action (e.g., President Nixon's visit to Peking), or be related to a unilateral decision (e.g., the U.S. policy to protect the position of the dollar), or involve a bilateral agreement of two out of the three parties. Although less visible than those held on the government level, consultations on the non-governmental level are also important. In all these consultations, if any party felt that it had been left out, misinformed or informed after the fact, this would be followed by an escalation of the diplomatic crisis.

To prevent the piling up of such aggravating factors, it is necessary to make efforts of the following kinds:

First, it is important to create and maintain a constant consultation process among as many internal actors as possible, so that no one vetos trilateral policy proposals out of resentment due to the feeling of being left out of the consultation process.

Second, a trilateral rule of conduct-making should be established that makes obligatory prior trilateral consultation about any unilateral or bilateral decisions that interest in any way the three partners. For example a NATO decision strictly related to intra-NATO military cooperation would not have to be an object of prior consultation with Japan, but a U.S.-Japanese plan for Asian development aid would require prior consultation with the E.C. countries to the extent that they are interested in the development aid to the Asian countries.

The negotiation process is complicated not only by the discrepancy of the definition of the responsibilities, mentioned above, but also by the fact that basic principles according to which trilateral issues have to be negotiated are perceived differently.

For example, the definition of *fairness* is not the same everywhere. There is a Japanese definition of what is fair that assumes that late-comers have the right to be accorded a "handicap" to make the "game" a fair competition. This definition of *fairness* is not acceptable to many Americans, who have traditionally believed in a free and fair competition without handicaps or restrictive regulations.

The principle that the Free World is the context within which issues must be discussed is consciously or unconsciously maintained by Americans, yet it is not necessarily accepted by all their partners. In certain cases, Europeans tend to assume that their supranational integration experience can be shared by their partners and make proposals that are not always accepted by their more nation-state centered interlocutors.

In view of the above and many other instances of a lack of shared principles among the three parties, it is urgent to initiate a joint study of those principles, to seek the formulation of common principles or at least to find a way to understand better each other's point of view.

Another problem in trilateral negotiations arises when demands are made and offers are proposed. It is the cultural differences in the bargaining process[21] which chiefly complicate the negotiation between Japan on the one side and her American or European partners on the other. The insistence of the latter to formulate the problems in specific terms and to seek the adoption of universally applicable rules is quite alien to Japanese negotiators, who have a tradition of avoiding too specific definitions of the problems and prefer case by case agreements that are flexible and revisable. This and other cultural differences create a margin of uncertainty about each party's real intention, which makes each side suspicious about the other's offer and unresponsive to its demands. The Japanese strategy that avoids taking an unambiguous position as long as it can be avoided, commonly accepted within the Japanese negotiation situation, is often irritating to her interlocutors.

Another complication is caused by the use of different bargaining strategies, such as the combination of different demands and offers into package deals. As the trilateral relations become increasingly complex, with more and more issues, economic, political or military, there is a tendency for some parties to seek a favorable deal by a combination of issues that are beneficial to their interest. The linkage between security and economic issues proposed by the United States is not welcomed by some European countries, like France, or by Japan.[22]

In view of the above complications, it is necessary to make efforts along the following lines:

First, to educate the negotiating parties so as to overcome cultural misunderstandings and complications.

Second, to make all possible efforts to prepare the negotiations informally by consultation and preparatory talks. (This should involve all three parties since otherwise the party left out feels greatly offended.)

Third, the use of different bargaining strategies detrimental to a reasonable solution of the issues should be avoided either by self-restraint or, better, through common agreement. Trilateral issues should be solved as much as possible in a technical manner, level by level, avoiding the mixing up of issues.

A further process that deserves more attention is the communication process within each of the three units. All trilateral issues and decisions that are taken up by the governments and the non-governmental actors are formed through a communication process where the different regional (in the case of the E.C.), national and local (on the state level in the U.S.) government agencies, political parties, interest groups, and mass media interact.

Any statement about trilateral issues made by a government official, by a business leader or by any other responsible person is bound to trigger a process in which the statement is welcomed or opposed by political parties, by interested pressure groups, or by press commentators. Sometimes government agencies contradict each other and a bureaucratic conflict follows. At other times, the mass media play a key role in mobilizing the as yet inattentive public against a foreign initiative and receive a counterattack from their counterpart in that country.

The mechanisms of such internal processes are often difficult for outsiders to understand. For example, the complex relationship that exists among different European institutions (governmental as well as nongovernmental), the mechanism of U.S. congressional politics with its pressure groups, crossparty alignment and committee politics, the Japanese intrabureaucratic competition or the LDP (Liberal Democratic Party)-Zaikai (business) relations—these are only a few examples of regional and national peculiarities in the communication process that are not easy to grasp and to calculate. The way the mass media react to these events and the way they shape public opinion is again a matter of uncertainty complicated by the different functions of the press and of public opinion in these three parts of the world.

In view of the above situation, it is necessary to take the following measures to prevent the complications of trilateral relations.

First, a thorough study of the communication process in the various sectors of trilateral relations must be made so as to clarify the major communicators through whom trilateral information is channelled and interpreted.

Second, the cognitive and evaluative frame of reference of these communicators must be analyzed so as to bring out the causes of diverging interpretations that are at the root of all conflicts.

Third, concrete measures aiming at facilitating the transmission of undistorted information must be taken. Here, it is necessary to begin with a systematic effort to channel more and more accurate information through more diversified channels so as to increase the reliablity of the communication system.

Fourth, it must be noted that even with the best communication system the fact that the various actors involved in the trilateral interactions (the governments, the business interests, the mass media, and so on) cannot be expected to hold identical interests. This is why better communication may sometimes increase tension, and trilateral relations can be stabilized only if institutional measures are adopted so that no actor can benefit from a noncooperative strategy. It is only when the rules of the trilateral game are well established that trilateral crises can become harmless for the three parties.

5. Trilateral Relations in a Global Context

So far, we have addressed ourselves to the problem of crisis diplomacy solely within the trilateral context. Clearly crisis management among the three parties is possible only if trilateral issues are solved in a way satisfactory to them. It also remains true, however, that the solution of a particular issue optimally satisfying to the three parties is not *ipso facto* optimally satisfying to other members of the global community. For example, a solution of the monetary crisis satisfactory to the industrailized countries may not be satisfactory to the Third World countries. If the reduction of the tension level inside the trilateral context is reached through a procedure raising the tension level between some or all of the trilateral partners and some actors outside this context, the crisis management cannot be judged successful. Therefore, a few remarks about the external effects of intratrilateral crisis management must be made before we conclude this section.

To use a concept widely accepted by economists, the problem boils down to one of externalities created by trilateral crisis management. If the process is accompanied by external economies, the global system will benefit from improved relations among the three partners. If, on the other hand, it creates external diseconomies for the global system, improved relations among the three parties are not a welcome phenomenon for the world community. To use in quite a loose way the prisoner's dilemma allegory, the former case is equivalent to a situation where the three parties reach a common agreement to choose together a noncooperative strategy vis-a-vis other countries, whereas separately they may have opted for a cooperative move.[23] Such a situation arises whenever a trilateral coalition guarantees that the power position of the coalition is so strong that no punishing countermove by the extratrilateral players is possible, whereas if such a coalition did not exist, each of the three parties would have to play safe and be cooperative for fear that the other of the trilateral partners would join a counter-coalition whose punishing move could be powerful enough to exclude the likelihood that none could benefit from a noncooperative option.

The latter case, on the contrary, occurs when each of the trilateral partners feels that as long as it has no guarantee that the two others will choose the cooperative option, it should play safe by selecting the noncooperative alternative. Thus an agreement among the three to play cooperatively (on the global level) motivates it to play that way. This happens whenever the cooperative approach is fruitful only when the three industrialized partners play together.

It is difficult to determine which issue produces external diseconomies and which generates economies. For example, the energy resources issue may encourage the three partners to cooperate to solve it. Theoretically, one sector where such a trilateral effort would have no externalities is that of a joint project to educate the citizens of the industrialized countries to adopt a less consumption-oriented life-style. In practical terms, the three partners seem to be more interested either in finding new sources of energy or in improving their bargaining position vis-a-vis the countries producing the presently most important energy resources, that is, oil. In the former case, joint development of new resources can be expected to create more external economies than diseconomies. If used competitively against oil, new energy resources may play the same role as that of synthetic products replacing natural products in depriving the developing countries of their market. In general terms the finding of new resources, must be viewed as an external economy (in the service not only of the industrialized countries but of the whole human family). As to the other approach, which consists of building a coalition of the three industrialized partners to build their bargaining power, it is clear that such a strategy amounts to having the three partners together play the noncooperative strategy against the oil-producing countries, who are themselves reinforced in their decision to play noncooperative. This is a typical case where the game-theoretic rationality of both parties' opting for a noncooperative solution is confirmed by the facts. The three partners, who separately may regard it as more reasonable to opt for a cooperative move, feel strong enough, together, to play noncooperatively. The net effect is counterproductive from the point of view of a reasonable solution of the energy problem in a global perspective.

This example indicates that for most issues there are alternative approaches that differ in their external effects. The problem boils down to knowing how the three partners can be encouraged to avoid creating external diseconomies, or, preferably, to generate external economies with the long range view that their move will be paid back by the other countries "some day."

Clearly, such an option requires a high sense of statesmanship on the part of the political and economic leaders of the industrialized countries. However, it is unrealistic to rely on their good intentions, and further measures should be adopted so as to make attractive the cooperative option to all three of the partners.

Theoretically the problem is simple. The three partners should cooperate with all the other regions of the world in order to internalize externalities through the setting up of efficient rules and institutions. To take again the energy question, a counterproductive polarization between the producers and the consumers can be avoided only if appropriate institutions are created to permit a solution globally as well as locally optimal for all parties. This is possible only if a multilateral forum and a neutral functional agency are organized—for example, within the framework of the United Nations. Otherwise, the bargaining process between the producers and consumers will only lead to a prisoner's dilemma game situation where the noncooperative solution prevails against everybody's best interests.

In reality, the problem is not that simple. The following complicating factors have to be taken into consideration. First of all, it is not a simple task to build a consensus within the trilateral setting about the necessity to avoid external diseconomies by the formation of a trilateral coalition. There is always the mirror-image effect, which works in favor of polarization. If the producers strengthen their bargaining position by forming a coalition, why should the consumers not do the same? This eye for an eye counteraction leads necessarily to an escalation of the crisis. We must learn the lesson of the bipolar conflicts of the past decades between East and West; otherwise we may find a similar conflict mounting spirally between North and South.[24]

Another complicating factor is the existence of various trilateral actors (and extratrilateral) who have special self-interests opposed to a globally oriented approach. If the industrialized nations improve their antipollution legislation, it is clearly less costly for certain industries to move their factories to Third World countries where such laws do not exist. The external diseconomies created by this exportation of pollution from the industrialized countries to the less-developed countries can be coped with only if international antipollution-legislation effort is made. It is, however, quite foreseeable that such efforts will meet strong resistance from the industries concerned, or even from governments of some less-developed countries that are too much interested in industrialization to bother about pollution. To overcome the resistance coming from the inside and the outside of the trilateral setting, it is necessary to improve the exchange of information, not only among the industrialized countries but between them and the other regions of the world. This is essential, because without accurate information no one can prove convincingly the existence of specific cases of external diseconomies, and without a minimal degree of mutual empathy it is impossible to create strong enough public support for a cooperative policy often "unrealistic" from a short term, self-interest point of view.

This leads us to the following final remark. Trilateral cooperation should be an open one—open to the other regions in the sense of being conscious of the need to avoid external diseconomies. Open, also, in a readiness to communicate multilaterally with the other regions of the world. Open, finally, in terms of seeking a global as well as local optimum acceptable to all, instead of pretending that the locally optimal solution for the three industrialized partners is in itself *the* global optimal solution.

Needless to say, it is much easier to build a trilateral coalition based on the self and the selfish interests of the three parties. This is why we must make speical efforts to avoid this unproductive path.

1. For a general discussion of the trilateral relations between Japan, North America and Europe, see: Duchene, Francois, Owen, Henry D. and Mushakoji, Kinhide, "The Crisis of International Cooperation: Report of the Trilateral Political Task Force to the Executive Committee of the Trilateral Commission," Tokyo, October 22–23, 1973.
2. An extremely interesting analysis of crisis diplomacy can be found in: Morse, Edward L., "Crisis Diplomacy, Interdependence, and the Politics of International Economic Relations", Tanter, R. and Ullman, R. H. (eds.), *Theory and Policy in International Relations* (Princeton, N. J., 1972), pp. 123–150.
3. The forthcoming Trilateral Commission Monetary Task Force Report contains a careful analysis of the problem as well as some concrete proposals.
4. Concerning one of the early trade-related conflicts between Japan and the United States, see: Nagai, Yonosuke, and Kamiya, Fuji (eds.), *Nichi-Bei Keizai-kankei no Seiji-teki Kōzō* (The Political Structure of Japan-U.S. Economic Relations) (Tokyo, 1972).
5. A classic in the field of U.S.-European trade issues is Servan-Schreiber, Jean-Jacques, *Le défi américain* (Paris, 1967). See also: Steuer, M. D., "American Capital and Free Trade", Johnson, Harry C. (ed.), *Trade Strategy for Rich and Poor Nations* (London, 1971).
6. The strategic use of oil resources made by the Arab countries in connection with the fourth Arab-Israel war had the effect of unveiling the divergence of interest

existing among industrialized countries. On the other hand, the United States initiative to create a consensus among the oil-consuming countries seems to work in
the direction of closer cooperation among the trilateral parties despite French reluc-
tance and Japanese caution. We will touch later on the global implication of such a
coalition.

7. Concerning technological gaps, see: Spencer, Daniel Lloyd, *Technology Gap in
Perspective* (New York, 1970). More specifically on the Japanese perception of it, see,
for example: Makino, Noboru, "Kokusai-ka to Nihon no Gijutsu" (Internationalization and Japanese Technology), Sekai Seito Kenkyu-kai (ed.), *Nijūsseiki kara no
Chōsen ni Kotaete* (Challege of the Twenty-first Century) (Tokyo, 1971).

8. It is important to have a realistic understanding of how aid to Third World
countries is used as a means to achieve certain foreign policy goals. It is probably in
this connection that the differences in the basic motivation for aid giving among the
three parties have to be studied. See, for example: Nelson, John M., *Aid, Influence,
and Foreign Policy* (New York, 1968).

9. Concerning North Atlantic relations see, for example: Kaiser, Karl, *Europe and
the United States* (New York, 1973).

10. Cf. Pierre, Andrew J., "Can Europe's Security Be 'Decoupled' from America?"
Foreign Affairs, 1973, p. 267.

11. See, for example: Saeki, Kiichi, "Juso-teki Takyoku-Kōzō to Nihon no Taio"
(The Multi-level Multi-polar World Structure and Japan's Position), Anzen-Hosho
Mondai Kenkyukai (ed.), *Asia no Heiwa* (Peace in Asia) (Tokyo, 1972).

12. An international conference on "Economic and Political Development in Relation to Seapower along the Routes from the Indian Ocean" was organized by the
National Security Program of New York University and the National Strategy Information Center, Inc., in London (May 25–28, 1972). The conference report is
forthcoming.

13. This is a general statement that needs qualification, since in all non-zero-sum
games there may be found noncooperative as well as cooperative solutions. In a
trilateral (three-person game) setting, it can be shown that depending on the pay-off
matrix there are not only cases where all three parties prefer to play cooperative or
noncooperative but also cases where two of the three prefer either the cooperative or
the noncooperative strategy depending on the others' choice. An analysis of the
trilateral relations using the multiperson prisoner's dilemma paradigm developed by
Thomas C. Schelling may prove to be a very interesting exercise in showing the
difficulties of the trilateral relations. For this approach see: Schelling, Thomas C.,
"Hockey Helmets, Concealed Weapons, and Daylight Saving: A Study of Binary
Choices with Externalities," *Journal of Conflict Resolution*, 17, no. 3 (1973): 381–428.

14. The difference in the role perception among the three parts of the trilateral
context can be expected to create cognitive dissonance. According to the theory developed by Leon Festinger such dissonance should be accompanied by a pressure on
all concerned parties to reduce dissonance. However, in a trilateral context the reduction of dissonance between two parties often increases the dissonance between the
two and the third party. This makes the trilateral dissonance reduction process a very
difficult one. A trilateral dissonance reduction experiment may help the analysis of
the actual relations among the three groups: Japanese, Americans, and Europeans.
    Concerning cognitive dissonance theory, see: Festinger, Leon, *A Theory of Cognitive
Dissonance* (Stanford, California, 1957).

15. The definition of Japan as a late-comer is rejected by some Japanese, who do not
like the pejorative implication of the term. They prefer to contrast Japan's dynamic
growing economy with the mature, but more static, economy of the U.S. and Europe.
Since the oil crisis of 1973, the Japanese have become extremely sensitive to the fact
that their country is among the three industrial units the most vulnerable in terms of
its dependence on resources coming from the Third World.

16. An interesting analysis of the problem of burden-sharing in security matters can

be found in: Olson, Mancur Jr., and Zeckhauser, Richard, "An Economic Theory of Alliance," Russett Bruce M. (ed.), *Economic Theories of International Politics* (Chicago, 1966), pp. 25–45.

17. In this connection, it is important to take a linkage political approach in order to avoid overlooking the various regional, national, and subnational units participating in the trilateral interactions. Concerning linkage politics see, for example: Rosenau, James N., "Toward the Study of National-International Linkages", Rosenau, James N. (ed.), *Linkage Politics* (New York, 1969), pp. 44–63.

18. A important contribution to the theoretical study of the French position is: Holsti, Ole R. and Sullivan, John D., "National-International Linkages: France and China as Nonconforming Alliance Members," Rosenau, James N. (ed.), op. cit.

19. These factors have been studied at a conference on "Japan's Emerging Role in the International System and Japanese-American Relations in the 1970's-1980's." Study papers are forthcoming.

20. A few examples of the governmental and nongovernmental consultations that took place in 1973 within the trilateral framework are the following:

May: Japan-U.S.-E.C. Businessmen's Conference (Monte Carlo) NONGOV.
May: Japan-U.S. Working Level Conference on Security Problems (Tokyo) GOV.
June: Japan-U.S. Policy Planning Conference (Tokyo) GOV.
June: Japan-E.E.C. Conference—a working-level trade negotiation (Brussels) GOV.
June: Regular Meeting of Japan Committee for Economic Development (C.E.D./Japan and C.E.D./U.S.), (Kyoto) NON GOV.
June: Annual Japan-U.S. Businessmen's Conference (Washington, D.C.) NON GOV.
July: Regular Meeting of C.E.D./Japan and CEPES/West Germany (Frankfurt) NON GOV.
July: Seven Nation Economic Conference—CED/Japan, U.S. Great Britain, France, Australia, West Germany and Sweden. (Frankfurt) NON GOV.
July: Tanaka-Nixon Summit (Washington, D.C.) GOV.
September-October: Tanaka's visit to Europe. GOV.
October: Trilateral Commission Conference (Tokyo) NON GOV.
October: Conference of Asian Pacific Study Group (CED/Japan) and the UN Association of the U.S. (Williamsburg, Va.) NON GOV.

21. Concerning cultural differences in the bargaining process, see the author's experimentation report: Mushakoji, Kinhide, "Negotiation between the West and the non-West: The Results of a Cross-Cultural Experiment" International Peace Research Association, *Proceedings of the International Peace Research Association Second Conference*, vol. 1 (Assen, The Netherlands, 1968), pp. 208–231.

22. The efforts made primarily by the United States to link security issues with economic questions into a single package deal is to be understood as a countermeasure against the disconnection of different issue areas that occurred as a consequence of the multipolarization of world politics. See Mushakoji, Kinhide, "Takyoku-ka no Riron" (A Theory of Multipolarization), Nihon Kokusai Seiji Gaku-kai (ed.), *Kokusai-Shakai no Tōgō to Kōzō-Hendō*. (Integration and Change in International Society), (Tokyo, 1972), pp. 1–11.

23. For a general discussion of the externality theory applied to international political problems see, for example: Wellisz, Stanislaw, "On External Diseconomies and the Government-Assisted Invisible Hand," Russett Bruce (ed.), op. cit., pp. 68–80. Specifically on the application of the prisoner's dilemma model to the analysis of external diseconomies, see: Schelling, Thomas C., op. cit.

24. In this connection, it is important to review all the studies made about conflict formation and conflict escalation in the bipolar context. Although the North-South conflicts take a completely different form as to the means to coerce the other party, precious hints may be found as to where we should orient our research efforts in our attempt to understand this new type of conflict. A basic reference may still be: McNeil, Elton B. (ed.), *The Nature of Human Conflict* (Englewood Cliffs, N.J., 1965),

and Kelman, H. C., *International Behavior* (New York, 1965). More specifically, the studies made by Robert North and his associates on the origin of the First World War deserve special attention. See, for example: Holsti, Ole R. and North, Robert C., "The History of Human Conflict" in McNeil, Elton B. (ed.), op cit., pp. 155–171. Another interesting approach based on economic models of conflict can be found in: Boulding, Kenneth E., *Conflict and Defence: A General Theory* (New York, 1962).

Kan Ori

Japanese Public Opinion and Sino-Japanese Relations, 1969-1972*

1. Introduction

Normalizing diplomatic relations with Communist China was one of the most debated topics in postwar Japan. Underlying the issue was the fact that it was closely interwoven with Japanese domestic politics; while all the opposition parties more or less favored the restoration of diplomatic relations with mainland China, the governing Liberal Democratic Party (LDP, conservatives) had traditionally been antagonistic to Peking and at the same time had been friendly with the Nationalist Chinese government in Taiwan. Concern over this matter, furthermore, had increased due to international developments, such as the Nixon announcement (July, 1971) of his intended visit to Communist China; the admission of mainland China, and the simultaneous expulsion of the Taiwan government, by the United Nations (fall of 1971); and more dramatically, the actual visit of Nixon to mainland China in February of 1972. Thus, the Japanese public seems to have been exposed more intensely to this issue of normalizing diplomatic relations with the Peking regime

*I am grateful to the Institute of International Relations, Sophia University, for providing me with unpublished data from its *Kokusai Shakaikan ni Kansuru Seronchōsa*, which was conducted under the direction of Professor Joji Watanuki in May–June, 1972. I further wish to express my thanks to Professors Roger W. Benjamin (University of Minnesota), Frank C. Langdon (University of British Columbia), Shigeki Nishihira (Institute of Statistical Mathematics), Kinhide Mushakoji and David J. Wessels (both of Sophia University) for reading an earlier version of this paper and for their valuable comments. Portions of the material presented here also appear in my "Die chinesisch-japanischen Beziehungen im Spiegel der öffentlichen Meinung Japans," *Die Waage* (1972), pp. 144–148.

in 1971–1972 than ever before, and the Japanese people and government seem to have responded to these events in a rather sensitive manner.

This paper attempts to describe and analyze Japanese views on Sino-Japanese relations. For this purpose public opinion polls conducted by major newspapers, news agencies, a broadcasting corporation, and academic institutes are examined. While some of the data used in this paper are not comparable, in a strict sense, with others presented, my intention is not so much to provide a rigorous statistical analysis of Japanese public opinion over time as to report the general trend of Japanese opinion regarding this issue on the bases of the combined direction of poll data examined. First, I shall compare surveys taken by the same agency (e.g., *Asahi Shimbun, Mainichi Shimbun,* and so on), though even these are not comparable in the punctilious sense, since questions were changed somewhat and often categories were not identical. Second, wherever possible, I shall compare results of sets of surveys, particularly as regards age and party identification. The former is useful in analyzing the trends of Japanese public opinion, and the latter is important because this issue had been related to Japanese domestic party politics throughout the postwar era. Furthermore, the latter must be taken into consideration because political power in Japan is not equally distributed

Table 1.   Composition of the House of Representatives, 1969

	Percentage of Seats	Percentage of Votes
Liberal Democratic Party	59.2	47.7
Japan Socialist Party	18.5	21.4
Komeito	9.7	10.9
Democratic Socialist Party	6.4	7.7
Japan Communist Party	2.9	6.8
Minor Parties	—	0.2
Independents	3.3	5.3
Total:	100.0	100.0

Source: *Shūgiingiin sōsenkyo kekka-shirabe,* 1970.

among the five main parties. The House of Representatives from December, 1969, to December, 1972, was elected in 1969 with the distribution shown in Table 1. Third, on the bases of these analyses, I expect to present a general picture of Japanese public opinion on the normalization question from 1969 to 1972.[1]

2. Comparative Analysis of Opinion Polls

When asked whether Japan should have formal diplomatic intercourse with mainland China, 64 percent of the Japanese people responded affirmatively, while 11 percent answered negatively (others, 5 percent, and no answer, 20 percent) in a nationwide survey conducted in June, 1970, by the *Asahi Shimbun*, one of the major newspapers in Japan. It is of interest to note that while 62 percent of the Liberal Democratic supporters (conservatives) felt it necessary to reestablish formal governmental relations with Communist China, the percentage was higher in the case of the opposition parties: Socialists (JSP), 70 percent; Komeito, 74 percent; Democratic Socialist (DSP), 74 percent; and Communists (JCP), 85 percent.[2] In terms of age distribution, it is to be observed that an overwhelming majority (80 percent) of males in their twenties favored the normalization of ties with mainland China, whereas in all other age-sex groups the support was lower.

A year later, the situation had changed considerably. The percentage of those favoring diplomatic normalization jumped to 73 percent, and of those opposed decreased to 5 percent, according to a poll taken by the same newspaper in May, 1971. Moreover, if we were to limit the respondents to those who expressed interest in China, practically everyone (93 percent) was for the restoration of diplomatic relations with Communist China. It is further to be noted that seven out of every ten Liberal Democratic supporters (and Komeito supporters) favored normalization, whereas eight to nine persons out of ten who support the Japan Socialist, Democratic Socialist, and Japan Communist parties advocated such a course of action. As far as age-sex differences were concerned, an overwhelming number of males in their early twenties, forties and fifties favored the normalization.

Another national poll was taken by the *Asahi Shimbun* in the same year(August–September, 1971), after the Nixon announcement of his intended visit to Communist China. In this survey, it was found that 63 percent of the Japanese population desired that immediate steps be taken to normalize diplomatic relations with the communist regime (opposed, 11 percent, others, 6 percent, and no answer, 20 percent). Interestingly enough, 74 percent of male respondents in their twenties were for immediate negotiation. Though a linear causal relationship cannot be established on the basis of data provided by the *Asahi Shimbun* survey, one of the reasons for this sense of urgency among the Japanese populace was undoubtedly the move taken by the United States to establish friendly relations with mainland China.[3]

The *Mainichi Shimbun*, another major newspaper, conducted a more focused survey on "China and Chinese" in the spring of 1970. Though the phrasing of the questions was somewhat different, and thus an exact comparison is not possible, the *Mainichi Shimbun* findings seem to confirm those of the *Asahi Shimbun* in 1970. Specifically, 16 percent of the respondents advocated the immediate normalization of diplomatic relations with mainland China, 47 percent were of the opinion that relations should be normalized as soon as possible, and 23 percent favored gradual normalization. Only 4 percent felt it unnecessary to restore diplomatic relations with Communist China (others and no answer, 10 percent). It is noteworthy that those who were younger (respondents in their twenties, thirties and forties) favored normalization more often than did older people, and Liberal Democratic supporters were much less keen on establishing governmental relations with the Peking regime than any of the opposition parties. In addition, more JSP, JCP and Komeito supporters asked for the immediate normalization of ties than their DSP and LDP counterparts. However, it must be stressed that even in the case of the LDP supporters, a comfortable majority (60 percent) supported immediate and prompt ("as soon as possible") normalization positions.

The 1971 (September–October) survey of the *Mainichi Shim-*

bun followed essentially the same pattern: 17 percent of the respondents favored immediate normalization, 40 percent were for normalization "as soon as possible,"and 25 percent advocated gradual normalization. In other words, more than 80 percent were in favor of normalizing diplomatic relations with the mainland government, whereas only 5 percent felt it unnecessary to do so (others and no answer, 13 percent). It is interesting to observe that the support for normalization was evident at this time in all age and party groups.[4]

The 1971 NHK (Nippon Hōsō Kyōkai, Japan Broadcasting Corporation) poll, which was conducted after the Nixon announcement of his intended visit to Communist China, corroborated the trend shown by the *Asahi Shimbun* and *Mainichi Shimbun* surveys regarding the normalization question. About one-fourth (25.1 percent) of the NHK respondents favored immediate normalization of relations, while 59.3 percent were gradualists. Only 4 percent felt it unnecessary to reestablish formal diplomatic relations with mainland China, and 1.3 percent opposed any attempt at normalization in the future (do not know and no answer, 10.3 percent).[5] Furthermore, it is of interest to note that even though the *Mainichi Shimbun* repeated the 1970 survey in the spring of 1972, after the Nixon visit to Communist China, it did not even bother to ask about the question of normalization. Perhaps, by that time, the normalization question was already a dead issue. That is, an overwhelming number of the Japanese would have favored normalization anyway, and thus the question was of no interest to the newspaper.

In both the *Mainichi Shimbun* and NHK opinion polls cited, respondents who favored the normalization position were also asked why Japan should restore formal diplomatic relations with Communist China. The findings are shown in the Tables 2, 3 and 4.

Since multiple answers were possible in the *Mainichi Shimbun* surveys and were not possible in the NHK survey, since the percentage results of these surveys are furthermore not comparable because the number and contents of their categories were different, a rank-order comparison is presented here. It is of considerable interest to observe that two major reasons mentioned for the normalization of Sino-Japanese relations, in terms of rank-order

Table 2.   Reasons for Normalizing Diplomatic Relations with Communist China (*Mainichi Shimbun* Survey, 1970)

Reason Given	Rank Order	Percentage of Support
"The same language, the same culture" and being a neighbor	1	50
Don't let slip a big economic market	2	47
Will lag behind the general situation of the world	3	31
Since the war is not terminated	4	15
Apprehensive of being attacked	5	10
In agreement with communism	6	2
Others and no answer		4
Total: (Multiple answers possible)		159

Source: *Mainichi Shimbun,* April 30, 1970.

Table 3. Reasons for Normalizing Diplomatic Relations with Communist China (*Mainichi Shimbun* Survey, 1971)

Reasons Given	Rank Order	Percentage of Support
Neighbor country with deep relations from the past	1	53
Need to expand trade	2	49
Other countries are recognizing China	3	21
War is not terminated	4	13
Necessary to defend country (Japan)	5	12
Status as a big country	6	11
Nixon's announcement of visit to China	7	8
Actually governing mainland China	8	7
Others and no answer		3
Total: (Multiple answers possible)		177

Source: *Mainichi Shimbun,* October 18, 1971.

Table 4. Reasons for Normalizing Diplomatic Relations
with Communist China (NHK Survey, 1971)

Reasons Given	Rank Order	Percentage of Support
Being a neighbor, having deep ties from the old days	1	35.5
Not be one-sided toward the United States (Need to be independent of the United States)	2	19.5
Being a big economic market	3	19.2
Actually governing mainland China	4	8.5
Better not to have a conflict with a big military power	5	5.6
To atone for the war	6	5.3
Will lag behind the general situation of the world	7	4.2
Others		0.3
Don't know and no answer		1.8
Total:		99.9

Source: *Hōsō-bunka* (December, 1971), pp. 68–69.

importance, were (1) cultural affinity (long cultural ties) and
geographical proximity (being a neighbor) and (2) the economic
market. Similar results were obtained in the May, 1971 *Asahi
Shimbun* survey, the two top reasons being geographical proximity
and the necessity of trade.[6] The significance of these findings will
be discussed in the concluding section of this article.

One of the most critical issues associated with the normalization question, particularly from the perspective of Communist China, was how Japan viewed the position of Taiwan. Is it an integral
part of mainland China, or do the Japanese take the position that
both the Nationalist government in Taipei and the Communist
regime in Peking should be recognized as legitimate? On this
question, more recent surveys conducted by NHK and the *Asahi
Shimbun* are instructive.

The NHK respondents were asked what Japan should do about
Nationalist China when diplomatic relations with mainland China

were normalized. The results are revealing. At the time of the 1971 survey (after the Nixon announcement of his intended visit to Communist China), only one out of ten was in favor of severing relations with the Taiwan government, whereas approximately 40 percent of the respondents took a more deliberate position, contending that Japan should consider carefully its relations with Taiwan in accordance with the international situation, though it should proceed to normalize relations with Communist China; about 30 percent felt that Japan should not sacrifice the Nationalist government, though it should proceed with the restoration of diplomatic relations with mainland China. On the other hand, only 3.4 percent were in favor of retaining the present relation with Nationalist China, even at the cost of jeopardizing future diplomatic relations with Communist China (others, do not know and no answer, 18.6 percent).[7]

The ambivalent attitude of the Japanese people regarding the Taiwan question is also attested by the *Asahi Shimbun* data. In June, 1970, the *Asahi Shimbun* respondents were asked their position on a proposition that "severing relations with Taiwan cannot be helped, in order [for Japan] to normalize relations with Communist China." Only 19 percent responded affirmatively to the proposition, and 46 percent opposed (others, 10 percent, and no answer, 25 percent). It is noteworthy that twice as many respondents opposed the idea of severing relations with Taiwan, and that one-third were neither for nor against the proposition, thus indicating that the Japanese people in 1970 were not quite ready to cut off Taiwan in order to normalize governmental relations with Peking. In May, 1971, however, one out of every three persons (33 percent) interviewed by the *Asahi Shimbun* thought it necessary to take the position that the People's Republic of China is the only government representing China, and that Taiwan is a territory of mainland China (i.e., a one-China policy), in order to normalize Sino-Japanese diplomatic relations, while one out of every five persons (22 percent) rejected such a view (others, 10 percent and no answer, 35 percent). It was also found that more men than women were for the one-China policy, and, moreover, one-half of the respondents in their forties and 40 percent of those in their fifties favored such a position. Furthermore, according to the *Asahi Shimbun* of January 3, 1972, 27 percent of the Japanese people favored the early restoration of relations with Communist China and dissolution of the same with Nationalist China, whereas 18 percent were for the early normalization of ties with Communist China, though they did not want to sever relations with Taiwan. The percentage of those opposed to severing relations with Nationalist China, and at the same time not supporting the early normalization with mainland China, was 12 percent. On the other hand, when asked (in the same survey) their opinion on the proposition that "in order to restore diplomatic relations with mainland China, we must proceed immediately in the direction of dissolving the relationship between Japan and Taiwan," 34 percent responded affirmatively, and 32 percent answered negatively (others, 6 percent and no answer, 28 percent).[8]

Another important variable in assessing future Sino-Japanese relations is the extent to which Communist China was perceived as a military threat to Japan. The question is relevant since the governing conservative party (LDP) in general (though divergent views are also available among LDP members) had then a different view from the opposition parties regarding this issue. In the 1970 public opinion survey of the *Mainichi Shimbun*, respondents were asked whether or not they were afraid of nuclear armament by Communist China. Close to one-half (46 percent) were very afraid of China's nuclear armament, while one-third (32 percent) were somewhat afraid. On the other hand, those who were not afraid of nuclear armament by mainland China were in a minority: 14 percent of the respondents were not very afraid of it, and only 3 percent did not feel any threat at all. If we were to make the percentages dichotomous, four categories into two, it would indicate that 80 percent of Liberal Democratic supporters were afraid of China's nuclear armament, while 16 percent were not afraid. The division in other parties was as follows: in case of the supporters of the Japan Communist Party, 60–36 percent; the Japan Socialist Party, 76–21 percent; the Democratic Socialist Party, 81–19 percent; and Komeito, 85–11 percent. No significant pattern was found among different age groups. It is to be noted that no similar or identical question was asked in the 1971 or 1972 survey of the same newspaper.[9]

Still another interesting question posed in various surveys was which country the Japanese consider to be the country with which they must be most friendly. Responses to this question are, perhaps, most revealing of recent international developments. In the *Asahi Shimbun* surveys, respondents were asked to name only one country. In 1969, the United States, naturally enough in view of the special Japanese relationship with it ever since 1945, was the top country with 40 percent of the Japanese respondents supporting while China was a poor second with 10 percent. We saw a considerable change in late 1970. According to a survey conducted by the same paper in November, 1970, the United States was still at the top with 42 percent support, and China was second. It is noteworthy, however, that the percentage of support for China doubled to 21 percent, though the percentage support for other countries had not changed much. Even though results of the survey conducted in May, 1971, did not produce significant changes (the United States was the top country with 39 percent support, and the second niche was held by China with 21 percent support) it is of interest to note that those who favored the United States were more numerous among females in the age range from thirty to fifty, and among those who are engaged in the primary industries. On the other hand, China was favored most by the male population in their early twenties and in their fifties and above.

The rank order of the countries was reversed several months later. In the survey conducted in December, 1971, and reported in the *Asahi Shimbun* of January 3, 1972, China became the top country with 33 percent support, and the United States became the second country with 28 percent. (The remainder were distributed as follows: all countries, 5 percent; other Asian countries, 3 percent; North Korea, 1 percent; USSR, 1 percent; and no response, 28 percent.) It is particularly significant that the percentage support given to China tripled that of 1969. This change of position between the two top countries, *viz.*, the United States and China, was perhaps due to the changes in the international environment surrounding Communist China: by the time the latter poll was taken, Nixon had already announced his intention of visiting mainland China, and Communist China's membership in the United Nations was a *fait accompli*. Those who favored China

JAPANESE PUBLIC OPINION, 1969-1972　47

came most frequently from males of all age groups, females in their twenties, clerks, managers, those in tertiary services, and blue collar workers. Moreover, major reasons given by the respondents why Japan should be friendly with Communist China are interesing; the top reason cited was China's geographical proximity with Japan (being a neighbor), and the second most important reasons were its being a big country and the necessity of trade with mainland China.[10]

Somewhat supportive of the *Asahi Shimbun* findings were those of an NHK survey (1971). NHK, in a nationwide survey, asked the Japanese public toward which country (among the United States, the USSR and China) Japan should exert the greatest amount of effort politically in the future. The country most often named by the respondents was the United States (51.2 percent), while only 4.6 percent of them considered the USSR to be an important country in that sense. It is significant that one out of every three Japanese (31.4 percent) regarded Communist China to be one of the most important countries to deal with politically in the future (do not know and no answer, 12.7 percent).[11]

What I have thus far discussed are the Japanese responses to specific current issues related to Communist China and future Sino-Japanese relations. Now, I wish briefly to examine the residual general attitudes of the Japanese people toward the Chinese and China, as these will to a considerable extent define Japan's future relations with mainland China. In this regard, it is of interest to find out where the Chinese people are ranked in terms of the Japanese preference scale. Recent studies done by the Institute of Statistical Mathematics show that usually Americans are "liked" most often, and Chinese, along with people of the Pacific, Russians and Koreans, are among those "liked" least often. In terms of most "disliked," Koreans ranked first (72 percent in multiple answers), Russians were second (58 percent), and Chinese were third (40 percent). Thus, it is clear that the Japanese populace shows a rather strong antipathy toward the Chinese as an ethnic group. The institute surveys also indicate which national groups are thought to be superior by the Japanese. While the Japanese, Germans and Americans were considered superior, the Chinese were among the least "superior" ones cited by the

Japanese respondents in polls taken in 1958, 1963 and 1968.[12] In a similar vein, Jiji Tsushin asked its respondents to name three countries they most "disliked." It is to be observed that in April, 1963, the first was the USSR (43.8 percent), the second place was held by Communist China (31.3 percent), and the third niche was occupied by South Korea (21.3 percent), while figures for other countries were insignificant. In March, 1967, for example, Communist China was the country most "disliked" (43.4 percent), the USSR, second (36.1 percent), and South Korea, third (30.8 percent). In February, 1971, the ranking was as follows: the USSR (30.5 percent), Communist China (25.2 percent), North Korea (24.1 percent), and South Korea (14.0 percent).[13]

3. Age and Party Identification

To corroborate the sometimes noncomparable public opinion polls reported above, I present the following data with appropriate controls based on a survey conducted by the Institute of International Relations, Sophia University, in May–June, 1972. First, it is to be noted that the IIR findings confirm the general trend shown in the *Mainichi Shimbun* surveys of 1970 and 1971.[14] Thirteen percent of the respondents favored immediate normalization of relations with Communist China, whereas 38.6 percent were for prompt ("as soon as possible") normalization and 33.7 percent were gradualists. Again, only 1.5 percent of those interviewed felt it unnecessary to reestablish diplomatic relations with Peking (others, 0.6 percent and do not know, 12.5 percent).

I will now examine a series of tables in which the relationship between some selected independent variables and the dependent variable, namely, various positions on the normalization question, is indicated. In the 1970 *Mainichi Shimbun* poll, it is to be recalled, those who were younger were more frequently in favor of normalizing diplomatic relations with mainland China than those who were older. In the 1972 IIR survey, we find slight variations among various age groups in the immediate normalization column

Table 5. Age and Normalization of Diplomatic Relations with Communist China (IIR Survey of 1972)

Age	N	Immediate Normalization	Prompt Normalization	Gradual Normalization	No Need to Normalize	Others	DK
15–19	337	15.7	37.7	36.5	2.1	—	8.0
20–29	756	13.4	41.1	33.7	1.3	0.8	9.7
30–39	801	15.2	37.3	36.5	1.5	0.9	8.6
40–49	554	11.9	40.4	32.9	0.9	0.5	13.4
50–59	442	10.6	41.2	32.4	2.5	0.7	12.7
60 above	414	9.7	32.1	29.0	1.2	0.2	27.8
Average %		13.0	38.6	33.7	1.5	0.6	12.5

Table 6. Age and Normalization of Diplomatic Relations with Communist China (IIR Survey of 1972)

Age	N	Immediate Normalization	Prompt Normalization	Gradual Normalization	No Need to Normalize	Others	DK
15–34	1,493	14.6	38.9	35.2	1.6	0.6	9.1
35–above	1,811	11.7	38.4	32.5	1.4	0.6	15.4
Average %		13.0	38.6	33.7	1.5	0.6	12.5

in Table 5. However, when we collapse age groups into two—prewar and postwar educated people—it is found that there is no meaningful relationship between age and positions taken on the normalization question (Table 6). Likewise, if we make positions on the normalization scale dichotomous, collapsing immediate and prompt ("as soon as possible") categories as well as gradual and "no need" categories, we find no significant differences among various age groups. The same can be said generally when we control for both age and sex (even though we see slight variations in the immediate normalization column, this is offset by other factors). Thus, age is found to be relatively insignificant in the IIR study, as was the case in the 1971 *Mainichi Shimbun* findings. Table 7 relates party identification and the normalization question. Here, LDP supporters show a clearly contrasting pattern in their responses to the normalization issue from the pattern shown by supporters of all other parties. For example, twice as many non-Liberal Democrats as Liberal Democrats advocated the immediate normalization of relations with mainland China, and conversely, twice as many LDP supporters as non-Liberal Democrats favored gradual normalization. It is further to be noted in this conjunction that results of the IIR findings are more discriminating than those of the 1970 *Mainichi Shimbun* survey but similar to the 1971 *Mainichi Shimbun* poll findings. Again similar patterns were obtained when the normalization question was measured against a much broader conservative-leftist dichotomy: 21.3 percent of the leftists, in contrast to 10.9 percent of the conservatives, favored the immediate restoration of diplomatic relations with the Communist regime in Peking, while twice as many conservatives (41.3 percent) as leftists (22.5 percent) were gradualists. Furthermore, considerably more leftists (49.9 percent) advocated

Table 7. Party Identification and Normalization of Diplomatic Relations with Communist China (IIR Survey of 1972)

Party Identification	N	Immediate Normalization	Prompt Normalization	Gradual Normalization	No Need to Normalize	Others	DK
LDP	985	9.7	35.6	41.3	2.3	0.6	10.4
JSP	539	18.0	49.5	26.2	0.6	—	5.8
Komeito	115	23.5	38.3	23.5	1.7	0.9	12.2
DSP	119	18.5	47.1	33.6	—	—	0.8
JCP	54	20.4	37.0	29.6	1.9	—	11.1
Others	9	22.2	66.7	11.1	—	—	—
No party to support	1,277	12.5	37.0	33.1	1.4	1.0	15.0
DK	206	7.3	29.1	29.1	1.5	—	33.0
Average %	3,304	13.0	38.6	33.7	1.5	0.6	12.5

the prompt normalization than conservatives (36.9 percent).[15]

Perhaps variables like education and levels of concern for international affairs are most closely related to the quality of public opinion leadership in external affairs, as only those who are informed and concerned about international affairs will have a potential influence on their government's foreign policy making. Tables 8 and 9 have been prepared to illustrate the relationship between these two variables and positions in the normalization scale. Data in Table 8 seem to confirm the proposition that the higher the level of education, the more progressive the respondents became in their position on this issue. In this respect, the *Mainichi Shimbun* findings are also very similar to those of the IIR. Likewise, Table 9 shows that levels of concern for international affairs are, as expected, significantly related to the various groupings on the normalization question. Obviously, Japanese opinion leaders in foreign affairs were in favor of taking more positive steps to normalize diplomatic relations with Communist China than those Japanese who had less concern for international affairs and/or were less educated.

Table 8. Education Level and Normalization of Diplomatic Relations with Communist China (IIR Survey of 1972)

Education Level	N	Immediate Normalization	Prompt Normalization	Gradual Normalization	No Need to Normalize	Others	DK
College graduate	262	18.7	46.2	32.1	—	1.1	1.9
High school graduate	1,301	13.3	40.6	36.4	1.4	0.6	77.7
Middle school graduate	1,430	10.8	35.2	31.7	1.8	0.6	19.8
Average %		13.0	38.6	33.7	1.5	0.6	12.5

Total "N" (3,304) includes 14 persons not applicable, as well as 297 high school and college students.

Table 9. Level of Concern for International Affairs and Normalization of Diplomatic Relations with Communist China (IIR Survey of 1972)

Level of Concern for International Affairs	N	Immediate Normali- zation	Prompt Normali- zation	Gradual Normali- zation	No Need to Nor- malize	Others	DK
Very interested	779	21.3	43.0	31.3	1.3	0.4	2.7
Interested a little	1,704	11.8	42.3	35.6	1.2	0.5	8.7
Hardly interested	562	8.0	32.4	35.8	2.5	1.1	20.3
Not at all interested	216	6.9	13.9	26.9	2.8	0.9	48.6
Average%		13.0	38.6	33.7	1.5	0.6	12.5

*Total (3,304) include 43 persons not applicable.

To reiterate, some independent variables such as party identification, conservative-leftist dichotomy, education and concern for international affairs are found to be significantly related to the normalization issue in the IIR findings. Despite these facts, however, it must be emphasized once more that in the IIR study (as well as others presented in this paper) a great number of the LDP supporters favored immediate or prompt ("as soon as possible") normalization with mainland China. The same holds true with reference to the left-right axis, age, sex, occupation, education, social class and concern for international affairs variables.[16]

4. A General Picture

Regarding the normalization of diplomatic relations with Communist China, there was a considerable shift in public attitude in the period covered in this study. This trend may be better ascertained by contrasting the data presented here with survey results of the 1960s. Several public opinion surveys conducted in the sixties show that the percentage of those favoring the normalization of Sino-Japanese diplomatic relations during those years was much lower than now, and in fact, the percentage has doubled in some cases.[17] It is to be added that much higher figures were obtained after the alteration of American policy toward China.

In a recent study, Professor George P. Jan reviewed 1951–1968 public opinion data on Sino-Japanese relations, and concluded that the majority of those who voiced an opinion on China were in favor of a two-China policy in general, and that while many of them felt the need to reestablish diplomatic relations with Communist China, few wanted to sever relations with Nationalist China on Taiwan.[18] We also found considerable change in this regard: this chapter shows, for example, that now practically one out of every three persons accepted a one-China policy in some form, with significant numbers of the respondents willing to sacrifice Taiwan in order to normalize relations with Peking.[19] Another salient aspect of the 1951–1968 poll data, according to Jan, was the large percentage of respondents who were in the don't know–no answer category.[20] It is of interest to note that the percentages in the don't know–no answer category decreased appreciably in 1969–1972 period as seen throughout this study.

Dr. Shigeki Nishihira of the Institute of Statistical Mathematics in Tokyo is of the opinion that this rather sudden increase of positive percentages toward friendly Sino-Japanese relations is most likely due to the unfolding of international events, especially recent initiatives taken by the United States.[21] I further feel that this shift of attitude among the Japanese public is related to its changing perception of US-Japanese relations. Hitherto, the reader will recall, the United States was the top country with which the Japanese wanted to be most friendly; but after the American rapprochement with Peking over the head of Japan, which traditionally followed the American policy toward China, the rank-order was reversed, and China became the top country.

Even with this shift in public attitude toward normalization, the future of Sino-Japanese relations may be thorny. First, as indicated in this chapter, residual Japanese attitudes toward the Chinese and China are not too favorable. Secondly, sources of possible future difficulties in Sino-Japanese relations may be found by an examination of the major reasons cited by the Japanese populace for the restoration of diplomatic relations with Communist China. It is to be recalled that the top reason was China's cultural and geographical proximity. Although such proximity is an objective fact, it is too simplistic a basis from which to predict future friendly relations between Peking and Tokyo. For one, the Japanese notion of "the same language, the same culture" may be illusory from the Chinese point of view. Furthermore, much of the Japanese image of China, I am afraid, is based on emotional feelings rather than facts. And to confound the problem, not many of them are aware of life in the new China after the revolution. More often than not, their perception of China is derived from their nostalgic knowledge of the old China. This is particularly true of those past their mid-forties who experienced the Sino-Japanese and Pacific wars. (It should be remembered that higher percentages of the male respondents in their forties and fifties supported the normalization of diplomatic relations with mainland China.)

The primacy of Japanese concern for economic matters in diplomacy is still another problem. The Japanese public wants to restore diplomatic relations with Communist China, as shown in this chapter, because China is potentially a good economic market for Japan, and at the same time could provide raw materials. In fact this was precisely the predicament of the China policy of the (conservative) regime of Eisaku Sato, who resigned in 1972. Since the early 1950s, the China policy of conservative governments was based on the "separation of politics from economics," but holding to this position became increasingly difficult, as Peking continued to ask for more and more political concessions, using trade as the inducement. Thus, Japan will be forced in the future to take a more definite political posture, beyond mere economic considerations in its attempt to normalize relations with Communist China.[22]

Throughout this study, it was found that party identification was significantly related to the respondents' position on the normalization question. In this conjunction, it is to be observed that Japanese opposition parties were particularly active in these years. In February, 1971, the Japan Socialist Party established a National Congress for the Restoration of Diplomatic Relations Between Japan and Communist China for the specific purpose of mobilizing the public. Of course, the party had been in favor of recognizing the Peking government and severing relations with Taiwan, since it regarded Taiwan as an integral part of mainland China. It is further to be noted that the Socialists had sent several official missions to Communist China since 1957, the last one during the summer of 1972.

More significant are the activities of Komeito and the Democratic Socialist Party. Komeito organized a National Council for Normalization of Relations Between Japan and Communist China, in December, 1970, to launch a nationwide campaign to improve Sino-Japanese relations. It also sent three missions to Peking in 1971–1972. These activities of Komeito are particularly noteworthy, because its position on Taiwan had previously been ambivalent. In the late spring of 1972, even the Democratic Socialist Party, which had hitherto lacked significant direct contacts with the Communist regime, sent a delegation to China. But, the Japan Communist Party, which was reported to be pro-Peking before 1966, was extremely cool toward China, even though it did not change its basic China policy, that is, favoring the normalization of Sino-Japanese ties and the return of Taiwan to mainland China. This perhaps explains the high percentages of support shown for normalization by JCP supporters, even though the future relationship between the People's Republic of China and the JCP is still difficult to predict. This is particularly so because in late August, 1972, the Peking government openly attacked the JCP as opposed to the normalization of diplomatic relations with it, grouping the JCP with the right wing forces in Japan.

On the other hand, until the end of the Sato regime the governing Liberal Democratic Party had not altered its basic posture toward Communist China, which it had held ever since 1955 (when the present LDP came into existence). Under Sato (i.e., from November, 1964, to July, 1972), governmental action (or inaction) to normalize diplomatic relations with mainland China lagged considerably behind Japanese public opinion. As a matter of fact, the Japanese public itself sensed this gap between its expectation and governmental actions.[23]

With the advent of Kakuei Tanaka as premier in July, 1972, however, there came a shift in the governmental position regarding the normalization of Sino-Japanese relations. As if to symbolize a new era, Takeo Miki, one of the factional leaders of the LDP who visited mainland China even while Sato was in power, joined the Tanaka cabinet (deputy premier); and both Tanaka and the incumbent minister of foreign affairs, Masayoshi Ohira, were eager to restore Japan's formal ties with the Communist regime. Tanaka and Ohira have visited Peking (the Peking government welcomed Tanaka's visit and officially invited him to mainland China in mid-August, 1972), and the Tanaka government restored governmental relations with Communist China, severing, at the same time, its official diplomatic connection with Nationalist China in Taiwan. Furthermore, the Japanese government reversed its "separation of politics from economics" policy. Even though this is a drastic change of China policy from the Sato era (and preceding conservative governments), Tanaka was capable of adjusting intraparty conflicts of interest over the China question.[24]

At any rate, one thing is clear: when Tanaka took action on normalization, his action was supported by the public. It is well to recall, as shown in this chapter, that a comfortable majority of the Japanese populace favored the restoration of relations with Peking, and even among supporters of the Liberal Democratic Party a great number of them desired to expedite the normalization process with Communist China. Moreover, indications are that the Japanese people, in so far as their opinions are reflected in public opinion polls, expected the government to alter its traditional policy toward mainland China and take more positive steps to restore diplomatic relations with the Peking government.[25]

5. Conclusion

The above portion of this chapter was written in mid-August, 1972, prior to the normalization of diplomatic relations with the People's Republic of China, which was accomplished through a dramatic visit there by Japanese Premier Tanaka and Foreign

Minister Ohira in late September, 1972. There was also a general election for the House of Representatives in December of the same year, the first such election confronting Tanaka since he came to power the preceding July. Results of the elections are shown in Table 10.[26]

Table 10. Composition of the House of Representatives, 1972

Party	Percentage of Seats	Percentage of Votes
Liberal Democratic Party	57.8	46.8
Japan Socialist Party	24.0	21.9
Japan Communist Party	7.9	10.5
Komeito	5.9	8.5
Democratic Socialist Party	4.0	7.0
Minor Parties	—	0.3
Independents	0.2	5.0

Source: *Shūgiingiin sōsenkyo kekka-shirabe*, 1973.

The survey of Japanese public opinion related to Sino-Japanese relations provided in this chapter (in sections I–IV) is a part of a larger and more comprehensive study of postwar Sino-Japanese relations within the theoretical framework of linkage politics.[27] Intended as the next project is a content analysis of major Japanese newspapers. News reporting and editorials of the *Asahi Shimbun, Mainichi Shimbun, Yomiuri Shimbun,* and *Nihon Keizai Shimbun* will be covered for the period from 1969 to 1972.

As a preliminary step toward such a study, Professor Kinhide Mushakoji (Sophia University) and I have completed a content analysis of one newspaper, the *Asahi Shimbun,* for a short period of sixteen weeks (July 7 to October 28, 1972). Even though we have analyzed only editorials thus far, the period under study includes three critical events: (1) the birth of the Tanaka cabinet on July 7—the beginning of the first period, (2) the official invitation of the Chinese government for Tanaka to visit Peking issued on August 12—the beginning of the second period, and (3) the actual visit of Tanaka and the subsequent normalization of diplomatic relations between mainland China and Japan on September 29—the beginning of the third period.

Our findings indicate that Sino-Japanese relations weve most frequently mentioned during the second period, and the attention level of the *Asahi* editorials to Sino-Japanese relations declined after normalization. On the other hand, the amount of attention paid to American-Japanese relations decreased sharply after Japan's restoration of diplomatic relations with the Peking government. In terms of the evaluational direction, it is interesting to observe that the negative image of the United States drastically increases in the second period (14 percent in the first period, 40 percent in the second period and 13 percent in the third period). At the same time, the plus-evaluation of Communist China steadily and manifestly gains strength throughout the three periods: of all evaluational directions, (positive, neutral and negative) only 4 percent was positive in the first period, whereas positive evaluations of Communist China jumped to 16 percent in the second period and further, to 50 percent, after normalization in the third period.[28]

While the tentative nature of our findings in this pilot study must be stressed, it is noteworthy that the normalization of relations between Peking and Tokyo seem to have affected both Sino-Japanese and American-Japanese relations rather significantly.

1. For a review of public opinion data on Sino-Japanese relations from 1951 to 1968, see George P. Jan, "Public Opinion's Growing Influence on Japan's China Policy," *Journalism Quarterly* (Spring, 1971), pp. 111–119. The same author also provided a general survey of the relationship between Japan's China policy and its domestic party politics in "Party Politics and Japan's Policy toward Communist China," *Orbis* (Winter, 1971), pp. 973–991.

2. This high rate of support among the Communists for the restoration of diplomatic ties with mainland China is interesting, as the Japan Communist Party had not been so anxious to normalize relations with Peking. See also the concluding section of this study.

3. The *Asahi Shimbun* surveys citied here were conducted in September, 1969, June and November, 1970, May, August–September, and December, 1971, and reported in the same paper on October 1, 1969, June 23, 1970, January 14, June 3, September 21, 1971 and January 3, 1972, respectively. Data are also reported in Shinji Futagami, "Seronchōsa kara mita wakai-sedai to chūgoku-ajia", *Asian Review*, Tokyo (February, 1972), pp. 88–95. The *Asahi Shimbun* used the stratified random sampling, interview method, covering all Japan above twenty years of age (sometimes including Okinawa),

and the sample size was three thousand each time. The percentages of valid returns for the surveys reported here ranged from 83 percent to 87 percent.

4. The *Mainichi Shimbun* polls cited here were conducted in March, 1970; September– October 1971; and April 1972 and reported in the same newspaper on April 30, 1970, October 18, 1971, and May 3, 1972. Its 1970 survey used the random sampling, interview method, covering all Japanese over twenty years old, with a 3,000 person sample, and 70.6 percent valid returns. The 1971 survey was based on the stratified random sampling of 5,578 persons above the age of twenty (interview method) with the 73 percent valid returns. The 1972 poll had a sample of 3,015 persons, and the percentage of valid returns was 74. It employed the stratified random sampling, interview method, covering all Japanese including Okinawans over twenty years old.

5. The NHK survey was conducted in September, 1971, and reported in *Hōsō Bunka* (December, 1971), pp. 68–69 as "Nihonjin no kokusaikankaku ni kansuru seronchō-sa". Its sample was 3,600 persons covering all Japan (the percentage of valid returns, 70.1 percent). It used the simple random sampling, interview method.

6. NHK, *ibid.*; the *Mainichi Shimbun, op. cit.*; the *Asahi Shimbun, op. cit.*

7. NHK, *op. cit.*

8. The *Asahi Shimbun, op. cit.*

9. The *Mainichi Shimbun, op. cit.*

10. The *Asahi Shimbun, op. cit.*

11. NHK, *op. cit.*

12. Institute of Statistical Mathematics, *Nihonjin no kokuminsei* (Tokyo: Shiseido, 1970), particularly p. 338, Table 128; *Nihōnjin no kokuminsei* (2) (Tokyo: Shiseido, 1970); and Research Report, General Series, no. 23, p. 154.

13. Naikakusōridaijin kanbo kohoshitsu, ed., *Seronchosa nenkan* (1964–68 editions) and Sorifu kohoshitsu, ed., *Gekkan seronchōsa* (April, 1971). The sample of the Jiji Tsushin polls was 1,250 persons. Its survey covered all Japanese over twenty years old, and its percentages of valid returns ranged from 75.9 to 83.4 percent for the study reported here.

14. The Institute of International Relations, Sophia University (Tokyo, Japan) survey was conducted in May–June, 1972. The institute used the stratified random sampling, interview method, with a sample of 4,000 persons covering all Japanese over fifteen years of age. The percentage of valid returns was 82.6 percent. Incidentally, the structured categories of the IIR survey on the normalization questions were identical with those of the *Mainichi Shimbun* survey of 1970.

15. The IIR respondents were asked to identify themselves on the conservative-leftist (progressive) axis, and this variable was crossed with responses to the normalization question.

16. Needed were more of the IIR type studies that are stratified by area, age, occupation, etc., asking identical questions replicable over time panels, in order to make meaningful time series analysis. For a detailed discussion of the importance of age as an explanatory variable, see Kenneth Prewitt, *The Recruitment of Political Leaders* (Indianapolis: The Bobbs-Merrill Co., Inc., 1970) and Kan Ori, "Amerikagashukoku ni okeru gunkenjishoku no seijıteki seikaku ichikosatsu," *Amerika Kenkyu*, Vol. 7 (1973).

17. See, for example, the Jiji Tsushin survey of 1964, which reported that 38.3 percent and 31.7 percent of its respondents were for Japan's recognition of Communist China in February and March respectively (Naikaku sōridaijin kanbo kohoshitsu, ed., *Seronchosa nenkan*, 1964, p. 220), as well as the 1967 survey of the Kyodo Tsushin, which showed that 33.6 percent of its respondents favored the "rather soon" normalization of relations with Peking (Naikaku sōridaijin kanbo kohoshitsu, ed., *Seronchōsa nenkan*, 1968, p. 419).

18. George P. Jan, "Public Opinion's Growing Influence on Japan's China Policy," *Journalism Quarterly* (Spring, 1971), pp. 111–119.

19. Likewise, it is noteworthy that according to the June, 1970, *Asahi Shimbun* survey 67 percent of its respondents were for the admission of Communist China to the

United Nations, and 9 percent opposed (others, 4 percent and no answer, 20 percent), whereas the December, 1961, Chūō Chōsa-sha poll cited by Jan showed that "33% favored the admission of Communist China to the United Nations, 8% opposed, and 60% did not know." (Jan, *op. cit.*, p. 117). The September–October, 1971, *Mainichi Shimbun* data show that 78 percent favored the admission of the People's Republic of China to the United Nations and 6 percent opposed (others and no answer, 16 percent).

20. Jan, *op. cit.*

21. Interview with Dr. Shigeki Nishihira on July 26, 1972.

22. Often neglected, in conjunction with this problem, is the possibility of Japan's having a conflict of economic interest with China in Southeast Asia. Professor Michio Royama thinks that this is one of the most critical areas in future Sino-Japanese relations. (See, Michio Royama, "Naze chūgoku o shonin subekika", *Chūō Kōron*, February, 1971.)

23. See, e.g., the *Mainichi Shimbun* surveys of September–October, 1971, and April, 1972. They showed that 61 percent and 68 percent of the respondents respectively felt either an extreme or a considerable gap between their government's China policy and their own (*Mainichi Shimbun*, October 18, 1971, and May 3, 1972).

24. Regarding the factional elements involved in the LDP's China policy, see Frank C. Langdon, "Japanese Liberal Democratic Factional Discord on China Policy", *Pacific Affairs* (Fall, 1968), pp. 403–15. On the factional nature of Japanese politics, consult Roger W. Benjamin and Kan Ori, "Factionalism in Japanese Politics", *Annual Review* (Tokyo: Japan Institute of International Affairs, 1969–70), pp. 76–91.

25. See, the IIR survey of May–June, 1972, in which its respondents were asked to identify how close they were to the following two contrasting views: (A) It is necessary for the Japanese government to change its previous actions (and policies) and to negotiate with the Communist government in China more earnestly; (B) Since the actions (and policies) of the Japanese government have not been incorrect, we will just wait for an approach to be made by mainland China. The results were as follows: close to the A opinion, 34.2 percent; rather close to the A opinion, 24.3 percent; cannot say either way, 14.4 percent; rather close to the B opinion, 4.2 percent; close to the B opinion, 3.8 percent; others, 0.7 percent and no answer, 18.3 percent.

26. In conjunction with this article, it is interesting that Komeito, which had been instrumental in the normalization of diplomatic relations with Peking, suffered a considerable setback in this election and that of three prominent proponents for prompt normalization within the LDP camp, two were defeated in this election and the third did not do well at all. As to probable reasons for this, we may hypothesize that foreign policy issues are not usually directly related to the electoral outcome in Japan and that at this election public concern shifted to other issues; however, we have no empirical data to corroborate or disprove these hypotheses.

27. See Abravanel, Martin, and Hughes, Barry, "Public Opinion and Foreign Policy Behavior: A Cross-National Study of Linkages," a paper presented to the annual meeting of the International Studies Association, Dallas, Texas, U.S.A., March 17, 1972. Cf. J.S. Hoadly and S. Hasegawa, "Sino-Japanese Relations, 1950–1970: An Application of the Linkage Model of International Politics," *International Studies Quarterly* (1971), pp. 131—157.

28. The August, 1972, survey of the *Asahi Shimbun* as to the country toward which Japan must be most friendly showed that China was the top country, with 38 percent support, and the United States continued to be the second country, with 29 percent support. It is to be noted that, while the support for the United States was almost identical in the previous survey of December, 1971, the support for China increased 5 percent, thus widening the difference between China and the United States (*Asahi Shimbun*, September 18, 1972). See also pp. 46–48 of this article. For content analysis of Japanese newspapers see Kokusaibunkakaikan (ed.), *Nichibeikankei no kenkyu* (Tokyo: University of Tokyo Press, 1970).

Yusaku Furuhashi

Evolving Japanese Policy Toward Inward Foreign Direct Investment in the Postwar Period

1. Introduction

"The growth of the Japanese economy in the past ten years has been one of the most extraordinary economic stories of all times . . . with the aid of an economic policy that has been singularly little studied in the West."[1]

"For American eyes Japan is now 'the last Garden of Eden for investment' . . ."[2]

"Japan is the country which par excellence has resisted foreign investment . . ."[3]

These quotes embrace the seemingly discordant elements of admiration, hope, frustration, and bewilderment of the Western-ers' business dealings with Japan. They involve the gist of the underlying issues with which the present article tries to deal. Specifically, it deals with five topics: (1) status of foreign direct investments in Japan as of fiscal year 1971;[4] (2) major policy developments in the postwar period; (3) the dominant current controversial issues; (4) key factors underlying Japanese attitudes; and (5) the future outlook.

2. Foreign Investment in Japan

With a large and rapidly expanding domestic market of its own and comparatively easy access to the other markets in the

Table 1. Introduction of Foreign Investment Validated [1]

Fiscal Year	Total	Acquisition of Stock & Proprietary Interest	Participation in Management [2]	Beneficiary Certificate	Debenture	Claimable Assets Arising from Loans	External Bonds Issued
(1949–1950)	3,150	3,150	2,572	—	—	—	—
(1951)	17,352	13,326	11,646	—	—	4,026	—
(1952)	44,751	10,123	7,166	146	25	34,457	—
(1953)	54,926	5,002	2,687	562	—	49,362	—
(1954)	19,307	3,970	2,467	58	—	15,279	—
(1955)	52,214	5,101	2,309	52	7	47,054	—
(1956)	103,302	9,520	5,360	115	15	93,652	—
(1957)	135,597	11,490	7,282	128	—	123,979	—
(1958)	272,967	11,350	3,698	116	28	231,473	30,000
(1959)	154,890	27,031	14,561	214	30	127,615	9,800
(1960)	211,658	74,151	31,593	555	20	127,132	—
(1961)	577,529	116,142	40,170	1,280	77	387,605	72,425

(1962)	678,823	164,668	22,619	650	86	358,419	155,000
(1963)	884,302	185,262	42,656	798	247	503,945	194,050
(1964)	912,784	84,845	30,645	1,828	851	650,760	174,500
(1965)	528,506	83,331	44,643	398	2,726	379,551	62,500
(1966)	457,097	126,735	39,812	390	261	329,711	—
(1967)	847,787	159,936	29,778	284	123	637,544	50,000
(1968)	1,836,645	670,008	52,701	253	32	947,372	218,980
(1969)	3,488,240	2,462,897	53,777	233	524	789,602	234,984
(1970)	2,525,913	1,542,228	75,272	335	25,108	838,557	119,685
TOTAL	13,807,740	5,770,166	523,414	8,395	30,160	6,677,095	1,321,924

NOTE: [1] Including reinvestments.   [2] Exceptions are cases where the total number of stocks held by all foreign investors is (1) 15 percent or less in the restricted industry group category, and (2) below 25 percent in the nonrestricted industry group category but where the ratio of the total number of stocks held by one foreign investor is 7 percent or less than the total stock issue and where in the above cases (1) and (2) acquisition of stock is made without participation by the foreign investor in the management by sending a director. (The above-mentioned alteration has applied since September 1, 1970. Note that the ratio of the acquisition of shares of stocks has been changed several times in the past as will be explained in the sections that follow.)

SOURCE: Based on the Bank of Japan, *Economic Statistics Annual, 1967*, p. 258; and *Economic Statistics Annual, 1970* (Tokyo: Bank of Japan, 1968, and 1971), p. 242.

Pacific basin area, Japan, the only highly industrialized country in Asia, offers many attractive features for foreign investors. A population of over 100 million people, a high degree of political stability and a remarkably vigorous and dynamic economy make Japan an undisputed major industrial country. The nation's GNP at about $200 billion has been second in the free world only to that of the United States since the late 1960's. Japan has a well-educated, highly trained, hardworking and well-disciplined technical and labor force. But despite these obviously attractive features that Japan offers to potential foreign investors, by Western standards and experience foreign direct investment played a comparatively minor role in the economy in the postwar years.

Magnitude of Foreign Investment in Japan

Since the reopening of Japanese markets to foreign investment in 1949, the induction of foreign capital has been carried out systematically. A number of laws, cabinet orders and administrative guidelines play significant roles in the orderly induction of foreign capital and technology into Japan. As seen in table 1, the cumulative book value of all types of foreign investment introduced into Japan since 1949 stood at $13,808 million at the end of 1970.

Several notable features may be observed from the table. Total "acquisition of stock and proprietary interest" amounting to $5,770 million accounts for 41.8 percent of the total foreign capital inflow during this period, with the rest in some form of loan. Particularly noteworthy is the amount of "acquisition with participation in management," with the total of $523 million accounting for 3.8 percent of total validated foreign investment. Such a limited amount of direct foreign investment in Japan is due largely to the highly restrictive policy that the Japanese government consciously followed throughout much of the postwar period (until recently). With the stepped-up program of liberalization of foreign capital investment in Japan started in 1967 and culminated in the implementation of the fourth and final round on August 4, 1971, it may reasonably be expected that considerable expansion in this category is foreseeable in the years immediately ahead. In fact, the rate of foreign capital influx registered since 1968 seems to indicate that the liberalization measures have begun to take effect, as can be observed in table 1.

In discussing the volume of foreign direct investment, we must include also the so-called yen-basis investments in subsidiaries, joint ventures or wholly owned branches made between October, 1956, and June, 1963. During this period residents of certain foreign countries were completely free to make yen-basis investments in nonrestricted industries, which, for all intents and purposes, were then treated like any resident-owned investments but did not enjoy transfer rights for income or liquidation proceeds. No permission was needed to bring in funds, and no records were kept, but, under a regulation of the Ministries of Finance and International Trade and Industry, foreign investors who had chosen this method were requested, in 1963, to submit data by the end of January, 1964, which revealed the existence of 289 yen-based branches with a total nominal capital of about $140 million.[5] No official information or estimate is available concerning yen-basis investment that might not have been reported, resulting in divergent views expressed by experts.

Another noteworthy feature is the zeal with which Japan has been introducing foreign technology in the postwar years. As seen in table 2, Japanese firms signed 13,228 patent and technological licensing contracts with foreign firms in the 1949–69 period, for which they paid a total sum of $2.2 billion. Until the initiation of the capital liberalization program in 1967, with a few exceptional years, Japanese firms paid substantially more for technological licenses acquired than foreigners paid for acquisition of stocks and proprietary interest in Japan. Introduction of foreign technology through licensing agreements undoubtedly played a critical role in the modernization of the Japanese economy and the development of highly technically oriented modern industries such as petrochemicals, chemicals and electronics.

Inward direct investment and the importation of intellectual property are nevertheless often linked. Although no clearly discernible trends are observable yet in the table, the share of foreign technology introduction via outright licensing agreements, as contrasted with some form of foreign capital participation, can be expected to decline due to the desire of foreign firms to partake in

Table 2.   Introduction of Industrial Techniques

Fiscal	Class A	Class B	Total	U.S. $ million
(1949–1950)	27	49	76	3
(1951)	101	87	188	7
(1952)	133	110	243	10
(1953)	103	133	236	14
(1954)	82	131	213	16
(1955)	72	113	185	20
(1956)	143	167	310	33
(1957)	118	136	254	43
(1958)	90	152	242	48
(1959)	153	225	378	62
(1960)	327	261	588	95
(1961)	320	281	601	113
(1962)	328	429	757	114
(1963)	564	573	1,137	136
(1964)	500	541	1,041	156
(1965)	472	486	958	167
(1966)	601	552	1,153	192
(1967)	638	657	1,295	239
(1968)	1,061	683	1,744	314
(1969)	1,154	475	1,629	368
Total	6,987	6,241	13,228	2,150

NOTE: "Class A" are cases where the term of contract or that of payments exceeds one year and payments are made in foreign currency (Law Concerning Foreign Investment). "Class B" are cases where the term of contract is one year or less, and if it exceeds one year, payments are made in yen currency (Foreign Exchange and Foreign Trade Control Law).

SOURCE: Based on the Bank of Japan, Statistics Department, *Economic Statistics Annual, 1967*, p. 258; and *Economic Statistics Annual, 1970* p. 242, (Tokyo: Bank of Japan, 1968 and 1971).

the fruit of their technology in the growing Japanese economy, expedited by the newly instituted capital liberalization program.

Motives for Foreign Investment in Japan

Some of the reasons for the abovementioned developments may be found in the motives for the introduction of foreign capital by Japanese firms as well as in foreign firms' motives for investing in Japan. A study among Japanese and foreign firms affiliated with companies with foreign equity participation as of June 30, 1967, conducted by the Ministry of International Trade and Industry (MITI) revealed such motives as follows:[6]

1. The predominant motive of Japanese companies for introducing foreign capital was "to acquire technology." Out of the total of 327 Japanese companies that participated in the study, 270 companies accounting for 83 percent of the total chose this as a motive and 195 companies or 60 percent of the total chose this as the leading motive.

2. The study points out that a high degree of correlation exists between the establishment of enterprises with foreign capital and the number of validated technological licensing agreements. Although Japanese companies might have preferred to acquire foreign technology through straight licensing agreements, the report postulates, many have yielded to the foreign companies' demand for capital participation as a prerequisite for the provision of their technology.

3. Two other significant motives mentioned, namely, "to secure domestic market position through the use of foreign firm's brand name," and, "to promote export through utilization of foreign firm's sales network or brand name," can be considered closely related to the introduction of foreign production technology. Use of brand name is often a concomitant to the use of a certain prescribed production technology to maintain a quality standard.

4. The predominant investment motive of foreign companies was the growth potential of markets in Japan in particular and, secondarily, the neighboring countries of the Far East. Out of the 411 foreign companies participating in the study, 326 companies representing 79 percent of the total cited "the Japanese market growth potential" as a motive, and 242 companies or 68 percent chose it as the leading motive. "To take advantage of the Japanese position in the growing Far Eastern markets" was cited as a motive by 160 companies or 39 percent of the total, and as the leading motive by 33 companies or 9 percent.

Some Salient Features of Enterprises with Foreign Equity Participation in Japan

Some of the salient features of enterprises with foreign equity participation in Japan may be briefly summarized as follows, based on the MITI data:

1. According to the Japanese government's definition of *gaishikei kigyo*, enterprises with foreign capital participation may be broken down as of June 30, 1969, as follows:[7]

a. *Jun Gaishi Kaisha*—companies over 95 percent of whose equity is held by foreign investor(s), excluding Japanese branches and offices of foreign firms: 196 firms out of the total of 653 firms that participated in the MITI annual survey or 30.0 percent of the total belong to this category.

b. *Gōben Kaisha*—companies owned jointly by Japanese and foreign shareholders from the time of incorporation: 408 firms out of 653 or 62.5 percent of the total.

c. *Gaishi Donyū Kaisha*—companies into which equity foreign capital is introduced: 49 firms out of 653 or 7.5 percent of the total.

2. The share of foreign capital in these enterprises as of June 30, 1969, was as follows: Out of 653 firms, 25 firms (3.8 percent) were in 20–29 percent category; 211 firms (32.3 percent) in 30–49 percent category; 171 firms (26.2 percent) in 50 percent category; 50 firms (7.7 percent) in 51–94 percent category; and 186 firms (30.0 percent) in over 95 percent category or *Jun Gaishi Kaisha* mentioned above.[8]

3. In terms of the amount of invested capital, the breakdown as of June 30, 1969, was as follows: Of the total of 653 firms, 153 firms (23.4 percent) had less than 10 million yen[9]; 179 firms (30.2 percent) more than 10 million yen

Table 3. Validated Acquisition of Stock and Proprietary Interest, with Participation in Management Classification by Kind of Industry

As of March 31, 1970 (In thousands of U.S. dollars)

Kind of Industry	Amount	Share
Chemicals	$117,198	24.3%
Machinery	113,826	23.6%
Petroleum	112,031	23.3%
Metals	47,507	9.9%
Rubber & Leather	19,527	4.1%
Foreign Trade & Wholesale	18,813	3.9%
Glass & Stone	12,742	2.6%
Spinning & Weaving	2,414	0.5%
Services	1,956	0.4%
Transportation & Communications	676	0.1%
Construction Works	439	0.1%
Warehousing & Storage	173	—
Others	34,341	7.2%
Total	$481,644	100.0%

SOURCE: Ministry of International Trade and Industry

Table 4. Validated Acquisition of Stock and Proprietary Interest, with Participation in Management Classification by Nationality of Foreign Investors

As of March 31, 1970 (In thousands of U.S. dollars)

Nationality	Amount	Share
U.S.A.	$312,503	64.9%
Switzerland	42,474	8.8%
United Kingdom	25,711	5.3%
Canada	12,663	2.6%
West Germany	12,396	2.6%
The Netherlands	10,332	2.1%
Panama	6,063	1.3%
France	2,870	0.6%
Hong Kong	1,706	0.4%
Others	54,926	11.4%
Total	$481,644	100.0%

SOURCE: Ministry of International Trade and Industry

but less than 50 million yen; 68 firms (10.4 percent), more than 50 million yen but less than 100 million yen; 172 firms (26.3 percent), more than 100 million yen but less than 1 billion yen; 58 firms (8.9 percent), more than 1 billion yen but less than 10 billion yen; and 5 firms (0.8 percent) had more than 10 billion yen of invested capital.[10]

4. As seen in the table 3, three industrial groups had almost three quarters of total foreign direct investment in Japan at the end of fiscal year 1969: Chemicals had 24.3 percent of total, followed very closely by machinery with 23.6 percent and petroleum with 23.3 percent.

5. In terms of the nationality of foreign investors, the United States dominated the scene with 64.9 percent of the total at the end of fiscal year 1969, although some indications of the relative decline of the U.S. share in the newly established enterprises with foreign capital participation have been observed.[11] On the other hand, some of the companies classified as originated in such countries as Switzerland and Canada are in reality subsidiaries of American companies.[12] A real share of the U. S. direct investment would be somewhat higher than the figures in the table above indicate.

6. Last, "world enterprise" is defined in the MITI study as those 200 top companies listed in "*Fortune's* 500 Largest Industrial Corporations in the United States" and the top 100 companies in "*Fortune's* 200 Largest Corporations outside the United States," as well as their international subsidiaries. "World enterprise affiliated company" is defined as those companies over 50 percent of whose shares are owned by a world enterprise. As of June 30,

1969, 78 firms out of 200 American companies (or 39 percent) had direct investment in Japan, while only 14 (or 17 percent) of 82 companies outside the U.S.[13] had direct investment in Japan.[14]

3. Major Policy Developments in the Postwar Years

Actual and potential foreign investors often claim that the general attitude of the Japanese government toward inward direct investment has been rather restrictive. Against the general background of spectacular postwar achievements, direct foreign investment is lagging in a way that seems surprising to the outside observer, whose first reaction would be that it has been deliberately neglected. Let us then briefly review the Japanese policy toward inward direct foreign investment in the postwar years.

Developments in the Early Postwar Years

With the promulgation of a government ordinance in March, 1949, concerning acquisition by foreign nationals of property in Japan, and another in January, 1950, regulating business activities by foreign nationals, the door was reopened for foreigners to engage in business and investment activities. On December 1, 1949, the Foreign Exchange and Foreign Trade Control Law was enacted to provide for the control of foreign exchange, foreign trade and other foreign transactions necessary to the proper development of foreign trade, and the safeguarding of the balance of international payments and stability of currency, as well as to ensure the most economical and beneficial use of scarce foreign currency funds. The law severely restricted remittances abroad that arose from external economic transactions.

At the same time, for early economic recovery from the devastating effects of the war, new technology and foreign capital were badly needed. Thus, on May 10, 1950, the Foreign Investment Law (FIL) was enacted and the Foreign Investment Council established as an institution attached to the Ministry of Finance. The purpose of the law was stated in Article 1:

To create a sound basis for foreign investment in Japan, by limiting the induction of foreign investment to that which will contribute to the self-support and sound development of the Japanese economy and to the improvement of the international balance of payments, by providing for remittances arising from foreign investment, and by providing for adequate protection for such investments.

More specific criteria were spelled out in Article 8 of the law, in both positive and negative terms, a part of which reads:

The competent minister shall apply the following standards on validating contracts prescribed in this law, and the priority shall be given to those which will most speedily and effectively contribute to an improvement of the international balance of payments:

1. Directly or indirectly contributing to the improvement of the international balance of payments, or

2. Directly or indirectly contributing to the development of essential industries or public categories, or

3. Necessary for continuation of existing technological assistance contracts concerning essential industries or public enterprises or for the alteration of the articles of the contracts concerned such as renewal.

The competent minister shall not validate contracts prescribed in this law that fall under any one of the following paragraphs:

1. Contracts the provisions of which are not fair, or are in contravention of laws and regulations.

2. Contracts that are deemed to be concluded or the alteration of articles of which such as renewal of the contracts is deemed to be made in a manner not free from fraud, duress or undue influence.

3. When deemed to have an adverse effect on the rehabilitation of the Japanese economy.

There were no published indications of precise meanings of these terms, however.

Another notable feature of the law is the prinicple concerning foreign investment stated in the Article 2:

Foreign investment in Japan shall be permitted to be as free as possible, and the system of validation pursuant to the provisions of this law shall be relaxed and eliminated gradually as the necessity for such measures decreases.

Thus, Japan upheld the principle of free international capital movement as a long-range basic ideal on the one hand and gave due recognition to the fact that the restrictions on foreign investment imposed by the law were undesirable, particularly in a long-range program for the Japanese economy.

The law also provided various safeguards for foreign investors. Once foreign investment contracts meeting the aforementioned requirements were validated, the law unconditionally guaranteed the remittance of profits as well as principal overseas, regardless of the country's foreign exchange position.

During the initial years after the enactment of the FIL, the Japanese government endeavored to comply with the three positive conditions mentioned above. The government reasoning then was that since the law unequivocally guaranteed homeward remittances of profits as well as principal, the greatest care should be exercised in validating only those investments that were sure to be beneficial to the Japanese economy; and that the law did not impose any restriction on foreign investors' activities in Japan, provided the investors did not seek the government's assurance of repatriation of their profits and principal.

In October, 1956, the system of yen-basis investment was formally introduced. Residents of such countries as Canada, Nationalist China, Finland, France, West Germany, Greece, India, South Korea, the Federation of Malaya, the Netherlands, Norway, Pakistan, Sweden, Switzerland, Thailand, the United Kingdom, the United States, and Yugoslavia could freely make direct investments, either starting afresh in the nonrestricted industries or adding new funds to earlier such enterprises. No licenses were needed, no questions were asked regarding the origins of the funds. On the other hand, neither income nor liquidation of the principal could be transferred abroad. The yen-basis companies were, for all practical purposes, ignored by the foreign exchange control authorities. The yen-basis provision came to an end in June, 1963, in anticipation of Japan's acceptance of Article VIII of the International Monetary Fund, which required all subscribing nations to guarantee repatriation of earnings and principal of foreign investors. In April, 1964, current earnings of yen-basis investments became transferable, although liquidation proceeds as well as any accumulated earnings prior to 1964 remained blocked. On September 1, 1969, the government further liberalized to allow remittance of accumulated profits of these yen companies.

With the reconstruction phase of the postwar economy nearly complete by the middle of the 1950s, and with the way cleared for self-directed development and growth, mounting sentiment in favor of a reexamination of the official policy toward foreign investment appeared. Of a series of slackening measures taken by the government, interesting to note was the liberalizing of restrictions on technological induction in the following areas:

1. The criteria for official approval were eased. Until that time, only cases coming under the provision of FIL of 1950 (Article 8) were approved. Under the new system, approval was to be given except in the following four cases:
    a. When domestic technology of the same type has already been industrialized, and the induction of such technology might hamper the growth of the domestic technology of the same type or it is clear that the latter is to be industrialized in the near future;
    b. When such foreign technology is feared to unreasonably oppress small enterprises;
    c. When such foreign technology markedly disturbs the good order of Japanese industry;
    d. When the outlook of the development of such foreign technological know-how in Japan is poor because of the inadequate preparedness of the recipient side.[15]
Thus, restrictions from consideration of the international payments balance, or regarding nonurgent or nonessential industries—including consumer goods—have been removed in principle, and restrictions have been left only on those types of technological know-how induction considered harmful to the sound growth of the national economy through the possible rise of excessive competition. In other words, the pivot of restrictions on the induction of foreign technology has shifted from the reasons based on the international payments balance to those based on the nation's industrial policy.
2. In addition, the autonomy of the changes of contract terms came to be respected and the procedures for obtaining approval were simplified.[16]

In the middle of 1963, concurrent with the elimination of the yen-basis investment, the Japanese government announced that direct investments as well as licensing agreements would in principle be approved, unless they are deemed to have conspicuously adverse effects upon the national economy. This was considered to represent some relaxation from the former requirement that a positive contribution to the Japanese economy had to be demonstrated. Criteria for such a determination were to be:

1. Extreme disruption of the industrial order;

2. Extremely adverse effect on domestic financial and economic conditions, as well as the balance of payments;
3. Unfair pressure on small and medium enterprises.[17]

In practice, however, this left a wide latitude for bureaucratic interpretation. Officials could set their own flexible, conflicting and confusing standards. Aspiring investors complained that their applications were needlessly and illogically delayed.

Since the abolition of the yen-basis investment option, it became virtually impossible for foreign companies to exercise 100 percent control of enterprises in Japan. Stockholdings in existing Japanese enterprises were limited by law to a maximum of 15 percent. Thus, the only avenue left for substantial management participation by foreign companies in Japan was through joint ventures with Japanese partners. As a general rule, however, the government did not approve joint ventures in manufacturing in which foreign ownership of the equity holding, or foreign management participation, exceeded 50 percent. Even a 50–50 joint venture was difficult to achieve. In nonmanufacturing, this rule was applied less stringently.

MITI had its own internal standards to be used in considering applications for foreign equity investment in manufacturing, as follows:[18]

1. Approval will be given, in principle, if the Japanese side has a stock ratio of 51 percent or more and will not be approved, in principle, if the Japanese side has 49 percent or less.

2. In the case of 50–50 joint venture, at least half the directors and auditors must be selected from the Japanese side, and the president must be from the Japanese side.

3. It is desirable that the Japanese side have the right of decision on important matters such as personnel, production and sales planning, fund planning, etc.; both sides, however, may share in deciding such matters, but a joint venture in which the foreign partner has the deciding voice in such matters shall be avoided.

4. In case of a capital increase, the percentage of stock held by the Japanese side shall not be decreased.

5. Specific limits shall be placed on the transfer of stock by the Japanese side.

Developments in the Early 1960s

Liberalization of foreign capital investment became a pressing issue in the early part of the 1960s because of the three major events: (1) Japan's acceptance of the obligations of an Article XI country under the General Agreement on Tariffs and Trade (GATT) on February 20, 1963; (2) her acceptance of the obligations of Article VIII of the International Monetary Fund Agreement on April 1, 1964; and (3) the beginning of Japanese participation in the Organization for Economic Cooperation and Development on April 28, 1964. As an Article XI country, Japan no longer was allowed to exercise import restrictions under Article XII of GATT. As an Article VIII nation of IMF, Japan no longer was permitted to apply foreign exchange controls for balance of payments reasons, and exchange controls were lifted from most trade, service and other foreign payments transactions. Controls on yen remittances abroad were also eased.

Upon joining the OECD, Japan made eighteeen reservations with regard to the obligations to liberalize capital transactions, including total reservations regarding direct investments, issurance of securities and acquisition of real estate in Japan by foreign investors. As to acquisition of Japanese stocks by foreigners, Japan maintained reservations where the ratio of stocks held by one foreign investor exceeded 5 percent. Member nations of the OECD accepted these reservations, but expressed the hope that Japan would proceed with removal of the reservations as soon as practicable.

With a sharp increase in the number of applications for establishment of joint ventures in Japan, and with the OECD looking over its shoulder, MITI was forced to consider a drastic overhaul of its policy for receiving direct investment from abroad. Broadly, MITI intended to strengthen its selective approval system for the establishment of joint ventures. Restrictions were to remain in cases of those industries in which domestic firms were still struggling to rationalize production and improve their markets. Thus, positive steps were to be taken in the establishment of joint ventures where (1) domestic industry appeared structurally solid, and (2) there was a need for the impetus that foreign capital could provide.

Demand for Japan's capital liberalization from overseas sources became notably intensified from the fall of 1965. In October, 1965, the OECD sent a study team to Japan with a view to further encourage her to accelerate capital liberalization. A report prepared by the team was presented to a country survey meeting on Japan held in Paris in February, 1966. At the fifth meeting of the U.S.-Japan Joint Committee for Trade and Economic Affairs, held in July, 1966, in Kyoto, the United States government reiterated its demand for Japan's liberalization of capital transactions.

It was reported that the United States and other member countries of OECD put heavy pressure on Japan for liberalization of foreign investments, particularly for the following reasons:[19]

1. Japan had been positive in inviting indirect investments such as loans. In contrast, restrictions on direct foreign investments were too severe. It was considered that direct investments were far more advantageous to Japan for improving the balance of international payments.

2. As a rare exception, extremely small-scale service enterprises by direct investment had been approved by the Japanese government since July, 1963. On the other hand, foreigners had been unable to acquire the right of management by a majority in newly established or existing Japanese enterprises.

3. In this connection, the abolition of the yen-basis system was taken to mark the tightening of restrictions on direct investments.

It was against this background that MITI reportedly decided to take the following three major steps in connection with the proposed liberalization:[20]

1. To set definite criteria for the screening of foreign capital investment under the provisions of the Foreign Investment Law. More specifically, capital liberalization will be progressively advanced, except in the major industries destined to be the keystone of Japan's future development, such as automobiles, electronics and petrochemicals.

2. To permit the holding of more than 50 percent of stock by foreigners when foreign companies establish joint ventures in Japan.

3. To accelerate procedures for the screening and approval of applications for foreign capital investments in the Japanese market.

The Japanese government as well as business circles were widely divided on the issue because of conflicting interests. One group definitely approved of full-fledged capital liberalization, while the other was extremely cautious.

Of the three governmental agencies most closely connected with liberalization of capital, namely the Ministries of Finance, International Trade and Industry and Foreign Affairs, the Ministry of Foreign Affairs, with more "internationalists" among its officials, took the most positive view, while MITI characteristically took a very cautious, negative attitude, as it was to be most directly connected with the brunt of liberalization. This latter adopted the basic policy that Japanese business and industry should still be protected against the unrestricted advance of foreign capital on the grounds that small enterprises have not yet been thoroughly rationalized and streamlined, and that even growth industries, such as automobiles, have not been thoroughly "capital equipped" for international competition on equal terms with foreign counterparts. However, MITI gradually took a more positive attitude and moved, by the middle of 1966, to draw up the basic policy for liberalization of direct investments.

In the business circle, Keizai Doyukai (Japan Committee for Economic Development) made a positive policy statement regarding capital liberalization, as follows:

Japan is now in a position to welcome increased investment made by foreigners in Japanese industries . . . we firmly believe that Japan's liberalization of capital transactions should be effected and that the present regulatory arrangements should be simplified . . . [21]

The prestigious Keidanren (The Federation of Economic Organizations) tried, in cooperation with the Japanese Business and Industry Advisor Committee to OECD, to draw up a list of industries that might be capable of accepting direct foreign investments. The list classified industries in three categories: those that could be open to immediate foreign capital entry, those where liberalization is difficult, and those where liberalization should be carried out in stages.

The group, advising a cautious attitude toward capital liberalization, gave such reasons as the following to justify its stand: [22]

1. With business and industry already having their hands full taking care of the mushroom rise of small enterprises, the additional entry of new enterprises through joint ventures would offer factors obstructive to industrial

reorganization through absorption, merger or interlocking of management.
2. Due to intensified competition, Japan would be converted into an arena for competition by mammoth international enterprises.
3. With domestic technical know-how already reaching a high level, domestic enterprises that were defeated in the Japanese market area would likely tie up with foreign capital, throwing industries concerned into unnecessary confusion.
4. Although key industries had become sufficiently competitive on the international market, some individual enterprises were still less competitive.

In addition, they called attention to the danger of unnecessarily arousing the sentiment of nationalism, fearing that a rapid advance of foreign capital into the country might provoke needless friction, which might not be advantageous to either side.

Nevertheless, even the most resolute proponents of the restrictions admitted that most of those peculiar conditions would disappear by degrees as the Japanese economy made further progress, and that the time would soon come for Japan to put its industry in order and accelerate the liberation of capital movement.

At any rate, by the middle of the 1960's the majority of the Japanese business community seemed to agree that the problem of capital liberalization had long since passed the stage of discussion and entered the stage of practical application. Capital liberalization had finally become accepted as the general trend of the world, and it appeared that they had adopted the policy of making the best of the general world trend.

Some signs of such a change in the Japanese attitude could be seen in the establishment of a joint-venture company, Nippon Scriptomatic K. K., with a foreign ownership of 84.5 percent. This was the first time that a joint venture in manufacturing with majority interest held by foreigners was approved by the Japanese government. In June, 1966, the Japanese government approved the establishment of another joint-venture company, Nihon Aircon, Ltd., in which the General Electric Company would have controlling interest with a 50 percent capital investment ratio.[23]

Developments Since 1967[24]

After lengthy consultation between government and business, and after the attitudes of different industries toward the forthcoming liberalization of capital were more or less definitely clarified, on June 2, 1967, the Foreign Investment Council (FIC) finally announced the draft of the plan on steps toward foreign capital liberalization. The draft plan included the following features:[25]

1. Capital transactions should be liberalized in a tentatively wide field of industries by the end of fiscal year 1971.

2. Domestic industries would be divided into two major sections (the liberalized section and the nonliberalized section) in case foreign companies establish new companies in Japan. The first section would be further divided into the first branch with the ratio of foreign capital investments automatically approved to the extent of 50 percent, and the second branch with the ratio automatically approved to the extent of 100 percent. In the nonliberalized section, such foreign capital investments would continue to be subjected to individual screening.

3. In already established enterprises, the ratio of stock to be acquired by foreign investors through automatic approval would be raised to 15 percent from 10 percent in the restricted section and to 20 percent from 15 percent in the nonrestricted section. The maximum limit of stock possession by a single foreign stockholder would be raised from 5 percent to 7 percent.

4. FIC reserved the right to screen foreign investments even in the "liberalized" industries if they intended to sell directly to consumers.

5. Concentration of foreign investment should be avoided.

6. Foreign investors should refrain from making unduly restrictive agreements with their parent companies.

7. As many Japanese as possible should be on the board of directors, and stocks should be placed on the open market.

8. Such firms should make every effort to avoid layoffs and plant shutdowns and should cooperate with existing Japanese counterpart companies in voluntarily maintaining industrial order when necessary.

The FIC, on May 31, also provisionally compiled the list of industries to be designated for capital liberalization: seventeen industries to be opened to unrestricted direct foreign investment, and thirty three industries to receive automatic approval of direct foreign investment up to 50 percent ownership.

On June 6, 1967, the Japanese cabinet adopted the council's recommendations in their entirety, effective July 1, 1967. In doing so, it emphasized its conviction that the implementation of liberalization programs should be based on the principles of equality and coprosperity. To be a responsible equal partner among the advanced industrial nations, Japan should expand the freedom of capital and other invisible transactions in the long run. At the same time, the order and interest of Japanese industry should be protected with care. It emphasized the need to take positive action in order to prevent confusion of the industrial order, and to create a basis on which Japanese and foreign firms could compete on equal terms. Thus, the government encouraged Japanese businesses to upgrade their competitive capabilities and to take a forward liberalization with a vigorous entrepreneurial spirit.

The most significant feature of the program was the automatic approval system that would be applied to direct foreign investments aimed at setting up new subsidiaries or joint ventures.

None of the seventeen industries that had been opened to 100 percent investment came particularly as a surprise. In many of them, Japan ranked among the world leaders and could effectively compete in international markets. Even the 50 percent equal partnership industries, in which the existing gap in competitive ability between Japanese and foreign enterprises was apparently a source of concern to some industries, were strong and appeared almost impervious to potential foreign investors.

Thus, it came as no surprise that there was only one case of application for approval among these liberalized industries during the first year after the liberalization. The application was that of CBS-Sony Record Company, which provided for a 50–50 joint venture. However, the application was not given automatic approval on the following grounds:

1. Sony had not been engaged in the same line of business as that of the enterprise being established; and
2. The new company's planned activities included the manufacture and sale of recorded tape, which was not among the industries liberalized.

The project was given approval, however, after an individual screening.

In a closely related area, the liberalization measure for technology was implemented in June, 1968:

1. All applications involving payment of $50,000 or less will be automatically approved by the Bank of Japan.
2. Induction of technology for the manufacture of aircraft, weapons, ex-

plosives, nuclear energy, space development, electronic computers and petrochemicals that will entail payment of more than $50,000 is to be approved on a case-by-case basis.

3. In all other categories, automatic approval will be given applications involving over $50,000 unless objection is raised by the appropriate ministry, if in its view the Japanese economy is likely to be seriously affected, not later than one month after the application is filed with the Bank of Japan.

A significant feature of this measure was that the government abolished its controversial administrative guidance on the price and duration of the contracts. Such details were now left entirely to negotiations between the companies concerned.

There were growing numbers of proponents of liberalization who were advocating that Japan should not continue to wait for the consolidation of domestic industry before liberalizing further but rather should endeavor to modernize and rationalize its industry by admitting foreign capital. They contended that if the scope of liberalization was to remain limited in the second round, such inaction would probably cause unfavorable external effects, while slowing down efforts to reorganize the domestic economy. They argued that even in those industries that would remain nonliberalized after the second round, it would probably be necessary to set clearer criteria for approval of investments or to make public the schedule for further liberalization.

The FIC held its first general assembly early in September, 1968, to study the second phase of capital liberalization. In mid-September, MITI announced that it planned:

1. to add some fifty industries to the list of liberalized industries (mainly, 50 percent category), and

2. to extend liberalization to industries that had been traditionally regarded as the special domain of small companies, and to the retailing and wholesaling sectors.

The FIC made the liberalization recommendation in February, 1969; it was adopted by the cabinet in its entirety, and the second round of capital liberalization went into effect on March 1, 1969. The new round affected 155 categories of industries, of which 135 were open to automatic approval of 50 percent foreign ownership (in addition to the 33 categories liberalized in 1967), and 20 were open to 100 percent foreign ownership.

The council in its report also suggested that special attention be given to the liberalization of the automobile industry. The council also proposed that decontrol be stepped up in the distribution industry, including department stores and supermarkets, to encourage modernization in that sector.

A far more inclusive capital liberalization was carried out in the third round of capital decontrol. At the request of the finance minister, the FIC submitted a detailed recommendation on the third round of liberalization on August 17, 1970. The cabinet, at its regular meeting on August 25, approved the report in its entirety, and the new program went into effect on September 1, 1970.

According to the FIC's recommendation, emphasis was placed on expanding the number of industries opened to foreign investment. Of the 323 industrial categories newly decontrolled, 315 were opened to joint ventures in which foreign onwership is limited to 50 percent, and the remaining eight were opened to wholly owned foreign subsidiary forms. In addition, the scope of the liberalized areas was widened in 44 categories, and 27 categories were shifted from 50 percent status to 100 percent status. Thus, there were 447 categories open for 50 percent foreign participation and 77 for 100 percent foreign participation, making a total of 524 liberalized categories. Among the industries liberalized were banking and security business, synthetic rubber, detergents, cosmetics, aluminum and the like, which appeared to offer some attractive opportunitites to foreign investors. Department stores and supermakrets were freed on the basis of one store per investor.

At the same time, the ceiling for "automatic approval of portfolio investment" in existing Japanese companies was raised from 20 percent to 25 percent of the total shares in any one company, but such investment in restricted categories remained unchanged.

The council also urged that the fourth round of capital liberalization be moved forward six months, to October, 1971. The council dealt with the matter of liberalizing the automobile and electronic computer industries, proposing that the liberalization of the auto industry be carried out before the fourth round of liberalization went into effect. As for the electronic computer industries, the council proposed to continue examining the possibility of liberalization.

The third round of liberalization seems to have indicated that

Japan was making a serious effort to internationalize its economy. The advancement of the future liberalization schedule was to show a consistent posture of launching Japan's economy into the international sphere.

On the basis of the recommendation on March 24, 1971, by the FIC, the decision was made by the cabinet on March 30 to carry out a special single-industry round—dubbed the "third and a half round"—of capital liberalization, effective April 1, 1971. It permitted foreign business interests to acquire a maximum of 50 percent ownership in Japanese firms that manufacture motor vehicles, including trucks and tractors. The five related industries, which were also opened to foreign investment under the same terms, are the manufacture of car bodies or attachable vehicles, car parts or accessories, piston rings for automobiles, electric appliances for internal combustion engines and electric bulbs for automobiles.

With the earlier liberalization of foreign capital investments in car distributorship, the capital liberalization of all industries related to automobiles was thus completed for the time being.

As to the fourth round, FIC recommended the following points to make it as internationally attractive as possible:

1. Adopt a "negative list" of uncontrollable business sectors (vis-a-vis the positive list of liberalized business categories in the previous rounds) but with care to minimize the negative list.
2. Do everything possible to transfer as many industrial sectors already decontrolled, but placed under the 50 percent foreign ownership, to the 100 percent foreign ownership.
3. To retain the past categorical and other classification of decontrolled business areas.
4. To study carefully the feasibility of relaxing the present limit of foreign ownership of any ordinary Japanese industrial enterprise.

In early June, the powerful Keidanren adopted a basic policy supporting the council's position and decided to work further for full liberalization of direct foreign capital investment in Japan, even after the enforcement of fourth round liberalization. The salient points of the basic policy were as follows:[26]

1. A negative list should be drawn up for the fourth round.

2. Industries incorporated in the negative list that are not those recognized by the OECD should be dropped as soon as possible after the institution of the fourth round.

3. The 50 percent principle should be maintained in the fourth round. However, efforts should be made after the round to liberalize them up to 100 percent.

4. The ceiling placed on possession of stocks by individual foreigners should be raised from the present 7 percent to 10 percent.

5. There is need to accord favorable consideration in screening industries on the negative list since the period of nonliberalization is left unfixed.

Both the government and the FIC decided, however, to refrain from drawing up a "negative list" for the fourth round of foreign capital decontrol in preference to listing non-liberalized industries under the title of "individual screening industries."

It was reported that they decided to use the new term because:[27]

1. The title "negative list" seems to imply permanently withholding the industries involved from liberalization; and,

2. "Individual screening industries" does not necessarily mean "nonliberalized industries," since the "individual screening industries" will be opened to direct foreign capital investment according to the nature of the investment, just as in the cases where the ratio of foreign investment sought exceeds a given limit of automatic approval.

In other words, both the government and FIC hoped that the new term and application of formula would amount in essence to the opening of all industries to foreign investment.

The fourth and final round of capital liberalization, begun in 1967, was put into effect on August 4, 1971, after the cabinet approved the FIC's recommendations in their entirety. The fourth round provided for the following steps:

1. Industries designated for individual screening will be limited to seven fields, as follows: primary industries related to agriculture, forestry and fisheries; oil refineries, distribution or sales; leather and leather products manufacture; sales or leasing of electronic computers and computer aided system; the information processing industry, including the computer software industry; retail trade operations with more than eleven stores; and the real estate business.

The government decided just prior to the fourth round that decontrol of the manufacture, sales and rental of main computer systems and related devices would be implemented in August, 1974.[28] In the oil refinery industry, almost all firms are involved in joint ventures with foreign oil interests; the screening in this area was intended to keep less than one-third of the market for purely Japanese-owned firms.

2. One hundred and fifty-one industries were newly opened for 100 percent foreign ownership. One hundred and forty-one of these categories were shifted from 50 percent to 100 percent status, while 10 moved directly from an individual screening basis to 100 percent foreign ownership. As 77 categories were already opened for 100 percent liberalization in the previous rounds, there are now 228 categories fully liberalized, about 30 percent of all liberalized categories.

3. The automatic approval ceiling for an individual foreigner investing in Japanese securities was raised from less than 7 percent up to (but not including) 10 percent. The ceiling for aggregate foreign ownership in a company remained unchanged at (but not including) 25 percent.

While the fourth round ended the Japanese government's foreign capital liberalization program started in 1967 ahead of schedule, the FIC attached a special memorandum of its views to its recommendation in which it hoped the government would continue to take active steps to achieve full liberalization after the fourth round, which would constitute a drastic departure from the official policy, held until then, that liberalization should end with the fourth round. The council's recommendation was reportedly based on the following considerations:[29]

1. The aims of the OECD's Code of Liberalization of Capital Movements emphasize 100 percent decontrol for new business ventures and additional decontrol as to acquisition of stocks of existing companies.

2. Feeling is strong in some countries, such as the United States, that the capital liberalization being carried out by Japan is not capital liberalization in the real sense.

If and when the Japanese government concurs with the FIC recommendation, a good possibility exists for complete government reassessment of its capital liberalization program in the near future. The statement issued by the finance minister upon the cabinet decision, on August 3, to put into force the fourth round of capital liberalization, strongly indicated such a mood, and read in part:

> The present measure completes a series of inward direct investment liberalization measures pursued since 1967 . . . It is, however, vitally important, in the light of the international and domestic economic situations, for our country to fulfill its responsibility in the international community, while attaining a further development of our economy, giving due consideration to international cooperation. With respect to inward direct investment in particular, it is necessary to promote further liberalization hereafter with renewed determination and a new concept, taking into account changes in the international and domestic situations.[30]

> Consequently, the government, in cooperation with various individuals and organizations, is determined to implement all necessary measures towards achieving this aim.

4. Some Controversial Issues Concerning Japanese Policy Toward Inward Foreign Direct Investment*

Some significant changes have been taking place in Japanese policy toward inward direct foreign investment in the postwar years, particularly since the mid 1960s. Highly restrictive policies toward inward direct foreign investment have been gradually, slowly, and at times grudgingly, relaxed. Both Japanese government and business circles appear to have adopted a more liberal policy, responding to mounting external pressures, as well as to internal forces that began to challenge the very tightly controlled, highly restrictive policy.

These measures of capital liberalization, however, have not been received with enthusiasm by foreign observers. They apparently have not met the expectations of Western observers for genuine reciprocity in Japanese economic relations with the rest of the world, particularly with those advanced nations of the West. Such a view of dissatisfaction and criticism of the Japanese attitude toward foreign business is stated succinctly as follows:

*This section is adapted from Furuhashi, Yusaku, "Issues in the Japanese Capital Liberalization," *MSU Business Topics*, Volume 20, Number 2, 1972, by permission of the publisher, Division of Research, Graduate School of Business Administration, Michigan State University.

Japan has a profound distrust, mingled with envy, of foreign business. Its basic attitude is that foreign capital invariably aims at dominating Japanese markets and should be permitted to enter only under strict surveillance. Foreign participation in the economy is generally subject to detailed bureaucratic screening, especially as to management control and future expansion plans . . .

Despite the fanfare accompanying these liberalizations, they are more attractive on paper than in reality, and foreign investors continue to face a number of obstacles.

The Japanese attitude to foreign investment is further hardened by the attempts of industrial groups, and the Ministry of International Trade and Industry (MITI) itself, to strengthen Japan's competitive position . . .[31]

Kogoro Uemura, former president of Keidanren (Japan Federation of Economic Organizations) and leading spokesman for Japanese industry, speaking in Washington in June, 1971, recognized such foreign criticism and described the situation in a more dramatic way as follows:

A growing number of people in your country apparently view Japan as an emerging super-economic power seeking to dominate world markets. According to this view, the Japanese government instructs and helps business interests to attack the overseas on a market-by-market basis, subsidizing exports while protecting its own market from trade and investment from abroad. The government is seen as an all-encompassing web of administrative guidance. Japanese announcements of (capital) liberalization are viewed as inadequate at best, and a mockery at worst. Japan, the criticism continues, aspires to dominate the U.S. economically and eventually the world.[32]

He expressed his sincere hope that the U.S. would not base its policy on such a distorted view of the realities of Japan, and pleaded for the shaping of a sound sense of realities on both sides of the Pacific.

Rikuzo Koto, senior managing director of Keidanren, discussing the same aspects of the Japanese attitude toward foreign investment in Japan, expressed his doubt about the restrictiveness of Japanese policy stating:

It should be kept in mind that current Japanese restrictions on foreign investment are by no means as onerous as might be supposed from the publicity on the subject. About 500 subsidiaries and affiliates of U.S. corporations are already established in Japan.[33]

These quotes contain some essential points of the controversy surrounding Japanese policy in her relations with the outside world. Some of the problems may be traced to the Japanese perception of the problems involved, the Japanese view of the world and the problem of meaningful communication regarding the reality and intent of its actions.

Lack of True Reciprocity

One of the current controversies encompasses the lack of true reciprocity on Japan's part. Foreign observers point out that a number of Japanese organizations, both governmental and private, are very aggressively engaged in the promotion of exports and the worldwide search for raw materials, at times via direct investment overseas. But when it comes to foreign interests coming into Japan, the Japanese seem to display a conspicuous lack of enthusiasm. In fact, many Japanese do not seem to accept even the overall long-run positive advantage to admitting foreign capital to their economy and society. The majority of foreign investments in Japan (with the exceptions of aforementioned yen-basis companies) until recently appear to have been made with the objective of obtaining essential materials or technology that would not have been obtainable through straight licensing or similar arrangements. Despite increasing foreign interest in investing in Japan, observers criticize, there has not been a corresponding receptivity to foreign investment on the part of Japanese in government or in business circles, few efforts having been made to attract potential foreign investors.

Differences in Perception of Competitive Power of Japanese Industry

Another criticism lies in the difference of views regarding the strength of Japanese business firms vis-a-vis those of the advanced nations of the West, especially the giant multinational business enterprises. The Japanese self-image may be that of a nation essentially a latecomer in economic development and international economic affairs (as well as its cultural singularity), as Dr. Saburō Okita has so pointedly put it:

The basic character of Japan's economic policy has been that of latecomer or 'catching-up' country. Highly-developed Western countries have relied on the workings of the market mechanisms to open up new economic frontiers. The economic policies of latecomer government can plan the course of development in advance and use the selective approach in promoting industrilization or in expanding export trade . . . .[34]

Thus, from the Japanese point of view, there is a tremendous gap in competitive power between Japan and the advanced Western nations, especially the United States. And Japanese, both in government and in a good portion of the business circles, want to continue maintaining some limitations on the introduction of powerful foreign competition, lest it become so strong as to disrupt harmony and have a disastrous effect on the Japanese economy in the long run. A widespread feeling also exists among Japanese that foreign corporations will not understand and operate with traditional Japanese methods. While Japanese have been extremely eager for years to acquire foreign ideas and technology wherever they are found, they have been highly selective and have placed a high value on Japanese ways of doing things.[35]

Many foreign observers are not always in agreement with such reasoning. Philip H. Trezise, assistant secretary for economic affairs of the State Department, touched on this issue directly while speaking about the Japanese automobile industry's competitive position:

It does seem from our point of view that Japanese industry is capable of standing on its own feet, of not only competing, as it does, successfully in the United States markets, but also competing in the Japanese market with American producers . . . The fear of the large American producer, it seems to us after all these years, is now very much misplaced . . . .[36]

Another astute observer of the Japanese scene, Dr. Herbert Glazer, made a perceptive statement, which put the controversy in quite a different perspective:

the foreign investor in Japan may find himself in a joint venture which is rather puny compared to the size of the Japanese partner firm. In addition, the foreigner is beset with a multitude of problems ranging from finances to language, most of which are quite different from those encountered in his previous American or European experience. The foreigner many times feels himself at the mercy of his Japanese partner and the governmental ministries, and quite powerless to affect the outcome of events bearing on the joint venture.[37]

Meaning of Capital Liberalization

Probably the most controversial points in the Japanese capital liberalization have been the substantial differences found in the perception of the true meaning of capital liberalization. The reading of the Japanese government's statement concerning its intention, as well as the actions taken so far under the capital liberalization program, indicates clearly the existence of a substantial gap between foreign and Japanese thinking and appreciation of what constitutes capital liberalization, and the proper role of government in the implementation of the liberalization program. The Japanese government's own interpretation of the nature and extent of its international treaty obligations concerning capital liberalization does not necessarily coincide with the original intention of such organizations as IMF and OECD, or with the way these intentions have been interpreted by the rest of the world. To foreign investors and observers, true "capital liberalization" means action by the government to liberate international investment transactions from formal or informal controls or regulation. To them liberalization should mean 100 percent decontrol for the entry of foreign capital. To the Japanese, 50–50 joint-venture companies promoted under government supervision constitute "liberalization" in the true sense of their perception.[38]

Thus, for most Japanese who consider the joint venture as a true form of capital liberalization, Japanese progress in capital liberalization has been truly remarkable. In fact, Japanese industries, with a very limited number of exceptions, are now open to foreign investment or, in their view, liberalized. However, for those who criticize the slowness of capital liberalization and the tightness of control that the Japanese government maintains over foreign participation in Japanese industry, it is the extent of ownership permitted (50 percent versus 100 percent) and the composition of liberalized industries, instead of the number of liberalized categories, that is most important. From the latter's viewpoint,

although the number of industries taken up for capital liberalization is indeed substantial, a foreign investors' participation in
Japanese industry is still greatly limited. Even after the much
lauded fourth round of capital liberalization, the bulk of Japanese
industry remains closed to 100 percent foreign ownership.

The Japanese government maintains its original stand of opposing *overall* 100 percent liberalization. In this respect, business
circles have been as cautious as the government. The number of
industries open to 100 percent foreign ownership has increased
significantly in the last few years. All indications show that more
will become open to 100 percent foreign ownerhsip. Nevertheless,
the basic policy appears to be that of joint venture with foreign
capital participation limited to 50 percent. The basic intent behind this 50–50 joint-venture approach seems to be to uphold and
maintain the interest of locally capitalized industrial enterprises at
an adequate level, and to provide protection from foreign pressure
to indigenously capitalized business firms on a semipermanent
basis.

The situation is even more restricted in the case of participation
in existing Japanese firms through stock acquisition, which is
limited to (but does not include) 25 percent. Such a restriction is
intended to prevent the possibility of an aggressive foreign business interest taking over the control of that company. The Japanese Commercial Code permits any business firm stockholder with
25 percent or more of its outstanding capital stock a cumulative
voting right to dispatch his representatives to the board of directors
of that company. Thus, without such restrictions, it becomes
possible for aggressive foreign business interests to be on the board
and attempt to take over control of an existing Japanese company.
This restriction is intended specifically to prevent such a possibility from becoming a reality.

In addition, under the present capital liberalization schedule,
the Bank of Japan, as an agent of the government, will, in principle, validate foreign investment in Japanese liberalized industries,
and, subject to certain provisions, applications for such investments are automatically approved by it, unless it is apprehended
that the foreign investment in question may have seriously detrimental effects on the Japanese economy.

Therefore, it should be noted that certain procedures must still be followed for obtaining an official approval under the new liberalization schedule. Capital liberalization in this context means that the screening of an application was abolished within a certain framework, and validation will be granted immediately, or within a fixed period, by the Bank of Japan if an application is correctly filed.

Furthermore, it was announced that the Fair Trade Commission (FTC) would enforce a new policy, effective October 1, 1971, requiring all foreign corporations possessing stocks of Japanese companies to file a report with it on the details of their stockholdings. The reason for this move was reportedly FTC's fear that powerful foreign interests, directly or indirectly, might come to dominate Japanese companies, unless carefully checked after the full implementation of the fourth round of capital decontrol.[39] Another reason was to ascertain the activities of, and to prepare for any possible contingency of, multinational ventures involving foreign banking companies possessing indirectly a considerable amount of Japanese stocks through utilization of their complicated European business networks.

Thus, Japan's capital liberalization does not mean complete decontrol of foreign investment; considerable restrictions still remain in force. All of these restrictive measures are naturally sources of great dissatisfaction for foreign investors.

Code of Good Foreign Corporate Behavior

Another point of controversy involves a set of rather confining guidelines for foreign investors issued by MITI in connection with the first round of capital liberalization program, in 1967, which is commonly referred to as "MITI's Ten Commandments":

1. Foreign investors should seek coexistence and coprosperity with our enterprises by preferring, for the time being, as a rule, joint ventures on a substantially equal basis.
2. Foreign investors should avoid concentrating their investments in specific industries.
3. Foreign investors should not suppress unduly our small and medium-sized business by coming into industries where most enterprises are small in scale.

4. Foreign investors should cooperate with our industries in their efforts to maintain order in their respective industries.

5. Foreign investors should avoid having unduly restrictive arrangements with their parent companies abroad, and they should not resort to unreasonable restrictions or engage in unfair competition.

6. Foreign investors should try to contribute to the promotion of technology in our industries and not hamper the efforts by our own industries and enterprises for their own technological development.

7. Foreign investors should cooperate with us in the improvement of our balance of payments by such means as the promotion of export trade.

8. Foreign investors should employ Japanese nationals as officers, and they should try to offer shares on the open market.

9. Foreign investors should avoid closure of plants or mass dismissals, and they should avoid unnecessary confusion concerning employment and wages by paying due regard to our prevailing practices.

10. Foreign investors should cooperate with the government in its economic policy.[40]

It is significant that this is the first time that the Japanese government officially disclosed the specific standards it uses for the screening and validation of applications. In a sense, therefore, this constitutes considerable progress over the vaguely stated criteria employed until then. However, foreign investors complain that it is not easy to satisfy all of of the "ten commandments," or other conditions required by the Japanese government, or the new code of good behavior reportedly being drafted in Japan as "a reflection of the joint aspirations of MITI and the Japanese business community."[41]

Although these guidelines belong to the realm of "administrative guidance" (informal guidelines, suggestions and admonitions communicated to business circles through frequent discussion and consultation, thus carrying only the force of moral suasion and no legal power) business firms could ignore them at their own risk, and their effect could be to restrict considerably the freedom that the business firms are supposed to enjoy under the letter of law.

Foreign investors and observers complain, therefore, that many detailed restrictive features still remain despite the fanfare accompanying the liberalization measures undertaken by Japan and regardless of whether or not the government refers to an industry as liberalized.

Current Regulations Briefly Summarized

Briefly summarized, the current Japanese regulations on inward foreign direct investments seem to include:

1. The Japanese government continues to retain control of foreign investment by screening:

a. Those industries designated for individual screening in the fourth round of capital liberalization of the program;

b. Any application exceeding the automatic approval levels both for newly established and existing Japanese firms;

c. Any application to form joint enterprises with Japanese firms in lines other than those in which the Japanese firms are experienced;

d. Any application to form an enterprise that intends to drastically change traditional methods of doing business in the industry involved, e.g., selling direct to consumers.

2. The Japanese government seems to set *some* upper limit on the foreign investments' production and market share, at least for those industries that are considered to be strategic in terms of Japan's national development. For example, in the fourth round of liberalization, oil refineries were reportedly retained on the list of industries designated for individual screening on the grounds that almost all firms in the industry were involved in joint ventures with foreign oil interests, and that the government intended to keep less than one-third of the market for purely Japanese-owned firms.

3. The government makes every effort to prevent take-over by foreign investors and to ensure that all ventures involving foreign capital remain under Japanese management control:

a. Japanese shareholders in a joint venture should have previous experience in the field in which the joint venture is to be organized.

b. The Japanese side should have at least half the directors and auditors, and provide for a Japanese as president.

c. The Japanese side must have dominant say or veto power in key management areas, particularly personnel and finance.

d. The ordinary rules of procedure prescribed in the Japanese Commercial Code should be followed in the conduct of joint-venture management.

4. Foreign investors are prohibited from using the proceeds and profits earned from local operations for purposes other than those for which they were originally granted permission by the government. This measure is specifically designed to prevent foreign investors from using their locally generated yen funds for the acquisition of Japanese companies outside of the Foreign Exchange Control Law.[42]

Japanese government and business circles emphasize their conviction in principle that it is necessary to make every effort for creating a firm relationship of cooperation between the Japanese

economy and those of other countries, and for expanding the freedom of international capital movement. But at the same time they
contend that many of Japan's enterprises do not yet have the
strength to compete against giant multinational firms on equal
terms, and thus the order and interest of Japanese industry should
be protected with care. From this viewpoint, government-regulat-
ed gradual removal of foreign investment and exchange controls
serves the long-run interest of both Japanese and foreign enterprises best.

One of the foremost authorities on Japanese affairs, former
Ambassador Edwin O. Reischauer, has commented on this ambivalent Japanese attitude:

> Intellectually, Japanese businessmen tended to agree with the criticism that
> came not only from the United States but from all Western countries. How-
> ever, emotionally, it was hard for Japanese to open up their country. Perhaps
> because of their old tradition of isolation, they had an instinctive fear of for-
> eign ownership of anything in Japan, and a powerful bureaucracy continues
> to guard the gates jealously. There was much talk of 'liberalization,' but
> little actual motion.[43]

5. Major Factors Underlying Japanese Attitudes Toward Inward Foreign Investment*

In the early postwar years, tight controls over all forms of international economic transactions were entirely justifiable, for the
economy was literally struggling for survival and trying to recover
from war damage and destruction. The economy was small, very
fragile and plagued by chronic balance of international payments
difficulties. The economy found itself lagging far behind the
advanced nations of the West in capital and technology. Such an
argument, whatever its intrinsic merit in the past, can hardly be
advanced today. Nevertheless, to Western observers (and an increasing number of Japanese, it might be added), Japan still maintains

*This section is adapted from Furuhashi, Yusaku, "Foreign Capital in Japan,"
Columbia Journal of World Business, Volume 7, Number 2, 1972, by permission of the
publisher, The Graduate School of Business, Columbia University.

a considerable array of restrictive measures toward inward direct investment, despite the phenomenal growth in its GNP and rapidly accumulating foreign exchange reserves. What might be the underlying reasoning for the Japanese brand of protectionism, and the go-slow, very careful approach to full capital liberalization and true internationalization of the Japanese economy? Let us examine some of the factors, which hopefully will illuminate this ambivalent attitude.

Political-Governmental Factors

One facet that might give some insight into Japanese behavior toward foreign investment can be found in the role of government and business, particularly big business, in economic matters. In the Japanese variety of the free enterprise system, the government's behavior goes far beyond the U.S. regulatory role, which calls for a minimum of governmental interference in business affairs. Although the Japanese have assimilated a great array of technology, business, trade and financial concepts, methods and organizations from the West, they have developed their own way of running and controlling their economy. Commenting on the Japanese economic system, Norman Macrae, the deputy editor of *The Economist*, has stated that "the Japanese like to say that theirs is an unplanned, free enterprise economy. But, in our Western term, it isn't. It is. . . the most intelligently dirigiste system in the world today." And he has quoted the advice given by the *Journal of the American Chamber of Commerce in Japan* to make his point as follows:

> . . . while business in Japan is highly competitive, it is not western style free enterprise . . . While much corporate and personal rivalry does exist, business, banking and government are all on the same team and probably function as a partnership to complement the policies and plans of the government.[44]

Business decisions in Japan are taken jointly with interested government agencies, indeed, with the government acting often as planner, arbiter and regulator. Thus, major investment decisions, such as substantial expansion of capacity in such critical fields as steel, chemical and petroleum, are typically made by companies within a working framework established after government-business discussion. And foreign firms "hardly fit easily into the web of relations between business and government that is so uniquely and elusively Japanese."[45] In this framework of economic operation, foreign firms are often viewed as not entirely reliable participants in the Japanese eye. Their basic commitments are not to Japan, but to executives and shareholders outside the Japanese system. Thus, there is a genuine concern that they may not act in an "orderly" fashion, might disrupt the system, and therefore, need to be excluded—or limited to a tolerably low proportion—from the total as well as from each of the sectors of the economy.

In the discussion of government-business relations in Japan, it should be pointed out that there is a basic assumption that goals and aspirations of government and business are essentially the same, namely, the maintenance of Japan's economic health, promotion of national interests and catching up and surpassing the Western economic powers. And government and industry work hand in hand toward these objectives, as expressed so well in the popularized term "Japan, Incorporated." In the words of John C. Lobb:

> In many ways the government is much more involved than in the United States. MITI has great powers. Literally, MITI plans are business strategy of Japanese industry in world markets. The Ministry decides which industries will expand, and it directs the Bank of Japan to provide funds to Sumitomo Bank, Fuji Bank or whatever the parent bank may be in order to permit expansion. There is no reckless competition for markets between Japanese companies in foreign markets. Only in Japan itself does free competition exist . . . Technology, manpower and capital are marshalled to invade world markets as a single entity. It is a fascinating and at the same time a frightening phenomenon. Only in time of war does the United States operate this way. . .[46]

The unanimity of objectives and actions among political parties, business and government, or even among various ministries implied in such an expression is *probably quite overly drawn*. And who is in charge of Japanese policies? Leon Hollerman has commented on it so aptly:

> If "the government" of Japan were actually a highly coordinated set of agencies, its powers could be applied with overwhelming force. Instead, partly

as a result of sheer ambition for status and partly as a reflection of divergent interests within the society itself, there is intense rivalry and jealousy among the ruling agencies and their personnel. In competing for power, they tend to neutralize one another's authority to some extent . . . An additional degree of freedom arises from the powerful influence exerted by big business on the political party in control. Indeed, it is often difficult to identify which is the master and which the servant, for they exchange roles from time to time in various situations.[47]

Nevertheless, in a sense, the Japanese government is the ultimate arbiter of economic relations, and it is an active participant in economic decisions in harmonious relation with business.

What makes this relation so workable is the fact that since the beginning of the Meiji era, the state took important initiatives and played the major role in Japan's very abrupt shift from a feudal system to a central national government and modern industrialization. This has resulted in the "development of a relationship of cooperation and trust between government and business, a sharp contrast with the American tradition of suspicion and hostility."[48]

Another reason for this symbiotic relation between government and business is the common social background, university education and training of top men in government bureaus and large business firms (as well as many of the political leaders). This tends to facilitate communication and understanding among these groups and to open up channels of communication for informal consultation and guidance. Of special significance here is the fact that there has been a tendency for the very best college graduates to take positions in prestigious government agencies in preference to business, since, as Richard Halloran puts it, "Japanese society assigns high prestige to the government official, making the bureaucracy attractive to the best brains in the nation."[49] They retain, however, options of entering either legislative politics or business later in their career.

Commenting on this harmonious relationship, Norman Macrae has stated that "the result is a cross-fertilization of opinions and a situation where some senior industrialists think of bureaucrats as 'those bright young men who are doing all that hard research work' (which is not how CBI regards Whitehall)."[50]

Such an attitude has a great bearing on the way various laws are administered. In fact, there is only a limited legal basis for the high degree of government involvement over so wide a front. Most involvement takes place in the form of "administrative" or "window" guidance, which is no less compelling than law, as William W. Luckwood explains it so dramatically:

> The hand of government is everywhere in evidence. The Ministries engage in an extraordinary amount of consultation, advice, persuasion, and threat. The industrial bureau of MITI proliferates sectoral targets and plans; they confer, they tinker, they exhort. This is the "economics of admonition" to a degree inconceivable in Washington or London. Business makes few major decisions without consulting the appropriate governmental authority; the same is true in reverse. The Ministries list 300 consulting committees for this purpose.[51]

Probably out of deference to tradition and habits, such administrative guidance is usually both given and taken. In fact, the majority of businessmen seem to favor dependence upon administrative guidance, because they tend to think, partly due to their traditional "foreign capital phobia," that the government can be used as an effective shield in their dealings with foreign business interests more often than it obstructs their normal business operations.

Foreign perplexity is further aggravated by the fact that, in Japan, government administrators seem often to believe that the laws may provide only the *minimum* safety measures to protect the interests of domestic industries, and, therefore, when the legal protection ends, they have a duty to step in as a guide and protector in order to direct the industries in the right course of action so that weak domestic industries are not exploited and dominated by strong foreign interests.

Although there is growing criticism from some business and political leaders against such bureaucratic interference, there is no denying that there is a popular feeling of respect and satisfaction toward the government that has managed quite well to maintain the nation's economic health and to blunt the mounting threat of large-scale foreign business invasion.

Economic-Industrial Factors

One of the basic themes of Japanese opposition to the rapid foreign capital liberalization goes like this:

> Postwar Japanese rehabilitation and growth have been too swift and sweeping to establish a strong, as well as well-balanced, industrial structure, and the ensuing weaknesses in rapidly expanding industries can easily become attractive targets for systematic exploitation by giant foreign multinational enterprises. Japan should proceed with great care in lifting protective shields from these industries, lest they become the victims of such unfair exploitation.

It is worth noting in this connection that many Japanese growth companies are undercapitalized and thus undervalued by the standards commonly employed in the United States. For example, the net worth ratio of industries has been on the average about 20 percent, and the ratio of outside liabilities to net worth around 400 percent in recent years.[52] Although the profitability measured in terms of return on sales has been comparatively low, sales growth of Japanese companies seems to have been maintained at an excellent level. For example, a ratio of profits to total capital employed in 1969 for 584 leading Japanese companies was 5.06 percent,[53] compared to the all-industry median of 11.3 percent for *Fortune*'s 500 largest industrial corporations,[54] although direct comparison of such figures is not very meaningful due to differences in accounting and reporting methods.

One of the indications of the rapid growth of Japanese companies can be seen in "The Fortune Directory of the 100 Largest Industrials Outside the U.S.," which first appeared in 1957, and, at that time, contained four Japanese corporations. [55] The directory was expanded to list 200 largest corporations in 1963, and 31 Japanese companies, including 14 among the first 100 companies, were listed. The 1971 directory lists 51 Japanese companies among the top 200 corporations, with 20 companies in the first 100. Thus, Japan edged past Great Britain to become for the first time the most heavily represented country in the 200 directory.[56]

Many of these companies undoubtedly are attractive candidates for acquisition by foreign investors. It comes as no surprise, therefore, that the Japanese government tightly controls acquisition of stocks in existing companies, guards against the possible take-over of joint ventures by foreign investors, and regulates the use of proceeds and profits earned from local operations.

Another point of significance here is Japan's phenomenal growth, accompanied by brisk investment activities, and the methods of financing such investments, as P. S. Stone has stated:

> Whilst almost every other feature of the Japanese scene can be accounted for in ways which are mutually contradictory, the fact of their high investment and its relation to economic growth is obvious and unarguable, and the really interesting question is how the Japanese arrange for this investment to be as high as it is.[57]

Aside from the apparently contradictory rationale (to foreign observers) for what has been referred to as "blind rush for industrial gadgetry," Japanese methods of financing industrial expansion are quite unorthodox in the Western norm. Since individual corporations could not possibly meet the amount of their desired investments internally through retained earnings and depreciation, they had to seek investment funds externally. The proportion of "direct financing" was 12–20 percent, and that of fund supply in the form of foreign capital inflow was 4 or 6 percent; and about 80 percent of the total funds obtained from outside were from financial institutions, primarily commercial bank loans (63–68 percent) and the government (11–16 percent).[58]

This preference given by Japanese corporations to bank borrowings over the other methods was due partly to the voluminous saving funds generated by the high level of personal saving, which reached 20 percent of disposable income in the late 1960s, and partly to other postwar developments that have pushed banks to the predominant position in the capital market.[59]

City banks, in meeting the brisk fund demand of business enterprises, have been chronically in the state of inadequate liquidity or "over-loan state." As a result, they have come to depend constantly on borrowings from the Bank of Japan for the supply of cash currency to meet with economic growth. Thus, the Bank of Japan, in addition to having the ordinary monetary tools, has come to apply what the Japanese have come to call "window guidance"—controlling the amounts, lengths of time and terms of loans made by commercial banks to business firms. This has had a great impact because the public money market has not yet been well developed in Japan.

Under these conditions, the economy is very vulnerable to sudden inflows and outflows of massive foreign funds. The kinds of "hot" money movements between different money markets of the West that have taken place off and on in the past decade would have devastating effects on the Japanese economy. And the Japanese government wants to avoid just such contingencies to the extent permissible within the constraints of its memberships in IMF, OECD and the Bank of International Settlements.

Another rationale of Japanese opposition to the rapid Western brand of capital liberalization has been along the following line:

> In order to achieve one of the main national goals, namely, the building of a high-welfare economy and society, which is truly affluent and stable, the Japanese should carry out a very intricate balancing act of consistent growth and prosperity without inflation. Internal price levels must be maintained at a level that keeps consumption low enough to support the massive capital formation required for the hoped-for continued high growth rate; excessive competition *(katō kyōsō)* must be contained, and the rationalization of industry must be carried out smoothly. This calls for the formation of a common national understanding and consensus and a united effort by the government, private enterprises and the general public to achieve the goal. And the kind of foreign capital liberalization that might cause radical changes in the role of foreign capital and participating management behavior in the Japanese economy should proceed, very carefully, at least for the time being.

Although it is not possible to recognize a simple trade-off relationship between economic growth and price increase, it is safe to state that the higher the growth rate, the higher the rate of increase of incomes and wages tend to be, resulting in a marked rise in the price level. In order to achieve both income growth and price stability at a higher individual standard of living, proper control of aggregate demand and various structural improvement policies must be vigorously pursued.

One cause of inflation is inflation "imported" through an increase in money supply resulting from a surplus in the international payments balance. Although external factors have been carrying an increasing weight in the money supply in Japan in recent years, the rate is still relatively small, compared with, for example, Germany.[60] Nevertheless, changes in the international payments balance through trade and long- and short-term investment accounts must be watched very carefully.

Introduction of foreign business into Japan undoubtedly contributes toward the accelerated (and forced) rationalization and modernization of Japanese industry. But it might lead to a higher degree of competition, resulting in *katō kyōsō* (excessive competition), which is regarded as wasteful. Although such an ambivalent attitude toward economic competition is difficult to justify, it should be pointed out that "what is known as excessive competition results from the fact that labor is an overhead cost rather than a variable cost in Japan."[61] And it is feared that the introduction of foreign business that might not understand such logic might have a disruptive influence on industrial structure and practices.

Another theme is that Japan's phenomenal recovery and growth in the last two decades has served only to compound the "dual structure" of the economy, since the emphasis has been placed primarily on the major industrial sectors of the Japanese economy. Many Japanese believe that in such a rapid growth situation it did not have enough time to make adequate adjustment of internal balances along the way, compared to the developed Western societies, which have many years of internal social and economic adjustment behind them. The upshot is that in almost every sector of the economy there are a few giant and powerful firms at one end of the continuum and a large number of small factories, stores and farms at the other, with a relatively small number of medium-sized companies in between. Differences found in the two end groups are extreme: one is as modern as can be found in the most advanced nations in the West, the other is in reality more like that of an underdeveloped economy.

Similar unbecoming features are also found in other areas of Japan. Former Ambassador Reischauer describes the problems as follows:

The prewar strategy of 'guns instead of butter' was supplanted after the war by a 'factory instead of butter' policy, which probably deprived the Japanese consumer too much in favor of a rate of industrial growth that was so fast it created dangerous social strains. In any case, the investment in social overhead was for long too small as compared with industrial investment. Japan became a country of some of the finest factories in the world and some of the worst housing, roads, and schoolhouses . . .[62]

Continued rapid economic growth has not solved these problems, although increasing attention is given over to the solutions of these problems, as evidenced, for example, by a heavy emphasis placed on the realization of a "truly affluent people's life" in a "high-welfare economy," in the Economic Planning Agency's *White Papers on Economy and People's Life*.[63] Thus, internal adjustments will be made in due time, but there has not yet been enough time for adjustment and realignment.

There are, then, the ever-present facts of internal political expediency. Small factory and store owners and farmers comprise a very sizeable group of voters who have vociferous spokesmen. Government action towards a wider liberalization may adversely affect them. This factor increases the political strains associated with liberalization. The Japanese government apparently feels that Japan needs more time to achieve the well-balanced maturity of its economy before it can open its door wide to outsiders.

Finally, all of these must be carried out in an international environment that is inextricably tied to political decisions. That is to say, the major trading partner has been, and most probably will remain to be, the United States. A major potential market could be the People's Republic of China. A major potential source of raw material supply could be Soviet Russia. The Japanese feel that they are discriminated against economically, notably by many of the European nations. Japan is the only member of OECD singled out for trade discrimination by almost all European countries, and has been a major target of U.S. attempts to establish "voluntary" export quotas. All of these are vitally important factors in Japanese economic growth and survival; each contains some elements of conflict with others at least for the time being, and all employ their foreign economic activity as an arm of the conduct of the foreign policy.

Under these circumstances, it is not surprising that the Japanese feel that they want to keep all control of the various interrelation aspects of their economy and society. Thus, the harmony and order among various sectors as the basis for the conduct of business and social relations must prevail. The contemporary Japanese business structure and behavior, while quite modern, are based on feudal tradition that often overrules logic. Whether foreign business can be trusted to participate in these deep-seated connections, duties and obligations that govern the relationships between various sectors of the economy, industry and society apparently remains a question in the mind of many Japanese.

Social-Cultural-Psychological Factors

There should be little question that there is a strong emotional and attitudinal basis for Japanese behavior toward foreign investment. Obviously, the nationalistic tendency of the Japanese plays an important part in attempting to limit the role of foreign capital in the economy. There seems to exist an underlying feeling that Japan is the unique and exclusive province of the Japanese, and that Japan should manage her economy as she sees fit without exposing herself to possible exploitation by foreign capital. Such attitudes are largely unconscious and usually taken for granted. Nevertheless, they constitute a real factor underlying the complex laws and regulations concerning foreign investment. Such attitudes and feelings have been nurtured by myriads of interacting elements, but a few of the outstanding ones may be pointed out.

Totally isolated from the rest of the world for several centuries, the sharp sense of separateness from other nations, as well as a deep consciousness of being Japanese and belonging to a special group, pervades the society, as Richard Halloran puts it:

> Among the most striking features of Japan is the profound sense of isolation and insularity that pervades Japanese society. The Japanese throughout their history have had less interchange with other peoples than probably any other "major" nation. This fact helps explain their unique qualities and the differences not only between them and Westerners but between the Japanese and other East Asians . . . [64]

The very reason for the start of industrialization a century ago was to prevent the entry of colonizing foreigners, and to avoid the humiliation and domination that Western powers had imposed throughout the rest of Asia. Foreign direct investment and participation in the process of industrialization were largely limited from the start to instruction in technology, a pattern that has been deeply imbedded in the Japanese view and persists to this day.

Then there exists a keen sense of national identity, unity and homogeneity. Indeed, as former Ambassador Reischauer describes it, "Japan constitutes what may be the world's most perfect nation-state: a clean-cut geographic unit containing almost all of the people of a distinctive culture and language and virtually no one else . . ."[65]

Thus, Japanese exhibit a very deep sense of identity and solidarity: there is a very clear-cut distinction between what is Japanese and what is not. Whatever the real causes, Japanese society exhibits a strong nationalistic feeling expressed in terms of *ware-ware Nihonjin* (we Japanese) as contrasted with "they, all non-Japanese." "So highly developed is the sense of national solidarity that the people have at times acted like one huge family with the Emperor as its head."[66]

Throughout history the deep Japanese sense of identity has been reinforced by developing cultural adaptability to things foreign without losing their own identity. John Whitney Hall has argued that:

> One of the outstanding features of the 'Japanese mind' throughout history has been its persistent inquisitiveness and flexibility in the face of new demonstrably superior intellectual system . . . In doing this, they have remained persistently eclectic . . . , so that the result has often been a distinctly Japanese adaptation of Western ideas or methods, an adaptation in which the Japanese have somehow been able to prove a modicum of their individuality.[67]

In short, it guaranteed its permanency and the continuity of its culture by always being ready to change and to assimilate the new and the foreign.

A salient product of the sense of isolation, distinctiveness, national identity and unity is the Japanese conception of history and their nation's destiny as something to be consciously determined by the nation's will. Despite the constant debate over the lack of national goals in the recent years, the Japanese seem to have adopted at least one common purposeful task: catching up with the most advanced nations of the West, "except that slogan has recently been changed to 'surpassing the West.' "[68]

This prevailing sense of unity and cohesiveness of Japanese society also has its manifestation in the prewar *Zaibatsu* or contemporary *kigyō shudan*, or enterprise growing, in economic organization.[69] Such relations as *kankei gaisha* (closely related firms), *keiretsu gaisha* (affiliated firms), *oyako gaisha* (parent-and-child firm relationship), powerful trade associations and the aforementioned "Japan, Incorporated" give rise to a web of intricate organic relationships. These unique setups fit well with the Japanese conception that Japan is a distinct nation whose institutions should be fitted to its own circumstances.

It is not surprising then that foreign business enterprises encounter a great amoung of difficulty at least in the initial entry period. Only when such enterprises can find a niche in this gigantic organism through successive adaptation can they fit into the Japanese social structure:

> In such an organic complex it is difficult for any foreign element not only to become accepted, but even to be accounted for. Only through long familiarization and assimilation can a foreigner (*gaijin:* "outsider") himself be seriously considered, as any foreigner who conducts business in Japan readily discovers . . .[70]

The other side of the strong nationalistic feeling is xenophobia and, specifically for our purpose, "foreign capital phobia." Such a fear of foreign control can be found partly in Japan's recent history. Unpleasant memories of Commodore Perry's "black ships" and the threat of foreign invasion and domination still live on. Thus, the Japanese consider themselves in a vulnerable position economically with regard to any influx of foreign direct investments. In fact, the Japanese have related recent outside pressures for foreign capital liberalization to the foreign exploitation of Japan following the forced opening of Japan a century ago, dubbing these outside pressures as "the second coming of the black ships." The "unequal treaties" imposed then on Japan by the Western nations through superior military power led largely to commercial exploitation. In fact, much of Japan's external trade was controlled by the Western trading companies of the day, until 1911 when

Japan became the first non-Western nation to win diplomatic equality with the West.

Translating this experience into modern terms, Japan can only look to Canada, Latin America and Europe to see what it considers to be a similar (more subtle, but nevertheless real) threat today in the example of the control of industries in these countries by giant multinational corporations. Thus, the Japanese have come to view foreign talk of equity and reciprocity as merely a cold legal cover-up for the real aim of foreign multinational firms—particularly U.S. firms—to invade and control strategic segments of the Japanese economy.

This deep-seated Japanese anxiety over foreign direct investments may be due to the country's insular tradition. Even today most Japanese reveal a state of general ignorance about conditions prevailing in the rest of the world. Furthermore, Richard Halloran states:

> Except for a superficial curiosity, the Japanese are seldom deeply interested in and rarely empathetic with the world beyond their shores. The people and the Establishment, with individual exceptions, do not understand how other nations function, why other people do what they do. The Japanese view of the world is misty and seen through the haze of their parochial insularity. More and more, Japanese businessmen and officials in recent years traveled overseas, and, as foreign exchange restrictions have been relaxed, more tourists are going on visits abroad. But they usually go in groups with other Japanese, stick close together, and absorb little of real life of the nation they visit.[71]

With insufficient international experience and knowledge, the Japanese tend to be provincial in their outlook. This led, on the one hand, to overestimation of the attractiveness of Japan to foreign investors and to skepticism of the true motives and modes of behavior of foreign business firms on the other. The Japanese rarely take things at face value, especially in their dealings with foreigners.

This anxiety is also due partly to the rapid pace of the postwar economic recovery and development and partly to the traditional Japanese inferiority complex against the strong, advanced Western countries. To a people whose land had never been conquered by an outsider in their recorded history, the defeat and subsequent occupation were great shocks, which left deep wounds on the Japanese psyche. In the midst of the postwar confusion and disenchantment with the past, they downgraded their self-image to that of a third-rate nation. Despite the remarkably rapid recovery and growth of the Japanese economy, regaining self-confidence came rather slowly. The real turning point in the psychological and emotional recovery came at the Tokyo Olympic Games of 1964, and the point of full recovery was reached with the Expo '70, held in Osaka in 1970. To outsiders, these were spectacular, highly successful international shows. To the Japanese, the symbolic meaning of these events was everything.

Nevertheless, the traditional Japanese inferiority complex probably still lingers on. In a way, some of the spectacular events of the past may be attributable to this inferiority complex and the intense feeling of being "on stage," as Michiko Inukai has stated:

> It was the desire not to appear inferior in the eyes of foreigners which . . . enabled them to carry through an astonishing modernization . . . In the same way, they build new roads . . . in order to present their nation in a better light to foreigners.[72]

Even today, the average Japanese is still unaware of the present wealth of his country, and still has what Saburō Okita calls "a GNP mentality gap."[73] Psychologically speaking, they still feel that they are poor and easily subject to the invasion and exploitation of powerful foreign capital.

It can be debated whether nationalistic feeling is on the rise in Japan. Indications thus far are quite mixed. But there can be little doubt about the fact that nationalism is strong, and that for the time being much of this feeling is focused on the economic sphere. And great tact must be used by foreign businessmen operating in Japan in dealing with this force.

Word of Caution

Obviously, these are only some of the major factors that as a whole will hopefully shed light on the ambivalent, ethnocentric Japanese attitude toward foreign capital and investment. Many of these factors are conflicting and contradictory. Nevertheless, these are used by different interest groups to arouse popular emotions and pressures for the short run. Thus, all these have an important bearing on the outcome of eventual national policy decisions.

In the Japanese brand of democracy, it is not the will of the majority that is critical in the final decision. To the Japanese, that would be "the tyranny of majority." It is rather how well the final policy decisions represent the best of the Japanese tradition of consensus, reached through an intricate and laborious process that may appear to Westerners as an endless series of compromises.

6. Future Outlook

The Japanese government is publicly committed to a continued easing of foreign investment restrictions in Japan. What then is the outlook for the future of Japanese policy toward capital liberalization? To begin with, it appears reasonable to expect that many of the direct and indirect mechanisms of control built into the present Japanese system will remain for many years to come. Specifically, it seems highly probable that the screening mechanism for foreign investments will remain in place, and that every effort will be made to ensure that new as well as existing business ventures remain under Japanese managerial control.

Furthermore, it is quite likely that the 50 percent joint-venture principle will be upheld as the cornerstone of Japan's capital liberalization program. It is based on the belief, widely accepted in both Japanese government and business circles, that, on the one hand, this principle offers a most reasonable and realistic way to achieve harmony with domestic interests and to avoid friction caused by nationalistic emotions. Thus, it will best serve the long-run purpose of ensuring *international equality and coprosperity* involving foreign investment. It is based on the belief, on the other hand, that jumping to a 100 percent liberalization policy on all fronts might cause unnecessary confusion in national economic policies and in business management, because economies, and ways of doing business, differ from country to country. For example, Toshio Doko, president of Toshiba (now president of Keidanren), has stated his view on this point as follows:

> 50–50 joint-business venture is the way internationalization of business should take henceforth . . . we cannot hope for a long-run success from now on without an attitude to cooperate with enterprises in the host countries. This will also apply to cases where Japanese enterprises go overseas . . . [74]

Naturally, from a Japanese perspective, the conduct of international investment, according to the conventional laissez-faire principles, in this age of widening gaps between the rich and the poor countries, is far from ideal in bringing about harmony and cooperation among the nations of the world. And many Japanese leaders believe that the 50 percent principle is the most workable international rule for the attainment of this goal, and should be incorporated as a cornerstone of a "world business charter," prescribing the mode of behavior of multinational corporations, especially in the developing countries. In fact, there are an increasing number of Japanese who feel that it is the mission of Japan to strongly advocate this Japanese view, since in former Ambassador Reischauer's words:

> Only Japan among important countries straddled *this triple chasm*, being the third largest unit on the side of the industrialized nations, but at the same time, the fifth largest population grouping on the non-Western, non-white side. This unique position, together with her special experience in modernizing herself, which seemed likely to prove more relevant for the non-Western world than the experience of North Americans, Russians, or Western Europeans . . . [75]

More specifically, referring to the case of Japan, Kogoro Uemura, former president of the Japan Federation of Economic Organizations (Keidanren) has stated that:

> . . . even where economic merit [of foreign investment] is proven, there is still a deep-rooted concern over a 'cultural takeover' of the Japanese way of life by a foreign way of life. Transnational investments are indeed transfer of the totality of managerial resources, and are bound to have influence on local business practice, employment patterns, working rules, community relations and the sense of participation among workers. This is a profound social and political hurdle in such a homogeneous nation as ours. This cultural and psy-

chological factor also explains the Japanese insistence on equal ownership. The principle is frankly based on the belief that foreign influence can be moderated by this formula. We ourselves want to proceed on this formula when we invest abroad.[76]

On the other hand, it appears highly probable that there will continue to be liberalization in the sense that an increasing number of industries will be designated for 100 percent foreign ownership. Among some of the important reasons for such a tendency despite Japan's adherence to the basic principle of 50–50 joint-business venture are the following:

1. As the Japanese economy is being drawn more and more into the mainstream of international business, a rapidly increasing number of Japanese are coming to recognize that their traditional unilateral actions in international economic spheres are becoming less and less acceptable abroad; and that if they are to avoid the possibility of catastrophe, brought upon them partly by the prewar political and military adventurism, they had better avoid similar adventurism in the realm of international economic relations. And the predominant basic international rule for capital liberalization of the advanced nations today, embodied in the OECD's Code of Capital Liberalization, is 100-percent foreign ownership.[77]

2. Some business leaders argue that the ratio of ownership is of secondary importance, and excessively heavy attention may have been given to this factor. For example, Minoru Segawa, chairman of the board of Nomura Securities Co., Ltd., states that "capital liberalization is basically the problem of the meeting of minds of people involved . . . Whether capital ratio is 50 percent or not is only a secondary problem compared with the critical question of whether the parties involved have trust in each other."

Yoichirō Makita, president of Mitsubishi Heavy Industries, also argues along the same line, but from the opposite perspective, stating that "it is essential that parties involved have a complete meeting of minds . . . If the partner is very good, 50 percent should be sufficient; if not, I feel uneasy even with over 51 percent.[78]

3. The Japanese business environment is so different that foreign enterprise can learn a great deal from the Japanese partner about local customs, etc., and, conversely, the Japanese has much to learn from foreign enterprises coming into Japan. As the process of assimilation proceeds, the degree of understanding and the meaningful communication increases to facilitate 100-percent foreign ownership on a much wider front.

4. There are many Japanese who believe that fears of foreign capital take-over of the Japanese economy are exaggerated, and that Japan needs the fresh ideas, methods and technology that foreign capital can introduce, feeling that the results will be healthy for the Japanese economy. Although the same result has been achieved fairly successfully thus far without 100-percent ownership, it may be becoming increasingly difficult to have the cake and eat it too.

5. Lastly, these attitudes reflect the bascially deepening self-confidence on the part of Japanese business in its international competitiveness.

Nevertheless, it is difficult to conceive of a time in the near future when the Japanese economy will be entirely open to foreign capital, in the sense that foreigners can invest without any essential restraint in any industry. But, on the other hand, mounting pressures, both endogenous and exogenous, for internationalization of the Japanese economy, will force it and its industries to evolve into an internationally viable and internally acceptable order. But that is more likely to be the result obtained "not according to consistent blueprint, but by means of a series of groping experiments."[79]

Another crucial aspect in the present discussion is the Japanese view on multinational corporations. Japan is not yet a country of multinational corporations. Many Japanese find it difficult to understand their motives and modes of behavior, resulting often in an exaggerated fear and concern over the impending domination of the economy by this relatively small number of giant corporations originated in a few foreign countries, predominantly the United States.

Japan does have a fairly large number of corporations engaged in international activities. However, their primary concern differs from more fully developed uninational or binational firms operating multinationally. Japanese corporations are in the embryonic stage of multinational corporate development. Their primary and predominant concern, until now, has been their domestic market share, with the aim that earnings from international operations assist them in being more competitive in the domestic market. Where this initial stage of Japanese multinational corporate development is seen, it is mainly in the early stages of production-marketing cycle. A truly multinational corporation is much more than the exportation of capital, encompassing the exchange of research and development, technology and management know-how. It, in fact, involves the entire spectrum of activities of industrial organization.[80] In such a sense of the term, Japan will probably remain outside of the true realm of multinational business for some years to come.

Regardless of whether the Japanese government or business leaders refer to the Japanese economy as liberalized or not, many restrictions will probably remain for many years to come. And to foreign investors and observers, the Japanese economy will remain a closely defended one, into which foreign capital can enter only with considerable frustration and difficulty and only based on very careful analyses and planning. It is not unreasonable to raise the question at this point of whether a foreign enterprise should bother to consider doing business in Japan. The answer certainly cannot be unequivocally affirmative at the present time. However, any view of the long-run future of multinational business can exclude Japan as a very critical component only at a grave risk.

In concluding this article, a point should be made explicitly concerning the future of the Unitde States-Japan relationship. It is unfortunate that the recent chain of events—such as Japan's slow approach to trade and capital liberalization, the impasse of the textile negotiation, and the "double-crossing by the United States," in the Japanese view, namely, President Nixon's visit to the People's Republic of China and his recent economic measures, aimed in the Japanese view, to a great extent at Japanese, on the twenty-sixth anniversary of Japan's surrender in the last war—seem to have sparked a deep distrust of the Japanese government and Washington among Japanese, and have placed United States-Japanese relations at the lowest ebb in the postwar era.

Former Secretary of State Rogers touched on a part of the causes in his speech before the Japan Society at New York in these words:

There is . . . a kind of perception gap arising from the phenomenally rapid growth of the Japanese economy. Among some Japanese there may be a tendency to view Japan as still struggling to make its way in a world of more economically powerful nations and thus requiring close government support of industry. Among some Americans the tendency may be just the reverse—to see Japan's economic strength as growing so massively that it has become a major threat to our own economic position . . . If, in both our countries, we can eliminate the stereotyped attitudes I have referred to, then the job of resolving the real issues that confront us will be much easier . . .[81]

Whatever the real causes may be, given such a close relation between the two countries politically and economically, as well as the general aspirations of the kind of world they both strive to build, it is inevitable that frictions do occur, and parties occasionally overreact to them. These periods of tension may have some beneficial effect in the long run: both sides are forced to carefully review each other's policies and attitudes and negotiate mutually accomodating policies between them, as well as with the rest of the world. The Japanese could take this opportunity to shift priorities, to devote more attention, as they have been doing increasingly in recent years, to various problems they has neglected at home: housing, health, living environment and other societal welfare problems.

The situation is a highly delicate one, partly because of the innate Japanese dislike for making quick decisions, or taking immediate action, and the Japanese tradition that the majority does not impose its will by force. Witness, for example, the Japanese government's short-lived, but stubborn, desperate attempt to keep the fixed exchange rate following President Nixon's announcement on August 15, 1971. It is hoped that the American government, business or other groups will not force the Japanese to rush into decisive actions. Such outside pressures could lead the Japanese to frustration and to giving up any hope of accommodation and could result in the creation of formidable barriers, animosity and the breakdown of communication. Such a sense of isolation may in turn force the Japanese to a feeling of impotence that they have failed to understand the world outside and that the latter cannot understand them.

Such a situation is clearly intolerable for both countries, since, as Herman Kahn puts it so perceptively:

The future is going to find the United States and Japan with many things to say to each other; they are further going to be closely related in a number of different projects, policies, areas, and they are going to be deeply concerned with each other's intentions and prospects.[82]

It is sincerely hoped that one beneficial outcome of the present tension will be the replacement of the conventional wisdom of Japanese business and government with a more realistic view toward international relations in the years immediately ahead, so that it can live in peace and harmony with the rest of the world.

1. Correspondents of the Economist, *Consider Japan* (London: Gerald Duckworth & Co., Ltd., 1963), p. ix.
2. Guillain, Robert, *The Japanese Challenge* (Philadelphia: J. B. Lippincott Company, 1970), p. 294.
3. Kindleberger, Charles P., *American Business Abroad* (New Haven: Yale University Press, 1969), p. 100.
4. There is no official Japanese definition of "direct investment." However two officials of the Incoming Section, International Finance Bureau of the Ministry of Finance, make distinctions among three forms of direct investment in Japan as follows:
    a. Establishment of subsidiaries and joint business ventures and participation in the management of existing enterprises;
    b. Establishment of branches;
    c. Granting of loans.
This division is to some extent reflected in the laws and regulations governing foreign direct investment. (Based on OECD, Committee for Invisible Transactions, *Liberalization of International Capital Movements: Japan,* (Paris: OECD, 1968), p. 13, quoting Mitsuru Katayama and Akira Nishigaki, *Investments in Japan, A Guide for Foreign Investors* (Tokyo: Institute of International Investment, 1964).
5. Katayama, Mitsuru and Nishigaki, Akira, *Investments in Japan, A Guide for Foreign Investors* (Tokyo; Institute of International Investment, 1964), as quoted in OECD, Committee for Invisible Transactions, *op. cit.,* p. 25.
6. Based on Ministry of International Trade and Industry, *Gaishi-kei Kigyo* (Enterprises with Foreign Capital), (Tokyo: MITI, 1968), pp. 31–36 and 274.
7. Based on MITI, *Gaishi-kei Kigyo no Doko* (Status of Enterprises with Foreign Capital) (Tokyo: MITI, 1970), pp. 3, 30 and 31.
8. *Ibid.,* pp. 2 and 30.
9. U.S. \$1 = 360 yen at the time of the study.
10. *Ibid.,* pp. 3, 30 and 31.
11. *Ibid.,* pp. 8 and 31.
12. See the list of companies, *ibid.,* pp. 87–157.
13. Out of the 100, 18 were Japanese firms and thus should be excluded.
14. *Ibid.,* pp. 3–4 and 9–10.
15. Based on "Foreign Capital Induction High," *The Oriental Economist,* October, 1961, pp. 589–590.
16. *Loc. cit.*
17. U.S. Department of Commerce, "Establishing a Business In Japan," *Overseas Business Report,* October 1966, p. 6.
18. *Ibid.,* p. 7.
19. "Capital Liberalization," *The Oriental Economist,* August 1966, p. 474.
20. "Liberalization of Capital," *The Oriental Economist,* May 1966, p. 253.
21. Keizai Doyukai, *Japan in the World Economy: A Statement on National Policy* (New York: Committee for Economic Development, 1963), p. 37.
22. "Liberalization of Capital," *The Oriental Economists,* May 1966, p. 253.

23. "Japan to Relax Control of Foreign Direct Investment," *United States-Japan Trade Council Report*, No. 58, August 19, 1966, p. 1.

24, Information in this section is heavily derived from the *United States-Japan Trade Council Reports* and *Japan Reports* unless otherwise specified.

25. "From Hotels to Steel, Japan Finally Opens Some Doors to Foreign Competition," *Business Abroad*, June 12, 1967, p. 9, and "Capital Liberalization & Industry," *The Oriental Economist*, June 1967, p. 385.

26. *The Japan Economic Journal*, June 15, 1971, p. 3.

27. *The Japan Economic Journal*, July 27, 1971, pp. 1 and 7.

28. *The Japan Economic Journal*, July 27, 1971, pp. 1 and 5.

29. *The Japan Economic Journal*, August 3, 1971, pp. 1 and 5.

30. *United States-Japan Trade Council Report*, No. 51, August 15, 1971, p. 3.

31. Business International, *Investing, Licensing and Trading Conditions* (New York: Business International, 1970), pp. 204–205.

32. "Challenge for Responsible Partnership," speech delivered on June 15, 1971, at Madison Hotel, Washington, D.C.

33. Koto, Rikuzo, "Japan in the World Economy: The View from Tokyo," *Columbia Journal of World Business*, March-April, 1970, p. 40.

34. Okita Saburō, "The Textile Negotiation: Japan's Point of View," *Columbia Journal of World Business*, January–February, 1971, pp. 74–75.

35. Koto Rikuzo, *op. cit.*, March–April, 1970, p. 40.

36. Assistant Secretary Green and Assistant Secretary Trezise Interviewed for Japanese National Television," *The Department of State Bulletin*, March 29, 1971, p. 453.

37. Glazer, Herbert, "Japan Unbars a Door," *Columbia Journal of World Business*, July–August 1967, p. 45.

38. See Glazer, Herbert, "Capital Liberalization," in Ballon, Robert J. (ed.), *Joint Ventures and Japan* (Tokyo: Sophia University, 1967), pp. 1–2 and 8.

39. "FTC Will Seek Report on Alien Stocks," *The Japan Economic Journal*, August 24, 1971, p. 1.

40. Business International, *op cit.*, p. 207.

41. "New MITI Code Being Drafted for Investors," *Business Asia*, August 13, 1971, p. 261.

42. *The United States-Japan Trade Council Report*, No. 51, August 5, 1971, p. 1.

43. Reischauer, Edwin O., *Japan: The Story of A Nation* (New York: Alfred A. Knopf, 1970), p. 332.

44. Macrae, Norman, "The Risen Sun," *The Economist*, May 27, 1967, p. x.

45. Luckwood, William W., "Japan's 'New Capitalism'," in Luckwood, William W. (ed.), *The State and Economic Enterprise in Japan* (Princeton, New Jersey: Princeton University Press, 1965), p. 490.

46. Lobb, John C., " 'Japan, Inc., '—The Total Conglomerate," *Columbia Journal of World Business*, March–April, 1971, pp. 41–2.

47. Hollerman, Leon, *Japan's Dependence on the World Economy* (Princeton, New Jersey: Princeton University Press, 1967), pp. 160–161.

48. Reischauer, Edwin O., *op. cit.*, p. 155.

49. Halloran, Richard, *Japan: Images and Realities* (New York: Alfred A. Knopf, 1969), p. 73.

50. Macrae, Norman, *op. cit.*, p. xxiii.

51. Luckwood, William W., *op. cit.*, p. 503.

52. The Bank of Japan, *Economic Statistics Annual, 1970*, pp. 211–12, and "Outline of Business Results of Leading Japanese Companies for the Latter Half of Fiscal 1969," *MERI's Monthly Circular*, November 1970, pp. 6–11.

53. *MERI's Monthly Circular, op. cit.*, p. 7.

54. "The Fortune Directory of the 500 Largest Corporations," *Fortune*, May 1970, p. 202.

55. "The Fortune Directory of the 100 Largest Industrials Outside the U.S.," August 1957, pp. 20–21.

56. "The 200 Largest Corporations Outside the U.S.," *Fortune,* August 1963, pp. 140–43, and August 1971, p. 155.

57. Stone P. S., *Japan Surges Ahead: The Story of An Economic Miracle* (New York: Frederick A. Praeger, 1969), p. 65.

58. The Bank of Japan, *The Japanese Financing System* (Tokyo: Bank of Japan, 1970), p. 13.

59. Terasawa, Yoshio, "Capital Market" in Ballon, Robert (ed.), *Doing Business in Japan* (Tokyo: Sophia University, 1967), pp. 97–101.

60. See, Economic Planning Agency, *Keizai Hakusho* (White Paper on the Nation's Economy) (Tokyo: EPA, 1970), p. 176–78.

61. Hollerman, Leon, *op. cit.,* p. 162.

62. Reischauer, Edwin O., *op. cit.,* p. 292.

63. See, EPA, *Keizai Hakusho* (White Paper on Economy: New Dimensions of Japanese Economy), 1970, pp. 189–269; and *Kokumin Seikatsu Hakusho* (White Paper on People's Life: Creating Rich Human Living Environment), 1970, pp. 149–85.

64. Halloran, Richard, *op. cit.,* p. 186.

65. Reischauer, Edwin O., *op. cit.,* p. 8.

66. Yanaga, Chitoshi, *Big Business in Japanese Politics* (New Haven: Yale University Press, 1968), p. 1.

67. Hall, John Whitney and Beardsley, Richard K., (ed.), *Twelve Doors to Japan* (New York: McGraw-Hill Book Company, 1965), p. 387.

68. Kahn, Herman, *The Emerging Japanese Superstate* (Englewood Cliffs, New Jersey: Prentice-Hall, Inc., 1970), p. 27.

69. See for detail, Yoshino, Michael Y., *Japan's Managerial System* (Cambridge, Massachusetts: The MIT Press, 1968), pp. 118–61.

70. Bairy, Maurice, "The Japanese Ways," in Ballon, Robert (ed.), *Doing Business in Japan,* p. 9.

71. Halloran, Richard, *op. cit.,* p. 189.

72. Inukai, Michiko, "Agreeing to Differ," *Japan Quarterly,* Vol. VIII, No. 2, p. 182.

73. Okita, Saburō, *op. cit.,* p. 74.

74. Freely translated from *Bessatsu Chūokōrōn: Keiei Mondai,* Fall 1970, p. 417.

75. Reischauer, Edwin O., *op. cit.,* p. 340. (Italics added.)

76. Speech given on June 15, 1971, at Madison Hotel, Washington, D.C.

77. Freely translated from *Bessatsu Chūōkoron, op. cit.,* p. 413.

78. Freely translated from *ibid.,* p. 421.

79. Yoshino, Michae Y., *op. cit.,* p. 194.

80. See, for example, Kindleberger, Charles P., *op. cit.,* chapter 1.

81. Rogers, William, "The United States and Japan: Common Interests and Common Problems," *The Department of State Bulletin,* July 19, 1971, pp. 70–71.

82. Kahn, Herman, *op. cit.,* p. 15.

(Professor Furuhashi finished his article before December, 1971, when ten-nation finance minister conference was held at the Smithonian Institute, the first of important events of international economy which was to come up in the course of four years. —Editors

Shunichi Takayanagi

Christology and Postwar Theologians in Japan[1]

1. Prewar and Postwar Backgrounds

The Christian theological scene in Japan reflects all the discussions in the West. We find the same themes are taken up by Japanese Christian thinkers with subtle mutations that indicate still existing intellectual and cultural differences. The Meiji period was for Japanese Christianity the age of charismatic leaders like Kanzo Uchimura (1861–1930). But when enthusiasm inevitably gave way to reflection, the perennial question arose: Who is this Jesus? The situation of Meiji Christian thought was something like that of early Christianity. Controversy arose between Danjo Ebina (1859–1937) and Masahisa Uemura (1857–1925) on the fundamental Christological issue under the impact of Unitarianism and Liberal Theology. Uemura maintained the traditional position on the unity of Jesus Christ God-man against the highly speculative Ebina, who developed the theory of cosmic Logos existing in the soul of Jesus the man and the souls of other human beings.

Christian missionary activities encountered more and more difficulties in the periods following the Meiji, with Japanese intellectuals growing more sophisticated and sympathetic towards Marxism. In the face of a number of desertions from the church and the indifference of the surrounding world, the young Christian intellectuals, who at first formed a Christian social movement under the influence of Troeltsch, responded enthusi-

119

astically to new Dialectical Theology. From the ranks of these men came most of the Christian thinkers, who dominated the theological scene from the early Showa period to the first decade after World War II. Their allegiance towards Barth was curiously combined with readiness to accept the philosophical thoughts of Nishida (1870–1945), Tanabe (1885–1962) and Seiichi Hatano (1877–1950).

Fundamental Problems in Christology (1934) by Yoshitaka Kumano (1899—), is the first major work in the field and a significant contribution to the prewar Christian scene. Maintaining the Barthian neo-orthodox position, Kumano puts Christology in the center of Christian thought.[2] Yoshizo Kitamori (1916—) is now well known in the West for his *Theology of the Pain of God*.[3] In another book he declares that the contemporary Japanese Christian situation requires Christology.[4] In *Theology of the Pain of God*, born out of theological reflection in the somber days towards the end of the war, he brings the idea of God's descent even further than Luther's position. But despite his efforts to keep Jesus Christ in central focus, Kitamori's Christology tends to volatilize.

Kitamori's *The Pain of God* occasioned heated discussions among Japanese Christian thinkers. Nobuo Odagiri accused Kitamori of a "docetistic tendency," and rejecting Kitamori's firm support of traditional Christological formula, Odagiri calls for the removal of all pagan Greek elements from Christian theology.[5] Protestant orthodoxy reacted violently against his position as "neo-arian". As part of the reaction Fujio Fujiwara (1900—) deepened the idea of kenotic descent and developed the theory on logos combining the traditional theology of the cross with that of glory as the former's consequence.[6]

Discussions of Kitamori's book had hardly subsided when controversy arose between two major figures. Both are nourished in Dialectical Theology, but there exists a definite generation gap between the one, intellectually brought up before the war, and the other, coming in contact with a new approach in postwar times. The controversy has all the ramifications of a battle between Barthians and Bultmannians.

2. Seiichi Yagi and Katsumi Takizawa: A Gap between Two Generations of Scholars

Seiichi Yagi (1932—), who studied in Göttingen between 1957 and 1959, considers that Jesus' proclamation of God's kingdom consisted of man's liberation from the oppression of social conventions and a return to the original roots of man's existence. Thus the heart of Christian faith is the historical event of Jesus the man. The Apostles' exclusive authority as the witnesses of Resurrection and the early Christian community's making this historical Jesus Christ-Logos suggest a typical human-religious process. Thus he proposes, based on the results of the history of religions, a hypothesis of three (A, B, C) early Christian communities in order to explain the crystallization of New Testament (religious) thought, with A's tendency towards emphasizing new freedom from the old Law, B's discovery of the event of Christ and individual existential commitment, and finally C's synthesis of the two in the ideas of love and communion, from which Yagi surmises that the doctrine of the Trinity and ecclesiology later developed. It was the less Jewish, less eschatological and soteriological B type of thought that started to evolve Christology on the basis of the doctrine of Resurrection.

Yagi regards the Christian dogmatic development as a type of universal movement of religious consciousness from unity to freedom and from freedom to synthesis. Christ is the result of this synthesis. He sees a dynamic relationship between Jesus as a historical being and Christ as a religious reality and triest of ace Japan's intellectual and cultural situation. For him the logos is the transcendental basis for human existence. The baptized, church and scripture are only different modes of the incarnation of the logos. Jesus of Nazareth is a human being, but the logos incarnated in Jesus (and as Jesus) is truly God and man. On the basis of indivisibility of the dynamic relationship, whose comprehension may very well suggest to the Western reader a peculiar maneuvering among many contemporary currents of theological and philosophical thought, Yagi accepts as a conclusion the traditional Christological Nicaean-Chalcedonian definition as a legitimate development of New Testament thought, but this definition has nothing to do with the historical Jesus of Nazareth. A historical reality can never be the basis for faith, Yagi proclaims. Faith has to do with human existence.[7] Yagi sees the event of Christ as underlying the religious experience of each generation of the church, which is to be the communion of personal existences in deep levels. Thus Christ is the communal experience of personal existences, and the church its manifestation: Christ speaks to me from within myself (Christ living in me), from within thee as thy word (Proclamation), and confronts me as the church. As the conclusion Yagi combines this Christ with Jesus of Nazareth: Jesus is the Gestalt of the subject of the church, which is Christ. Yagi closes up the circle in this manner with a significant remark on the eschatological nature of human existence. Man as a religious being in this world always feels that this synthesis is never to be realized and lives in eschatological hope of God's kingdom, and his faith consists in his participation in Christ's work.

Yagi's most important work is *The Formation of New Testament Thought* (1963). He always speaks of human existence or ultimate reality. He begins his book avowedly as a critique of Bultmann and emphasizes that his method of investigation is of a neutral *geistes-wissenschaftlich* nature. Therefore, with the customary distinction between faith and religion, he claims that the Christian faith is an eminent religious phenomenon.[8] He remarks that although he owes much to Bultmann on the unity of existence and thought, he came to realize through his acquaintance with Buddhism the fundamental correspondence of Christianity and Buddhism: Christian existence is just one possibility of human existence, the appearance of Christianity being an event in human existence. Naming his own position a *pro-se* one, he accuses Bultmann of a stringently individualistic *pro-me* attitude. In other words, Yagi desires to share human existence or ultimate reality with other human beings, those of other faiths—as the ultimate communion in Christ before God.

Thus scholarly (objective) investigation is to turn into a *koinonia* in the spirit of love. For that purpose the New Testament documents should first be looked at as human documents. Yagi remarks that the nineteenth-century German Liberal Theology united religion and culture on the same level, whereas the Dialectical Theology of the first half of this century dissociated Christian faith from culture and made the divine inimical to the human. Kerygma (which in Dialectical Theology is identical with faith) is for Yagi essentially human, as a product of human thought. But it must transform itself into the divine through the religious experience of personal existences.

Katsumi Takizawa (1909—), who studied two years under Karl Barth before World War II and wrote his first theological book on the German theologian in 1939, took issue with Yagi. The latter's view on the possibility of investigating New Testament religious thought on a neutral basis brings forth ultimately an insufficient analysis of the person of Jesus Christ, according to Takizawa.[9] Nevertheless, Takizawa endorses Yagi's idea of the common existential basis between Christian faith and Buddhism. He points out that Yagi is a born Christian, whereas he came to know Christ after his philosophical career, and recounts an autobiographical episode. Nishida, his teacher, who was well-versed in Zen Buddhism, recommended him to study under Barth when he went to Germany. Takizawa interprets this fact as indicating Nishida's conviction on the fundamental agreement between Christianity and Zen Buddhism.

Yagi's standpoint in Takizawa's view is self-contradictory and self-defeating, since his categorization of the religious thought of three early Christian communities is in itself a value judgment, and Yagi takes his position in regard to the proclamation of Jesus as Christ. It is, furthermore, impossible to construct an existentialism while preserving one's neutrality. The authentic existence, which Yagi uses repeatedly, always offers itself to be answered. In Takizawa's understanding, Yagi identifies this authentic existence with the religious existence of the historical Jesus, but Jesus as the Son of God, Christ, is the discovery of the early Christians from the Resurrection, which involved a higher stage of interpretation of Jesus's redemptive death. In other words Yagi's view is according to Takizawa a serious challenge to the traditional Protestant doctrine of redemption.

In order to answer Yagi's challenge, Takizawa tries to clarify the nature of Apostolic witness on the person of Jesus. Man in his concrete existence is in union with God despite insurmountable distance and the irreversible order from God to man. This was the basis for the coming of Christ the Saviour, who really suffered on the cross, died, resurrected, ascended and will come at the end of this aeon. Concrete human existence in its origin derives from God and is in this sense divine (Takizawa calls this the fact of Immanuel). The disciples saw in the historical Jesus the divine man who fully realized the Immanuel-nature and identified and proclaimed him as Christ the Redeemer. Thus *Immanuel* expresses the unity between God and man, but it is nonsensical to speak of this unity only in abstract terms. Immanuel is the complete union of the symbol and the symbolized—the thing itself. Yagi's authentic existence, according to Takizawa, therefore fails in great measures to see historical convergence between the divine-radical and the human-historical, which is the dynamism in the Bible fulfilled on the cross.

As a direct reply to Takizawa's critique, Yagi wrote *Christ of the Bible and Existence*.[10] He admits that he did not come to the awareness of the fundamental fact of Immanuel and now proposes to prove the inseparable unity of Christology and existentialism. He notices some significant differences between Barth and Takizawa. In his understanding Takizawa's Christ is the foundation of self-realization; he is the contact-point of God and man that is universal to all men. Yagi, however, critically adds that Takizawa's Christ has no personalistic side of calling the faithful with "thou," as does the Christ of the New Testament, and is simply posited as the fundamental relationship of God and man. Yagi condemns Takizawa's ontological character, which is much stronger than in Tillich. Oddly enough, Yagi is now against a divisionist Christology. Takizawa is said to divide Jesus and Christ by identifying Jesus with Immanuel without qualification. Jesus according to Yagi is the one that has realized Immanuel, and among the New Testament writers a clear distinction was made between Jesus Christ according to flesh and according to spirit. In Yagi's view one has to distinguish between Jesus the man and Immanuel as the foundation of self-realization, though in actuality they are inseparable.

Yagi takes up Takizawa's Immanuel, which he regards as the great contribution of the latter to theology, derived though it may be from Barth, and interprets it in his own light. Since Jesus is a man just like all of us, his relationship with Immanuel is fundamentally the same as with ours. But he is the normative man, who exhausted the possibility of Immanuel-nature. This Immanuel was discovered by Jesus' disciples only after the Resurrection through reflection on his deeds before death. The New Testament is the result of these reflections. Immanuel therefore is not only the expression of what Christianity calls Christ but of religious existence common even with Buddhism. This distinction answers the question of historical Jesus in terms of mediation of religious existence in Jesus. The disciples realized that the foundation of Jesus had been Immanuel, and this is also their own and explicitly formulated as Risen Jesus Christ. Yagi accuses Takizawa of an undifferentiated exegetical method that does not distinguish between Immanuel itself and its realization. Immanuel is still a living force. The absolute identification of Jesus with Immanuel in the faith after the Resurrection is still alive among the faithful, who are Christ's body. Yagi further accuses Takizawa of failing to develop a phenomenology of Immanuel in terms of which a man's realization of Immanuel in his life in relations with fellow men can be analyzed. He insists that Immanuel works in the community of men. What is lacking in Takizawa, Yagi remarks, is ecclesiology as the legitimate consequence of Christology. Against Takizawa's criticism that he lacks theological-ontological reflection, Yagi replies that Takizawa himself is not too clear on the ontological determination of Christ; his method is at best intuitive, with his special linguistic system intolerant of other systems.

3. Collections of Studies on Christology: Faith and Historical Scholarship

The controversy between Yagi and Takizawa came to its formal end in the fall of 1971.[11] Looking at the discussion between Yagi and Takizawa, one has the impression Japanese theologians can tackle problems skilfully in the systems of language constructed by European theologians and translated and modulated by those of Japanese philosophers. But for these systematic interpretations and speculative theological discussions there should exist a rather extensive background of scholarly works of historical nature on the Christologies in the New Testament, Patristics, Middle Ages and contemporary theology. The very fact that the previous two theologians discussed their problems in terms of Barth and Bultmann underlines the high degree of their theological sophistication. Often enough it is extremely difficult to dissociate historical works from systematic speculation. They are not only the basis for theological speculation but also are entangled in the fabric of the genuine theological ideas of their authors. In the case of Gnostic understanding of Jesus or of Arian controversy, problems may seem quite remote from present theological discussion, but they form an important part of the background for the question of the historical Jesus.[12] The essential connection of speculative works with historical investigations is shown by several collections of essays, three of which are explicitly contributions to the problems of Christology.

Nobuyuki Tajima grasps Paul's Christology as a *Kyrios* Christology after Deissmann and Bousset.[13] Although the position maintained by these two biblical scholars that the title "Lord" (Kyrios) originated in the Hellenistic Gentile communities is untenable today, the identification of Jesus with the Lord, which is less prominent in the Gospels than the Son of God, shows definitely the deepening of understanding of the event of salvation. For Tajima the *Son of Man* Christology lays stress on the future and suggests a line extending forward. The title has as its background Old Testament apocalyptic materials. The Son of Man in the Book of Enoch has a typically apocalyptic character. Thus the Son of Man Christology is also apocalyptic with its eschatological Christ. The *Kyrios* Christology of Paul is a synthesis of point (present), line (future) and space (universe). Thus Christ is the Lord in the universe who is to come as the Risen Lord at the coming *parousia*.

Interesting also will be Yoshio Noro's article in the same collection with Tajima's article, which tries to bring "an existentialist approach to the redemption."[14] He is interested in approaches made by Nicholas Berdyaev and Miguel de Unamuno on the suffering love of God. But Noro considers that they as well as Kitamori and D. M. Baillie concentrate too much upon the suffering love of God as past event, and they all have a tendency of patripassianism. Noro too distinguishes the event of Christ from that of Jesus. "The event of Christ is the event which happened to Jesus, because of Jesus' obedience to the will of God, but it is still happening in the present in which we are personally and existentially involved."[15] Nevertheless, he recognizes an existentialist element in the traditional concept of redemption (and Kitamori's pain of God is taken as the sharpening of this concept) in the sense that God loves the unlovable. The event of Jesus on the cross is the symbol of God's turning towards us because of Jesus' obedience to the will of God. But for Noro, God's suffering is only one note of the entire event. Here he emphasizes the Resurrection as victory, which confirms the present existentialist I-thou relationship between God and man. But the Resurrection, as well as the Incarnation of the eternal logos and others contained in traditional Christology, is fundamentally a myth, to proclaim that God's word given in (the event of) Jesus determines our existence till the end of human history. Thus for Noro the forgiveness of sin is also central in that message. But he tries to mitigate the austere impression of traditionally conceived redemption. "The existential understanding of Christianity consists in finding the absoluteness of Christianity not in Christology in the traditional sense but in the very quality of God's love symbolized in Jesus Christ." All other considerations like life after death are not the concern of theology. "It is sufficient that we believe the event of Jesus as Christ is the Word of Love from God which makes us really exist."[16]

In *Evangelism and Theology*[17] Noro further develops an existential understanding of the Eucharist based on his existential Christology and soteriology. The Eucharist is there for us to experience the existential side of the Christian faith. There impossibility in the event of the cross. God conquered on the cross the impossible situation. The Eucharist makes us experience the infinite power of God in overcoming the impossible, and the faithful participate in this overcoming—and thus happens a wonder in the Bultmannian sense. Keiji Ogawa's discussion of Barth's second edition of his commentary on the Romans is also important.[18] He emphasizes as Barth's central theme that God's Word is intelligible only through the cross. Barth understands strictly the supremacy of God's Word over human existence. There is no human existence that stays outside of the salvific economy. Its essence is clearly manifest under the light of God's Word. Thus Jesus Christ is boldly proclaimed to be my existential *ego*.

Junichi Asano edited a number of collections of theological essays. *The Problems of Christology*[19] is one of them. Asano himself wrote the first article, "Christ in the Book of Job," and sees in Job a witness of Jesus Christ.[20] He contrasts the Wisdom literature with the Prophets and Law in the Old Testament. Wisdom in the Old Testament is unhistorical, having to do with man's existence itself. The central problem for Wisdom writers is in general that of the individual's faith and experience. Since Wisdom is not primarily concerned with a particular race, there is no concept of chosen people in the Wisdom literature. Central in the Book of Job is thus the suffering of Job himself. In the Prophets and Law there is an emphasis on God's Word as His commandment, and a man can have the choice to obey and receive life or disobey and face death, while in Wisdom a man can question if God's commandment is just, and this judgment derives from his experience. Thus Asano sees here the growth of man's self-conciousness even in a primitive form. The Wisdom in the Old Testament is God's wisdom according to Asano but is also human wisdom, and what constitutes this is human experience. Asano emphasizes in this connection the emergence of human self-consciousness through experience.

The human person as the center of self-consciousness is a drama in which man's own concept of righteousness is tried by God's justice and undergoes the process of purification in man's bitter and ununderstandable experience. Out of this the longing for the Mediator appears. Thus although Job's experience and his crisis have primarily nothing to do with history and time, time is personally experienced by Job in his experience of faith as crisis. The Christ of the Book of Job can first justly be considered with the background of Job's personal crisis-faith, and this Christ transcends the time of the Old Testament to that of the New Testament.

Asano remarks that Job's eschatological faith agrees fundamentally with that of Old Testament prophets, especially Jeremiah.[21] Jeremiah (and with him the Old Testament concept of servant of God) is limited to the history of Israel. Asano's estimate of the Old Testament prophecy in this matter is rather negative. Job has in a way universalized the human situation, setting it free from the bonds of covenant. However, precisely this covenant has an essential place in the Christology of Paul and the author of the *Hebrews*. In passing it must be therefore mentioned that Asano should examine his distinction between Wisdom, and Prophecy and Law in the Old Testament; recent scholarship suggests a more intimate connection, or at least according to it the early Christians saw it between them.[22] Kenichi Kida examines the concept of covenant as the background of the Covenant Christology of Paul and the *Hebrews,* based chiefly on G. E. Mendenhall.[23] In the history of the concept of covenant there had gradually come to the surface the idea of God's forgiveness, which is the central notion in Jeremiah, and this takes a central place in the new Christian faith.

Ken Ishihara analyzes thought in John's Prologue.[24] Its structure, as he sees it, was formed on the basis of the beginning of new understanding of Creation and Redemption as new Creation in the divine Logos. The beginning is for the Evangelist no relative *berischeth* but the absolute aetiological beginning. He sees God's glory through the appearance of Christ. What the Gospel sees central therefore is not the constituting of nature called Creation but the completion of spiritual glorification through the Logos. Thus the transcendent Logos' role is explored in the Prologue as the preexistent, which is ontologically over and above all the created as the *sophiological* Being. The appearance of this Logos on earth does not presuppose *harmartological* human history since the Creation, but it happens out of the necessity of its inner essence. Consequently this is the revealer of truth. The Logos' role is further contrasted with that of Moses. The Logos fulfills what Moses could not. The Evangelist wants to show that Jesus is a historical person but at the same time has divine origin. He is not so much interested in history as in the sign-nature of Jesus' existence. The Incarnation of the Logos is therefore the best possible way to bring his thought to expression. John's Logos Christology turns into the light-of-the-world Christology, based on the contrast between *nomos* and *logos,* Moses and Christ. Christ is *Mystagos,* spiritual initiator into the Mysterion of rebirth, although the Fourth Gospel contains a reaction against Gnosticism. The historical person of Jesus in flesh is *ipso facto* the Logos as the Light in the world.

The problem of the self-consciousness of Jesus is analyzed by Isaburo Takayanagi, and it is brought to conclusion on the person of Jesus.[25] Jesus had also no clear-cut notion of his life and mission from the beginning; he had no sureness about his own Messiahship and the consequence of the proclamation and spread of the Kingdom of God as the result of his experience of his intimate relationship with the Father as the Son at His baptism. That made him refrain from explicitly stating his Christ-nature. The identification is the contribution of the early Christian community, who realized the meaning of this incomparably original person. Its foundation was that God was in Christ, but "Jesus is the Lord" continues to be the confession of the faithful through the Holy Spirit.

Using Bultmann and other exegetical materials Seigo Yamaya endeavors to clarify the biblical identification of Christ and hope and draws consequences for ecclesiology.[26] The early Christian community's expectation of the nearness of the *parousia* is frustrated, and a new interpretation has to be invented. The identification of Christ with hope indicates the coming of a new type of Christianity. Christ as our hope is no immovable essence in heaven; he is the Lord who comes near to us. Hope is related with the future. Man hopes on the future event (Rom. 8, 24–28), but when it is difficult to be convinced about the hope's realization, a crisis in faith sets in. Thus hope must be presented not merely as an ideal but as a dynamic living force, which has a direct connection with us. Hence Christ must become the Christ who comes to us: i.e., the *parousia* of Christ in every moment of history as presence. Yamaya considers that we are in the second (phase of) history of salvation, in which time flows to us from before us, from the eschaton of Risen

Christ. He stresses the necessity of placing hope in the stream of time coming from the future to the present. Thus the situation of the Old Testament in which Christ is the coming Messiah is reversed; the realizer of Christian hope is the Christ of glory.

As the last piece of the collection on biblical Christology, Hiroo Sekita writes on the significance of the geneology of Jesus in Matthew and Luke.[27] They develop geneological Christology. Their geneologies have different theological outlooks and motives. Matthew concentrates on the history of salvation coming down from the Old Testament and Christ as Son of David. Thus his is the Son of David Christology. Christ is the Son of David because he is the Messiah, not vice versa, while for Luke the history of salvation has a worldwide perspective and thus his is the Second Adam Christology.

There are two articles on Christology from the point of view of history of dogma. Tetsurarō Ariga's article has indeed no direct connection with the content of Christology itself, but he examines the internal necessity and process of formation of dogma.[28] He seems to consider that this process already had an inner principle in Jesus himself, and rejects the viewpoint of Martin Werner, Harnack, and Seeberg, which takes Hellenizing of Christianity as a purely external process. Sasagu Arai treats the *Shepherd of Hermas* and gives a picture of Christology in the background of the history of researches on the letter.[29] The equal setting in the letter of the spirit and the son of God brought forth an endless discussion on whether Hermas' is an Adoptionist Christology or an angel Christology. Arai places Hermas in the context of *de-eschatolozing* process or prolonging the end of the world to the future, and seems to suggest that Hermas' is an angel Christology.

Yoshio Noro attempts in this collection an existentialist Christology, stimulated by the Christological controversy between Kitamori and Odagiri.[30] As a personal note he writes that he makes a new theological start, since he sees now that there is no possibility for reconciling his Bultmannian existentialism and the mystical ontology of F. von Hügel. The latter has made him maintain a conciliatory stand towards traditional theology, but mystical ontology cannot be reconciled with the personal God, who confronts us with the urgent demand for our decision. Thus he says he has to reinterpret in an existentialist manner what is mystical within himself. He begins with the analysis of Barth's critique of Bultmann's Christological position. Bultmann's Christology is, as he himself admits, a doctrine of justification. Barth criticizes that in Bultmann's theology Christology is merged with soteriology. This Bultmann himself does not take as criticism. It expresses precisely what Bultmann's Christology is. The author comments that with Bultmann Jesus is more emphasized in the event of Jesus Christ, whereas with Barth Christ is more stressed. Bultmann emphasizes more the event, which is a great difference from Barth. Thus it is more the meaning of this event than the essence of the person of Jesus that counts in Bultmann's thinking. The Christological definition of Chalcedon is therefore nothing but hindrance for a man's decision. What Jesus means to our decision is for Bultmann more significant than small historical facts about Jesus. Bultmann's existentialist theology is not a monologue of man, as Barth and Tillich see it. It affirms that God works within the world, not outside the world. Existential decision is required by God and is the result of God's working. Christology and the doctrine of the Trinity must and can be existentially rethought. Christology must therefore be a meeting of God and myself. After the event of the cross and the Resurrection, we can no more meet God except through what is presented in the Bible, and this God, as described in the Bible, is the God who demands our decision. Thus the Resurrection is no historical fact but an existentialist-historical event. The empty grave is no longer for Noro a matter for theological inquiry.

The second collection of essays on Christology is entitled *The Living Christ*, edited by Kanō Yamamoto.[31] The book is divided into three parts, "The Light of the World," "Christology in the New Testament," and "Christology in Modern Theology." The volume is meant not as a purely theoretical book on Christology, but tries to apply Christology to missionary activites. Masatoshi Fukuda develops the Johannine theme of Christ as light of the world.[32] For him too Christology is no theory but requires decision of faith. Faith is thus an existential attitude, and approach to Jesus cannot be made apart from this attitude. There are only two possibilities: faith or scandal before Jesus Christ. Jesus Christ in history is an existential reality that we dare to gain through faith. The way of scandal is ultimately depersonalization and estrangement from humanity. Christ is the true light; i.e., he is the light not lighting this world from outside. This light is in the world through his Incarnation. He is the light of life. Thus Jesus Christ is no teacher, prophet or social reformer or religious reformer. He is the Salvation itself for human existence. He is the *autobasileia*, and thus his biography is not to be written. His mission is to reconcile men with God and restore them as sons of God; he is in this sense the ground of human existence, its meaning, end and hope. He fought most radically against human self-righteousness. Man can be saved only through breaking his self-justification. Christ is the light to illumine in concrete terms Divine and human truth. Fukuda is influenced by Barth and Kierkegaard in his understanding of Christ. Mikita Takagi analyzes the deep spiritual exhaustion of the modern masses, and concludes that Christ is the only fulfilling answer for modern man's feeling of unreality.

According to Hideyasu Nakagawa, who examines New Testament Christology in light of Bultmann and the post-Bultmannian generation, Christ's names and titles in the Bible are no simple descriptive terms, but those which confess Jesus and show what a function Jesus has for our history of salvation.[34] They tell us about *"Christus pro me"* but not his nature. They tell us of the urgency of our decision by making clear the new situation for men and the world. Thus Jesus' names and titles all express him as the eschatological event. Thus in the horizon of the understanding of Christ exists that of history. Takeo Yamanaga summarizes the historical, cultural and intellectual backgrounds of the Christological controversy at Nicaea; he sees in the conflict between Athanasius and Arius the confrontation between philosophical speculation and conviction of faith, human wisdom and God's foolishness.[35] The living Christ was what Luther and Calvin emphasized, remarks Naomichi Kodaira.[36] But paradoxically in order to grasp the living reality of Christ as our own reality the Jesus crucified must be presented not sentimentally but theologically and soteriologically. The risen Christ must be proclaimed as the surest guarantee for our righteousness. This faith in the living Christ through the Resurrection is given by the working of the

Holy Spirit. The faithful are to live in this living Christ through the faith given by the Holy Spirit. Christ makes us live a new life in salvation.

Toshio Sato traces Christology up to that of Dialectical Theology in modern times with background of intellectual history.[37] He divides it into three stages: (1) the destructive criticism of the Enlightenment and the presentation of Christ merely as *Vorbild*, (2) German Romanticism and Idealism with its emphasis on Christ as *Urbild* and (3) Positivism as the criticism of speculative Idealism with the life of Jesus researches. And he sees in this stream theology's efforts to unify Jesus and Christ. The theological thought of a Swedish theologian, Gustaf Aulen, is also introduced to Japan by Yasuo Furuya in the present collection.[38] Furuya bases his article mainly on *Christus Victor, an Historical Study of the Three Main Types of the Idea of Atonement* (1931), and *The Faith of the Christian Church* (1948). Aulen classifies the doctrine of the Redemption into (1) the objective Latin type of Anselm, Reformers and traditional Christians, (2) the subjective humanistic type of Socinius and Liberal theologians and (3) the type of Christ as Victor, which though classical has not received attention (I Cor., 5, 19). According to Aulen the third type was maintained by many Church Fathers. Thus the Redemptive work is regarded by Aulen as victory. The author too stands on the traditional unity of Christology and soteriology together with Aulen and quotes the words of Melanchton, "Christus cognoscere est beneficia eius cognoscere." But Furuya proposes Jesus Victor instead of Christ Victor. He criticizes George Hendry in his *The Gospel of the Incarnation* (1958), saying, that Aulen has made Christ's victory over sin and devils too much a *fait accompli* and thus deprived humanity of its significance in the order of Redemption.[39] Christ is the only Victor among men, but if he is from his essence the divine Victor, there seems to be no necessity for the Incarnation. Furuya thinks that most sermons in Japan center around Christ's victory. This is not because Aulen's thought is known in this country; it is the result of Barth's influence. Barth has at least a tendency to ignore evil and sin when he talks about the absolute victory of Christ. The author suspects Barth's neglect of the problem of sin, since according to him there is no independent harmartology in his

Dogmatics. In the intellectual climate of the West there is the consciousness of evil and sin, but in that of Japan this consciousness is almost nil. Thus it is better to emphasize Jesus Victor in Japan, according to Furuya. He considers that this is based on the doctrine of the Incarnation; he tries to see more significance in Jesus Christ who is homoousious with us.

Seiichi Yagi has also a short article on the double nature of the concept of the Kingdom of God in Jesus.[40] The idea of God's Kingdom in Jesus is partly derived from John the Baptist—the apocalyptical vision of the sudden coming of the Son of Man from heaven in future—and partly from his own experience—the presence and growth of God's Kingdom among the faithful united in love and koinonia. Jesus himself believed in the imminence of the *eschaton,* but it did not arrive. Thus the thought rooted in Jesus' own personal experience assumes more importance, which urges us with the metahistorical content of truth to our decision, and it is actually possible to arrive at God. Here Yagi considers that a Christological moment is contained.

Kanō Yamamoto's contribution seems by far the most important in the collection he himself edited.[41] He surveys the theological thought of the century of Japanese Protestantism and emphatically places Christology in the center of theology and missionary activities. It all depends on what kind of Christ has been proclaimed in Japan: dead Christ or living Christ? Ideologized Christ or Christ who speaks God's Word to us as new humanity and new reality of the world? The Christ of the dogma or the only true real Christ? This is an actual question for Christology. The history of Japanese theology is the reflection of Western trends. In the Taisho period Jesus the man received most attention, and there were published a number of lives of Jesus. The theology of the early Showa period attained its high standard under the influence of Brunner and Barth; Kumano's *Fundamental Problems of Christology* is the representative work of this period. But there are dangers in these two forms; the one Ebionistic Christology and the other Docetistic Christology. We must ask whether our Christology is a real confession of biblical Christology or Christ's divinity, or that of either of the previous two heresies. Japanese Christology has never grasped, according to Yamamoto, Jesus Christ of the New

Testament. Christology is for him no play of speculation with concepts taken from old days. It is the beginning, key, center and basis for theology that tries to be real theology. The present danger for Japanese theology is docetism. In the thirty years since the introduction of Barth, Japanese theologians are inclined to interpret docetistically Barth's radical insight into *vere Deus vere homo*. There is some docetistic tendency in Barthianism, or at least the suspicion of it. As a reaction there emerges an ebionistic existentialism, and the Barthians venture to correct Bultmann with Barth. The New Testament Christology stands on the following two statements: "Jesus is Christ—Jesus of Nazareth is God's Word or God's Son," and "Christ is God's Word or Jesus." Christology must always try to renew these fundamental biblical statements. Yamamoto takes up the history of the problem of the historical Jesus as an example of this. The problem is again seriously discussed in the post-Bultmannian generation of biblical scholars and theologians but their motive in the approach to historical Jesus is essentially different from the so-called *Leben-Jesu-Bewegung* in the nineteenth century. The new generation wants to hear again the New Testament witness of the humanity of Christ–the divinity of Jesus. Thus Yamamoto suggests the necessity to return to the New Testament for Christology, based on the three mysteries of Incarnation, cross and Resurrection.

Studies on Christology dedicated to Odagiri is until now the most voluminous book on the subject.[42] It contains the articles of scholars of contemporary renown, that have already appeared in the course of our discussion. The topics covered range from the New Testament to our times. Yoshihata Sakaeda mentions in the preface that the meaning of the event of Christ Jesus (his life and death in human history) can never be determined univocally by human understanding. Thus there is no other way to Christology except through dialogues and discussions among the faithful. Christological problems should be discussed with open-mindedness. Where there is no such spirit, Christological discussions turn into polemics.[43] In his dedication, Yamamoto reiterates his view on the importance of Christology for Japanese Christianity, which must be based on the deepening of understanding of the biblical witness of Christ and the mystery of the redemption in the person of Jesus Christ and his Cross and Resurrection.[44] Throughout all the phases, trends, and moods in theology in Japan, there has been no time that does not reflect directly or indirectly the problem of understanding the mystery of Christ. The scholars here assembled formed a study group on Christology under the initiative of Odagiri. There are naturally differences in theological positions, but they all endeavor a dialogue with the Bible and biblical Christology and try to understand more deeply the person and work of Jesus Christ. Even the authors of the history of Christology cannot ignore modern hermeneutics and deal with their problems from the points of view of modern theology, and the writers of the contemporary scene of Christology must be biblical and aware of all historical problems that lead to their contemporary problems. The volume is therefore meant to be a contribution to the contemporary understanding of Jesus Christ.

Akira Takamori investigates the connection between Old Testament and New Testament Christology and takes up as an example Rom. 5, 12–21, where Paul develops his typology of Adam as a figure of Christ.[45] The parallelism between Adam and Christ summarizes the need of man's salvation and its actual happening, and thus this passage is integrated in the theology of the West. Takamori examines Peter Lengsfeld's work[46] and his criticism of Barth from a Catholic position. As an answer Takamori thinks that Luther's critique of scholastic typology is still relevent. In the Scholastic conception of typology all Old Testament events find their absolute fulfillment in Christ, figures are integrated in the history of salvation with Christ as its zenith, but the way to it is a gradual process, and the process itself is more important than the revelation of figures as figures in the light of Christ. With his Christology based on the theology of the cross, Luther stresses not the gradual process but the tensional difference between figures and their fulfillment, and the preliminary nature of figures.

Kenzo Tagawa expresses the view that one should not try to read into Mark Christology constructed from a few places in the Gospel on the Son of God, or the Servant of God.[47] He had neither the *Son of God* Christology nor the *Servant of God* Christology. Mark unified for the first time the Logion and miracle stories and produced the Gospel genre. This construction itself is a strong Christological declaration on the part of Mark. He had the concept of Jesus as the one with absolute authority, but this authority is to forgive sin on earth and not in reference to transcendence. Thus Jesus confesses ignorance as to the last day's arrival. This understanding of Christ cannot be set in the Gospel without consciousness of being with Jesus. Thus Mark's is the *with-Jesus* Christology. Jesus' authority and ignorance indicate that his total concern is in this world; even if he is called the Son of God, he is no God but Jesus.

Christ for John is the revealing medium of God, who is the source of existence for the faithful, according to Yagi, who writes on the Christology of the Fourth Gospel.[48] Thus the starting point for John's Christology is the existence of the individual. It is a seeking after his own ground of life and existence. The individual stands as the center of relations, and his individual existence is contained in the generic existence. Christ is the generic existence, which determines each and every human existence, and in this determination Christ receives determination from God and is sent by God and does the work of God. To do the work of God determines Christ's existence, in this sense Christ is the one with God; Christ is determined by God, and God is in turn determined by Christ. Yagi emphasizes the importance of the image of light in effectively bringing out Christ's function in this regard.

Soteriological significance in the Passion story is emphasized by Kinji Hidemura; Jesus' Passion and death open the way for the salvation of mankind.[49] Theologically this Redemptive death should be strictly distinguished from that of other religious heroes, he remarks, quoting Odagiri. Paul's Christology is treated by Jisaburo Matsuki, who stresses that Paul's proclamation and theology centered around Jesus Christ.[50] Paul's Christology has been discussed in different intellectual contexts like the life of Jesus theology, Jesus and Paul, and historical Jesus and the proclamation of the early Christian community. The author would like to see the historical Jesus on earth in Paul's Christology. Paul's knowledge of Jesus is a matter of his own experience where living and thinking are unified. Bultmann sees in Paul's use of Gnostic motifs their demythologization as the basis of his existentialist interpretation. Jesus interests Paul not as an ethical or religious character but as centered on the Cross. Jesus is the Word of the Cross. But this has simultaneously the Christological turning-point of Resurrection from among the dead. This turning-point is to be realized again within us in baptism. Thus it must be emphasized that for Paul Cross and Resurrection constitute one event.

Hideyasu Nakagawa deals with the famous hymn on Christ (Col. 1, 15–20).[51] He thinks in agreement with other scholars that the hymn is an answer to the so-called Colosian heresy. In the first part of the hymn Christ's cosmological role is set forth, while in the second Christ as Redeemer enters into history, brings peace in his suffering and makes all the created reconciled (soteriological role) with God. Thus the hymn deprives the world of its magical powers and sets it free from pseudo-divine powers, so that human existence becomes rationalized.

The Christological motif in the twelfth chapter of John's Apocalypse is analyzed by Akira Satake.[52] Christologically important are Christ's death and glorification in the passage, which is the adaptation of two sources. Christ's glorification is intimately related with his death, but this death has soteriologically an important place. The characteristic Apocalytic soteriology stresses that salvation becomes reality only with the faithfulness of the believers, and this faithfulness is the one even unto death; they are to be related with Christ's death through their own death.[53] In order for Christ's universal victory to become reality each Christian should remain faithful unto death.[54]

According to Jiro Shimizu, Paul's *Letter to the Romans* contains the tension in the process of Christology's encounter with the Western Roman society and its assimilation of Paul's Gospel, which is Christological.[55] The *Letter* as a whole contains more the history of salvation with its Christological center than the traditional Protestant basis of justification by faith. Christology's battle for admittance is brought to Rome. The *Letter* is therefore Paul's Christology deeply rooted in history. Paul's Christological message to the Romans is no social theory, but he declares that the Risen Christ turns towards Rome and Paul must do so too.

Katsumi Matsumura ventures an evaluation of ancient Christology from the point of view of contemporary theological issues.[56] The beginning of Christology is to analyze the fact that historical

Jesus of Nazareth is Christ the Saviour. Christology becomes for the first time a conscious question, when Jewish and Hellenistic traditions become one and the Christian church comes to possess a common ground with Hellenism. Ancient Christology maintains a middle position between Adoptionism and Docetism, but the history of formation of Christological dogma indicates that emphasis and interest were put more and more on Christ instead of Jesus. Christology is to deal with Jesus Christ, but the name itself already shows a certain accent shift in Christian conscious-ness. It should be called properly "Jesuschristology." The author's conclusion that Christology must always be in a living relation-ship with Jesus of the New Testament can be accepted, but his rather negative attitude towards the formation of Christology as dogma reminds us of narrow biblicism.

Kumano's position as regards the formation of dogma, at least in so far as is it seen from his discussion on *Filioque,* seems to be positive, in comparison with Matsumura.[57] The expression *Filioque* divides the Western church from the Eastern. The Eastern church wanted to preserve the *monarchia* of the Father concentrated in him, but the later development in the theology of the Western church was to concentrate on the concept of God as the Father. But this leads easily to pneumatology and in the end to the anthropotheology of the Renaissance. By grasping in a true way the *Filioque* we can do justice to the dialectical tension of spirit and letter; the Spirit is present in the world in its essential relationship with the Incarnated Eternal Son. The *Filioque* has established the connection of eternity and time. The presence of the Spirit in the world is the constant intervention of eternity in time, but it is for the fulfillment of the time of Christ.

Ken Ishihara tries to bring out Luther's image of Christ in his *Book of Consolation.*[58] In a sense the book is in the line of the *ars moriendi* genre, and Luther uses many symbols and expressions of medieval piety, but he already sought to contrast his position with that of tradition. On the cross is the glory of the Resurrection, and suffering and joy of victory are one. Here Ishihara sees the foundation of Luther's theology of the Cross. Masatada Odagaki traces the history of Christological thought from John Wesley, Fichte, Hegel, Schleiermacher, Bauer, Hermann, and Troeltsch to

Kierkegaard. Under the impact of the Enlightenment, modern theology till Liberal Theology speculated on Jesus Christ exclusively in the context of human thought.[59] Thus the question has appeared in twentieth-century theology: who is this Jesus Christ?

Odagaki's article is followed up by a discussion of Kierkegaard's understanding of Christ by Akira Kitagawa.[60] With Kierkegaard the idea of moment occupies a significant place in his thought. The moment is the encounter of two entirely different spheres: eternity and time; and thus for him one who lives fully in the moment becomes important. The human being is for him therefore a synthesis of the infinite and the finite. In contrast to Hegel, who saw the necessary process to Christ, Kierkegaard concentrated solely on the event of Jesus Christ, and for Kierkegaard other events were uninteresting. This event is for him the absolute event. He distinguishes secular history from sacred history. In the history of Jesus Christ, which is sacred history itself, there is always presence, for nothing in this history is transient. What is decisive in this history is Jesus' life and death. Thus Kierkegaard distinguished clearly between the history of Jesus Christ and that of world events. In Jesus, God becomes a man, and this is the center of his understanding of Christ. Christ's is the only existence that as an individual transcends individual existence. The Incarnation as humiliation of God takes place because of God's love. He contrasts sharply between human love and divine love. There is no compromise or synthesis between the two. Divine love therefore is revealed with its clash with human love in Jesus Christ's suffering on the cross and through this heals men, for it exposes human sin and gives men scandal. The history of Jesus Christ exposes truth about men, when they confront it. Such is the event of Jesus Christ. Kierkegaard sees thus the contemporaneity of the event of Jesus Christ with our present situation. But this contemporaneity is, according to Kitagawa, limited for Kierkegaard to sacred history. Existentialist theology expands this to the structure of history in general.

Takizawa sets out his position in this collection of essays.[61] He locates his Immanuel as the fundamental divine-human relationship in the stream of the history of modern theology and contemporary issues. In positions taken by Barth and Brunner that take strictly "Jesus is Christ," the word *is* has not yet met an exact analysis; theologians like Käsemann and Gollwitzer turn again to the problem of historical Jesus. But for Takizawa the relationship between absolute transcendence and the content of historical Jesus as object of historical scientific approach is still unclear even with them. In Barth Takizawa cannot recognize the necessity of connection between Immanuel as fundamental transcendent reality that is not to be ascertained by human thought and the concrete perceptible words of the Bible or the living content of historical Jesus; he depends upon both, but takes them as something self-evident. Barth thinks that Immanuel is God's absolute decision, which needs no premise, but at the same time that this Immanuel is possible only with the appearance of Jesus of Nazareth in human history. Here again for Takizawa Jesus is a manifestation of fundamental reality called Immanuel, though we know this fundamental reality first with Jesus. The Bible describes Jesus from a hidden eternal core.

Kanō Yamamoto summarizes here Barth's Christocentric qualities.[62] His article is again a dialogue with Barth from the missionary situation of Japan. He tells how he met and assimilated Barth's Christocentric view in the course of his preaching and theological career. According to him Japanese theology until now has been anthropocentric theology; it appealed strongly to the Cross or the doctrine of the redemption, but all the trends lacked their Christological basis and therefore could not enter into dialogue with the cultural and intellectual life of modern times. This type of theology is typified in Tokutaro Takakura's theology. The author's theological maturing process according to the author himself consists in his reading Barth against his master's advice. Kumazawa deals with Brunner's Christology.[63] Brunner's theological starting point is Jesus' absoluteness as revelation in his suffering, death and Resurrection. God is absolutely apart from man; man can come to God only through Jesus Christ. In the Incarnation God takes his absolute initiative; it is grace because God accepts man. Brunner speaks of the humanity of the Son of God. Thus Jesus Christ is Mediator as revelation and reconciliation. Brunner's Christology develops from person to deed. He sees truth in meeting; it is a personal encounter between God and man in Jesus Christ, and this is further to become the setting-up of a personal relationship between God and man in which consists God's reign. Thus Brunner's Christology has the character of an answer to God's revelation, which is Christ.

Kikuo Yamaoka treats Bultmann's Christology.[64] He grasps the characteristic of Bultmann's Christology as the existentialist interpretation of biblical eschatology. Thus it is a demythologizing Christology. This the author tries to set in a dialogue situation with Max Weber and dialectical materialism over the question of secularization. Masatoshi Doi is engaged here with Tillich,[65] whose Christology is based on his analysis of historical existence. Tillich sees man's historical existence as estrangement in the sense that he is separated from the ground of his own existence, the world and fellow men. But ironically he has no freedom to act outside the universal destiny. There is the structure of destruction within himself, and when a man exercises his freedom, he falls into this estrangement. Thus man's condition is despair, and God is the God of wrath. Christ is for Tillich the New Being, which overcomes the estrangement. The Incarnation is the revelation of the essential God-manhood in historical existence. This is in a sense a paradox, for the essential existence appeared in historical existence. But Tillich fundamentally understands faith as participation in this New Being. Thus the cross shows the subjection of essential being to history, with the Resurrection its conquest.

Recent Christology according to Yoshio Noro has not abandoned its concern with what ancient Christology strives to express in its culmination of Chalcedonian definition.[66] What it did intend to express is now expressed in the different languages of today's theology. As Daniel D. Williams remarked, two histories, not two natures, must now be combined: the history of man's struggle for liberty in which Jesus of Nazareth lived and died, and the history of God's creation in which God tends towards man and acts creatively and redemptively, and its height is also Jesus of Nazareth. With this perspective Noro discusses Barth, Pannenberg and the *death-of-God* theology represented by Thomas J. J. Altizer and William Hamilton. Noro traces Barth's position to the Antiochian position at the Council of Chalcedon, for Barth takes the Incarnation not as identification but as confrontation between two histories. Pannenberg's Christology is for Noro Alexandrian in that God penetrates into human history, since he supposes, on the basis of revelation as history, the apocalyptical eschaton in the future with Christ as its sign. The *death-of-God* theology is also fundamentally Alexadrian in that it sees the union of two poles in the death of God. In Ferre's theology Noro sees an Antiochian effort to construct a language on God as a dialogue with the *death-of-God* theology. The author's sympathy is naturally with the Antiochian, Barthian position. He would like to take Christology as confrontation.

Saburo Takahashi's book starts with his concern about the growing tendency to regard the historical Jesus not as Son of God.[67] He sees nothing new in such a position, but to limit the work of Jesus to the past and think that it has no relevance to contemporary history is fatal. This is the position of the politically minded leftist new theology of radical students, who regard the question of historical Jesus as solved in their favor and do not listen to the orthodox Protestant position. Behind this new theology, Takahashi sees Yagi and Kenzo Tagawa. Yagi, according to him, considers that Paul's theology is not based on the thought of historical Jesus. The author challenges Yagi's statement: "The theory of the cross as redemption stands on a false premise." Takahashi discusses the question ultimately in terms of the question of Jesus and Paul; his position is evidently that Paul interprets Jesus correctly and legitimately as the Son of God, Christ. He considers that Yagi's position is from the outset frustrated by I Cor. 15, since Yagi lacks the doctrine of justification, and the victory of the cross for him remains only the problem of so-called religious existence, of attitude towards life. This Takahashi concludes is the abandonment of the Gospel of Christ. What relates Jesus as a historical figure with us today is the acknowledgement of the fact that the Risen Christ of the cross and the resurrection, yea, Jesus' entire life on earth, has a fundamental relationship with the present. He sees the church as Christ's body, the union between the historical existence of Jesus and us. Thus Takahashi puts the *Letter to the Romans* in the center of theology and encounters Yagi and Tagawa. His theological view is naturally strongly redemptive and shows all the characteristics of the orthodox Protestant position.

Takahashi's Christology is thus strongly Pauline. Christology can be discussed objectively without the consciousness of the problem of our sin, but this objectification ultimately deprives Christian faith of its vitality, as is shown in ancient Christological controversies, e.g., with Arius, he thinks. Purely Christological questions were discussed by Paul in relation to a more significant issue. Christ was the Lord as the battle cry against the emperor cult in the Roman world. In the subsequent history of Christianity Paul's issue had been forgotten only to be discovered by Augustine and the Reformers. Present Japanese Christians should rediscover Paul's issue in order to proclaim Jesus as the Lord.

Christology is man's growth with Jesus Christ towards God in history. In the last one hundred years Japanese theologians have shown their remarkable capacities in tackling the ever-remaining problem in a sophisticated manner and with a high degree of integrity and commitment. Although there has not yet appeared a theologian of the caliber of Barth or Bultmann, many Japanese theologians are scholarly able men, and their writings indicate their concern with the cultural and intellectual situations of Japan and of the West. Perhaps in the future Japanese theologians must overcome their prejudice towards ontology and analyze the ontological structure of the Incarnation in a radical manner and combine their results with the history of salvation.[68]

There is already in Japan the Christology of non-Christians manifested in many literary works. It would be interesting to investigate this non-Christian Christology and compare it with the Christian development of Christology in Japan.[69] It would show the impact of Christian theology even in an indirect way.

---

1. This article takes up the period after that which was surveyed by my brief treatment in German, "Christologie in der japanischen Theologie der Gegenwart," *Theologische Berichte* 2 (1973): 121–133. For the "Kirishitan" Period, see Appendix 1.
2. Cf. appendix 2.
3. English translation.
4. *Shingaku Nyūmon* (Introduction to Theology), (Tokyo, 1969), pp. 119ff.

5. *Kirisutoron, Doitsu no Tabi* (Christology—after a Journey in Germany), (Tokyo, 1964). Cf. Appendix 3.

6. *Logos-Kotobaron* (Logos-Word), (Tokyo, 1963). Cf. Appendix 4.

7. *Kirisuto to Jesu* (Christ and Jesus), (Tokyo, 1969), p. 84.

8. *Shinyaku Shiso no Seiritsu*, pp. 333ff. Yagi's position reflects the major trend in Japanese biblical studies among young scholars. Cf. Kenzo Tagawa (1935—), who studied in Strasbourg and is now in Göttingen, *Genshi Kirisutokyō no Ichi Danmen— Fukuin-Bungaku no Seiritsu* (An Aspect of Primitive Christianity—Formation of Gospel Literature), (Tokyo, 1968).

9. *Seisho no Jesu to Gendai no Shii* (Jesus of the Bible and Modern Thought) (Tokyo, 1965), pp. 56–65. Yagi in his turn tells us about his *non-church* family background, growing doubt about faith in the cross, interest in exegesis and search after the essence of Christian faith (*Kirisuto Kyo wa Shinjiuruka, Honshitsu no Tankyu*, Can Christianity be believed? A Search after the Essence, Tokyo, 1970), pp. 12–56.

10. *Seisho no Kirisuto to Jitsuzon* (Tokyo, 1967), esp. pp. 49–81.

11. K. Takizawa's article in *Fukuin to Sekai* (Gospel and world), Oct., 1971, pp. 65–75, and S. Yagi's in *ibid.*, Nov., 1971, pp. 84–87.

12. Arai, S. *Die Christologie des Evangelium Veritatis* (Leiden, 1964), and *Genshi Kirisutokyo to Gnosis-shugi* (Early Christianity and Gnosticism), (Tokyo, 1971); F. Sonobe, *Arius-ha Ronsoshi* (History of Arian Controversy), (Tokyo, 1969).

13. "Paul no Kirisutoron no Ichi Kosatsu—Kyrios Kirisutoron—" (A Consideration on Paul's Christology—Kyrios Christology—), in J. Asano (ed.), *Paul Kenkyu* (Studies on Paul), (Tokyo, 1961), pp. 73–86.

14. "Shokuzairon no Jitsuzonronteki Rikaihoko" (Existentialist Approach to Soteriology," *ibid.*, pp. 209–238.

15. *Ibid.*, p. 221.

16. *Ibid.*, English summaries at the back of the book, p. 32.

17. *Senkyo to Shingaku* (dedicated to J. Asano), (Tokyo, 1964). "Seisan no Jitsuzonronteki Rikai," (Existentialist Approach to the Eucharist"), pp. 401–446. This volume contains a bibliography of Asano's works and a significant assessment of "Lives of Jesus" in Japan by Isaburo Takayanagi (pp. 195–214). Western scholars like Walter Eichrodt, Günther Bornkamm and Carl Michalson contributed articles to this volume.

18. "Kami no Kotoba to Ningen no Jitsuzon" (The Word of God and Man's Existence"), *ibid.*, pp. 447–479.

19. *Kirisutoron no Shomondai* (Tokyo, 1959).

20. "Job-ki ni okeru Kirisuto" ("Christ in the Book of Job"), *ibid.*, pp. 1–36.

21. *Ibid.*, p. 4.

22. Cf. e. g., Christ, F., *Jesus Sophia: die Sophia-Christologie bei den Synoptikern* (Zürich, 1970); Suggs, M. J., *Wisdom, Christology, and Law in Matthew's Gospel* (Cambridge, Mass., 1970); von Rad, G., *Weisheit in Israel* (Neukirchen, 1970); Skehan, P. W., *Studies in Israelite Poetry and Wisdom* (Washington, D. C.); Whedbee, J. W., *Isaiah and Wisdom* (Abingdon, Virginia, 1970).

23. "Keiyaku Shisoshi no Nisan no Mondai" (Some Considerations on the History of the Covenant-Idea in the Old Testament), *ibid.*, pp. 37–56.

24. "Dai Yon Fukuinsho Prologue no Kaishakugakuteki Kenkyu—Johanne Bunsho Kirisutoron e no Josetsu to shite" (Exegetical Study on the Prologue of the Fourth Gospel), *ibid.*, pp. 57–86. (The volume itself is dedicated to Ishihara.)

25. "Jesu no Jiishiki ni tsuite" (The Self-consciousness of Jesus), pp. 87–108.

26. "Shinyaku ni okeru Kibō ni tsuite no Ichi Kosatsu" (Concerning Hope in the New Testament), pp. 109–130.

27. "Jesu no Keizu no Kenkyu" (A Study on the Geneology of Jesus), pp. 131–164.

28. "Kyogishi ni okeru Hossokuten no Mondai" (When and How Did the History of Dogma Begin?), pp. 165–186.

29. "Hermas no Bokusha ni okeru Angelus interpres Josetsu" (Angelus interpres in the Shepherd of Hermas: An Introduction), pp. 187–215.

30. "Jitsuzonrontekina Kirisutoron e no Kokoromi" (An Attempt at an Existentialist Christology), pp. 243–276. C. Michalson and K. Löwith contributed articles on Christ and history. Cf. "The Event of Jesus as Christ" (Kirisuto to Shite no Jesu no Dekigoto), in *Jitsuzonronteki Shingaku* (Existentialist Theology) (Tokyo, 1964), pp. 231–252; 426–33.

31. Japanese title: *Ikeru Kirisuto* (Tokyo, 1961).

32. "Yono Hikari" (Light of the World), *ibid.*, pp. 3–24. This volume is obviously inspired by the theme of the New Delhi World Congress of Churches: Light of the World—Jesus Christ.

33. "Taishu e no Kirisuto" (Christ for the Masses), pp. 49–68.

34. "Shinyaku seisho no Kirisutoron—Bultmann no Kaishaku o Chyushin to shite" (Christology in the New Testament—Mainly on Bultann), pp. 69–90.

35. "Nikaia Kirisuto Ronso" (The Strife on Christology at Nicaea), pp. 91–108.

36. "Shukyokaikau-sha ni okeru Ikeru Kirisuto—Luther to Calvin o Chyushin ni shite" (The Living Christ in Reformers—with Emphasis on Luther and Calvin), pp. 109–128.

37. "Kindaishingaku ni okeru Kirisutoron" (Christology in Modern Theology), pp. 129–146. Cf. the author's *Kindai no Shingaku* (Modern Theology), (Tokyo, 1964).

38. "Shorisha Jesu" (Jesus the Victor), *Ikeru Kirisuto,* pp. 147–166.

39. *Ibid.,* p. 149. The author benefits from George S. Hendry's critique of Aulen (The Gospel of the Incarnation, 1958).

40. "Nazare no Jesu" (Jesus of Nazareth), pp. 167–186.

41. "Gendai Shingaku ni okeru Kirisutoron" (Christology in Contemporary Theology), pp. 187–237. Cf. also the author's preface, where he emphasizes the significance of Christology for mission.

42. *Kirisutoron no Kenkyo* (Tokyo, 1968). The volume has a bibliography on Christology from both Western and Japanese sources, compiled by Y. Amagai. The part on Japanese sources was published (rearranged with selections, additions and short notes) under the supervision of Y. Kumazawa in *The Northeast Asia Journal of Theology*, 2 (1969): pp. 117–134. The same issue contains also an account of Christological materials in Korea, pp. 111–116.

43. *Kirisutoron no Kenkyu*, pp. 2–3.

44. *Ibid.,* p. 6.

45. "Kirisutoron to Kyuyaku Seisho—Roma-jin e no Tegami 5, 12–21 o Chyushin ni shita Shinyaku Seisho ni okeru Yoteiteki Kaishaku o megute" (Christology and the Old Testament—Typological Interpretation in Rom. 5, 12–21), *ibid.,* pp. 5–32.

46. "Adam und Christus: Die Adam-Christus Typologie im Neuen Testament und ihre dogmatische Verwendung," *Koinonia* (Essen, 1965).

47. "Marco no Kirisutoron—Soreo tou-koto no Imi" (Christology in Mark—the Meaning of its Search), pp. 33–56.

48. "Johanne Fukuinsho no Kirisutoron" (Christology in the Gospel according to John), pp. 57–88.

49. "Jesu no Saiban—Jesu Junanshi no Rekishiteki Kosatsu" (Law Process against Jesus—Historical Consideration on the Passion), pp. 89–112.

50. "Paul no Kirisutoron—Iwayuru Shiteki-Chijono Jesu o megute" (Paul's Christology—So-called Historical Jesus on Earth), pp. 113–150.

51. "Korosaijin e no Tegami 1, 15–20 ni okeru Kirisutoron ni Tsuite" (Christology in Col. 1, 15–20), pp. 151–176.

52. "Johanne Mokujiroku 12 Sho ni okeru Kirisutoronteki motif ni tsuite" (Christological motif in Apoc. 12), pp. 1771–96.

53. *Ibid.,* pp. 147ff.

54. *Ibid.,* p. 111, note 48. (Cf. Kirisutoron Doitsu no Tabi, p. 339).

55. "Roma Teikoku to Kirisutokyo" (Roman Empire and Christianity), pp. 199–234.
56. "Kodai Kirisutoron no Hyoka—Konnichi no Shingakuteki Kadai to shite" (The Evaluation of Ancient Christology—as Problem for Today), pp. 235–254.
57. "Chichi to Ko yori" (qui ex Patre Filioque procedit), pp. 255–263.
58. "Shukyokaikakusha Luther no Nagusame no Sho" (Religious Reformer Luther and His *Book of Consolation*), pp. 263–270. As the editors of the volume admit, its weakness lies in the Middle Ages. Cf. e.g., Ingu, T., "Juniku to Shokuzai" (Incarnation and Redemption,) *Fukuin to Sekai* (Gospel and World), December, 1964, pp. 79–109.
59. "Kindai ni okeru Kirisutoron" (Christology in Modern Times), *Kirisutoron Kenkyu*, pp. 271–298.
60. "Kierkegaard no Kirisutoron" (Christology of Kierkegaard), *ibid.*, pp. 299–323.
61. "Rekishi no Jesu to Shinko no Kirisuto" (Jesus of History and Christ of Faith), pp. 327–352.
62. "Barth no Kirisutoron—Kyokai Kyogigaku ni okeru Kiso to Tenkai" (Barth's Christology—Foundation and Development in His *Dogmatics*), pp. 352–398.
63. "Brunner no Kirisutoron" (Brunner's Christology), pp. 399–418.
64. "Bultmann no Kirisutoron—Shakaikagaku to no Taiwa o fukumu Oboegaki" (Bultmann's Christology—Note including Dialogue with Social Sciences), pp. 419–454.
65. "Paul Tillich no Kirisutoron" (Paul Tillich's Christology), pp. 455–478.
66. "Kirisuto to Rekishi" (Christ and History), pp. 479–516.
67. *Kirisuto Shinko to Honshitsu* (Essence of Christian Faith), (Tokyo, 1971).
68. I mean by that some similar efforts made recently in *Mysterium Salutis*, III/1 (E. Klinger, "Formaler Vorentwurf und geschichtliche Einführung," pp. 9–46; D. Wiederkehr, "Entwurf einer systematischen Christologie," pp. 477–648).
69. Cf. e. g., Tetsuro Watsuji, *Genshi Kirisutokyo no Bunkashiteki Igi* (The Significance of Primitive Christianity in the History of Culture), (Tokyo, republished 1971). Interesting in this connection would be Catholic novelist Endo Shusaku's recent novel *Shikai no Hottori* (By the Dead Sea) and his *Life of Jesus*, which indicate the novelist's grasp of modern biblical scholarship and its integration into the stream of consciousness and search motif. Endo's novel belongs to the last phase of the history of Christ motif in fiction, as indicated in Theodore Ziolkowski, *Fictional Transformations of Jesus* (Princeton, 1972). Cf. for the critique of Endo's positon Arai, Sasagu, " 'Dohansha' Jesu" (Companion Jesus), *Fukuin to Sekai*, Dec., 1973, pp. 14–22, etc. The following books are among more important theological publications after the completion of this article: Kojima, J: Fukuinsho no Kirisutoron [Christology in Gospels], Tokyo, 1971; Murakami, K: Kirisuto Kyusairon [Christ-Soteriology], Tokyo, 1971; Hamabe, T.: Takizawa Katsumi to Barth Shingaku [Takizawa Katsumi and Barth's theology], Tokyo, 1974.

Appendix 1
The Idea of Christ in the "Kirishitan" Period

Japan's first contact with Christianity occurred when Francis Xavier landed on August 15, 1549, in Kagoshima in southern Kyushu. He travelled eventually to Kyoto, then the capital of Japan, and his followers had a tremendous success in spreading the Christian faith as well as Western knowledge among the Japanese till the former came to be prohibited and a period of intensive persecution began, which led in the end to the closing of Japan's doors to the Europeans for a period of two hundred and fifty years. Thus not only a great expectation for Christianity but also many possibilities of fruitful cultural syntheses for Japan and the world were totally extinguished until the Meiji Restoration, which set forth the forces of modernization. Xavier himself had a high regard for the industry and intellectual capacities of the Japanese people. But for about thirty years after his arrival in the country of the rising sun, till the arrival of Alessandro Valignano as Visitor, no genuine efforts were made to recruit clergy from the new baptized. The tendency was to discourage the Japanese from studying theology in a systematic way and reaching priesthood. Valignano reversed this position and introduced to the young growing Christianity a school system leading up to sacerdotal ordination.[1] His decision had not only a significant impact on the missionarizing method but also on the deeper recognition of the Japanese nation. Thus the missionary attitude hitherto represented by Francisco Cabral, who was highly suspicious of Japanese as Christians, was rejected by Valigniano at the conference of missionaries in 1580–81; Cabral was removed to Macao. But it took ten years to implement Valignano's decision. The missionaries were heavily engaged in spreading faith, and the actual organization of schools and books seems to have been delayed in the face of demand for actual preaching and shortage of manpower.

The year 1587 saw the first sign of difficult times ahead for missionaries and Christians. The missionaries were ordered to be expelled, and many churches were pulled down. But this first persecution was ironically beneficial for speeding the work of compiling the theological textbook, since the missionaries were allowed to stay if they did not come out conspicuously. The plan, which had been in the process of materialization, came finally to be completed. The only systematic compilation of European theological, as well as scientific, knowledge in the sixteenth century on the Japanese soil was the *Compendium Catholicae Veritatis, in Gratiam Japonicorum Fratrum Societatis Jesu, Confectum per Rdm Patrem Comezium V.P.S.J. in Provincia Japonica.*[2] The *compendium* consists of three parts: astronomy, the summary of Aristotle's *De amima* and theology (summary of *Catechismus Tridentinus*).

Since this was the only professionally theological work, we have to take a look at it in order to obtain a view of the Christology in the sixteenth century on Japanese soil.[3] In general this Christology does not manifest any originality. Its theological frame is doubtless that of the New Scholastics of this century. However, it is interesting to observe the structure of the system of knowledge and the place the Christological discussion occupies. Astronomy, a most popular science, which was called for in Asia, is the foundation; then significantly interest is focussed on man, his soul and its immortality,[4] and finally as supernatural knowledge comes theology. The Christological part occupies the third place in theology. Jesus is the only son of God, our Redeemer and Saviour, Christ and our Lord. But particular attention seems to have been focussed on Passion, Resurrection and Ascension. Thus every item is followed on the basis of the *Credo*, and finally Christ's coming and the end of the world are discussed.

In many ways the ideas and the manner of their treatment in the *Compendium* are followed by many popular books on Christian faith.[5] The Passion occupies here a central place, and there were already official translations from four Gospels to be read in the Passion Week. These germinal ideas were quickly disseminated among the populace by the printing machines brought to Japan in 1590. In *Dochirina Kirishitan* the cross is regarded to be the highest value. It calls for the deepest devotion for the cross, which frees man from sin.[6] Christ's life on earth is ethically the most perfect one, since his person is that of God. It is therefore the model for Christian life. Thus it is necessary to read, know and meditate on his life. One must see God's work of love in Christ's life as a man. Many passages from the devotional literature of this period try to bring to readers the existential nearness of Christ's life on earth. This is nothing particular from the trends in sixteenth-century Europe. We may say that this tendency derived from the so-called *Devotio Moderna*, a spirituality, which places man in the center of religious sensibility.[7] The important fact is that this existential Christology became the living force behind the spirit of the Japanese Christians of the sixteenth century, which did not flinch before martyrdom. Christ's Passion is considered as victory in Resurrection and Ascension. Moreover, Christ is the Judge above all human judges. The brave are promised to become adopted sons of God and heirs of God's glory. The *Kirishitan* printing machine produced more than fifty books extant and lost,[8] and a few of these were copied during the two hundred-fifty years of persecution and remained among the hidden Christians.[9]

1. Cieslik, H., "The Training of a Japanese Clery in the Seventeenth Century," J. Roggendorf (ed.), *Studies in Japanese Culture* (Tokyo, 1963), pp. 41–78.
2. The work remains only as a MS., Regina Lat 426, in the Vatican Library. On the work, cf. S. Obara, "Kirishitan-jidai no Kagakushiso" (Scientific Thought in the Kirishitan Times), *Kirishitan Kenkyu*, 10 (1965): 126–135.
3. Prof. Obara is engaged in the study on this *compendium*. He has tentatively translated its astronomy into Japanese (Cf. *ibid.*, pp. 179–273). I am indebted to him for the unpublished table of contents on the theological part. The text is now in the process of being read and translated.
4. On *de Anima* in the *compendium*, cf. S. Obara, "Kirishitan Kyoiku ni okeru Ningenron—Pedro Gomez'no de Anima—" (Anthropology in the Kirishitan Education), *Kirishitan Bunka Kenkyukai Kaiho* (Reports of the Society for Kirishitan Studies), 14 (1971): 1–15.
5. Cf. M. Sugiura (ed.), *Kirishitan-Rangakushu* (Kirishitan and Rangaku Collection), in *Nihon no Shiso*, 16 (Tokyo, 1970); A. Ebizawa et al. (ed.), *Kirishitan-Haiyai Shu* (Kirishitan and Anti-Kirishitan Collection) in *Nihon Shiso Taikei*, 25 (Tokyo, 1970).
6. *Kirishitan-Haiya Shu*, pp. 225ff.
7. Cf. H. Cieslik, "Kirishitansho to sono Shiso" (Kirishitan Books and Their Thought), *ibid.*, pp. 577–580.
8. *Ibid.*, pp. 559.
9. Oddly enough the life of Jesus received the first full treatment by Arai Hakuseki in his *Seiyokibun*. Cf. I. Takayanagi, "Lives of Jesus in Japan, "*Senkyo to Shingaku* (Evangelization and Theology), (Tokyo, 1964), pp. 198ff.

Appendix 2
Yoshitaka Kumano's Christology

In his Christological book, Kumano tries to show the claim for modern relevance of the ancient Christological dogma preserved by the church, and further its eternal significance based on its modernity.[1] He sees the strictly dogmatic or theological issue of Christology has been somewhat avoided by modern theology. At least dogmatic Christology is considered to have no direct connection with our daily living faith, which receives personal influence from the historical divine person of Christ as Jesus of Nazareth without the mediation of speculation. Kumano introduces here the concept of the church and, while admitting some truth in this position, maintains that when the church speaks of Jesus Christ, it is not the Christ of private trust or of personal, mystical experience, but it relies on a special language to confess him officially and "catholically" in the most radical sense of the word. Thus despite historical and speculative elements, which are nonessential, historical Christology is still to be "the logic of historical-ecclesiastical nature," and our faith is fundamentally made possible on the basis of Christological structure. Kumano emphasizes that Christology is no ideology, after alluding to the interdependence between the special logic of Christology and logic as the self-development of human speech. Kumano's fundamental premise is again eschatology; it is only through eschatology that Christology can further maintain its specific system, liberated from the logic of ideologization. This has great implication for the understanding of the relationship between church and culture.

Harnack's emphasis on the historical (and therefore the influence of Jesus' personality in history) Jesus makes in its consequence Jesus a legendary figure. The Gospel must be understood as historical fact as well as metahistorical significance. Otherwise faith in the historical Jesus becomes a human faith, faith in ourselves. Since the Gospel is historical as well as metahistorical, it cannot be analyzed only with historical science or psychology. It requires a specific discipline, which is Christology. Christology deals with Jesus Christ, who is not only a historical figure but also someone who has been proclaimed in history to demand of us our decision of faith. Thus according to Kumano, Christology presupposes necessarily contradiction in history.[2] This "contradiction in history" is described by Kumano as a disjunctive, non-historical element, which can be grasped only by eschatology. Thus he calls eschatology "Urbildchristologie." For eschatology has always dealt with the presence of the nonhistorical, the eternal in history. Thus the speech for the presence of the eternal in history, in our case the presence of Christ in history, has been formulated by eschatology. The eschatological relationship between eternity and perishable human history is made possible by the living Christ. Christology based on eschatology must be brought to the present through pneumatology. The living Christ is to be experienced historically as the Holy Spirit, whose function is not only to revive in memory Jesus Christ, historical figure, but also to make it possible to speak of him in the present language as the continuation of Jesus Christ's work. Since it is the essence of the work of the Holy Spirit to continue the redemptive work of Jesus Christ's cross, Christology, pneumatology and soteriology have one single basis, although the latter two disciplines contain richness of materials to constitute themselves as disciplines. Kumano sees Protestant Christology to be more dynamic than Catholic Christology, which establishes the place of Jesus Christ in terms of Greek metaphysics. He is therefore interested more in the soteriology of Christ's work than in the Christology on the divinity and personality of Christ. But in order to grasp soteriology, it is essential to investigate the person of Christ and place the Incarnation in the center of Christian faith. Only by establishing radically Jesus of Nazareth as the Son of God can we make the Gospel most powerful in its communication. Soteriology is never to legitimatize and rationalize subjective, immanent, personal soteriological experience and understanding, but to describe the meta-experiential, meta-sensual event. Thus soteriology both conditions and is based on Christology.

Kumano cites Pascal, who has said that man can know neither God nor himself. Theism is therefore conditioned by Christology, not vice versa. Christian theology is not based on some subjective mystical experience but on a historical being called Jesus Christ. It requires a specific logic to recognize Jesus as Christ. One may call this the logic of the Divine Word's Incarnation. The event of the Incarnation means already the judgment of history. Thus Kumano thinks that eschatology is the *Vorfrage* for Christology. That Jesus Christ is Mediator between God and man means for Christian faith that Christ is the Self-interpretation of God, and that the Self-interpretation of God is also that of Christ himself. Logos incarnatus solves the contradiction within human existence and history and proves in clear terms the eschatological nature of human culture and thought. Kumano sees the history of Christian faith as nothing but the history of Christology. Strictly theological Christology itself is the activity of Christian faith. The history of the church is the series of Christological events.

Christ as the object of Christian faith refuses historical description, and Kumano follows Bultmann and remarks that in order to speak with Jesus Christ as historical existence we have to directly communicate with him in today's language. Jesus Christ with whom our faith has to do is no historical figure but the Christological existence.[3] This statement must not be taken as ignoring the historicity of Jesus Christ. It is the result of our thinking on the relationship of historical existence and the presupposition of faith. Thus the life of faith based on Jesus Christ forms necessarily Christology, and the Christian transforms his existence in Christology. An ideology presupposes the transformation of anthropology, but Christology puts an end to it. In this sense Christology is all the more eschatological and is thus a theory to show the eschatological structure of the world. There is no objective Christological description for Kumano. One is faced with the decision for Christology or non-Christology. There is at any rate no neutral Christology. This Kumano sees from the wider perspective of the history of Christian faith in connection with cultures. Man asks about himself by asking about Jesus Christ. The terminology of Christology is fundamentally dependent on Christ's self-proving (Selbstprüfung). Jesus of Nazareth is believed as the coming Christ, and the Word of this self-proving denies the position of man. Thus Christology is no systematic science. The Incarnation of the Divine Word is not to be considered as a past event but with the eternity of the Incarnated. The Incarnated Word refuses the development of the human logos and in so doing reveals God's plan for the world. Thus when every age speaks about Him with its own speech, it simultaneously exposes its own inner contradiction. Thus the development of Christology reveals the deadlock of the cultural Zeitgeist. It does not, however, mean mere self-destruction on the part of man. The Incarnated Word carries with itself the disjunction and creation of history, by indicating the event of salvation. Kumano sees in this aspect of creation the continuation of Christology as development in history. The history of Christology shows therefore the failure of cultural thought and human speech to comprehend and speak Christ. It is no accident for Kumano that the New Testament does not contain any dogma of Christology. What is contained there is not *Christusverständnis* but *Christusglaube*. Dogma as Confession is contained in the New Testament. The New Testament appeals to us with such a living force because of its decisiveness of revelation: it is the radicalization of revelation, and this decisiveness contains human words as confession of faith, from which later the dogma of Christology has developed.

The miracle of miracles of the New Testament is the Risen Christ. Christology starts therefore with the empty grave. The Risen Christ is the coming Christ. Here again Kumano recognizes the eschatological situation of world and history, and Christology is the reflection of this situation. With this viewpoint the church separated herself from Judaism. Kumano emphasizes therefore the Resurrection faith of the disciples.[4] The Christ of this Resurrection faith demands a place greater than a mere historical figure. Thus Jesus Christ has been from the beginning "dogmatic existence" for the church.[5] Kumano sees a paradox in his insistence that it is a mistake to search for the dogma of Christology in the New Testament and his conviction that Jesus of Nazareth is Christological existence. Kumano further sees dynamic evangelical Christology in the New Testament, which is a forerunner for that of Luther and the Reformers. He traces the Christological development of the ancient church and considers the definition by the Council of Nicaea most decisive for the

Evangelical truth. This was the growth of consciousness about the soteriological conditioning of Christology. Reflection on the person of Christ arose not only out of sheer interest in the past but was also given to the church as one of the most serious questions. Through this process the Incarnation of God is to be testified as the event upon which the logic of Incarnation is to be established. The Nicaean definition is to be crowned by that of the Council of Chalcedon. He sees in this definition the radically religious basis as the declaration of the place of man. The insufficiency of Greek terminology used by the ancient church in defining Jesus Christ reveals in clearest terms the truth and power of the radical Evangelical content for the church. Kumano regards Augustine very highly in the history of Christology, for it was he who established the Christological *apriori* as the starting point for theology. Augustine places the Incarnation in the center of his soteriology. Kumano never underestimates the medieval Christology represented by Thomas Acquinas but feels some dissatisfaction in its making Christology static. Anselm's question "Cur Deus Homo?" was the only radical search for the Christological basis of soteriology. And this fundamental attitude was further intensified by Luther. What Luther intended therefore is no dissolution of dogma but change of Christology towards the Evangelical core. Against modern Protestantism Kumano upholds this position of early Protestantism. He proposes to take Christology theologically in the exact sense of the word. The modern anthropology of Feuerbach mythologizes man, but his situation is not something that liberalist culture wishfully imagines. Anthropology must begin with the fallen nature of man and should be an effort to free him therefrom. In this sense Marx-Engels critique of Feuerbach is valid but not radical enough.[6]

Kumano further considers Jesus Christ's significance as *the* revelation. Here Bultmann's influence is more remarkable than in other parts of his book. Christ's Incarnation, Death and Resurrection as his revelation expose the constitutive elements of human existence. Before this revelation man is to decide for life or death. The divinity of Jesus Christ is for us no speculative question. Here in this connection Kumano quotes Emil Brunner ("Was hat uns Gott in ihm zu sagen?") and concludes that the mode of existence of Jesus Christ in history is in itself already the revelation. We are not to proceed to know God through the person of Jesus Christ, but to be urged right in his person to decision. The Divinity of Jesus Christ is the pressure or solemn religious judgment upon humanity and history. Jesus Christ's existence in history is in itself judgment to condemn human history. The Incarnation is primarily an event in which God's sovereignty establishes itself as the grace of supernatural salvation.[7] One is not to see it as harmony between the natural and the supernatural. The Logos incarnatus does not reveal the progress and harmony of human history (Hegel) but declares God's justice by showing its division, fall and coming destruction.[8] It is not through the Incarnation that the eternal one becomes a person, but He becomes historical through the Incarnation. Thus without preexistence the person of Jesus of Nazareth cannot be adequately explained. The immaculate birth of Jesus is no construction of the ascetic ideal; it is fundamentally a derivation of Christological dogma. The meaning of the Incarnation is the transformation of the whole of history through the "historization of the eternal one." Kumano insists on eternity in the Incarnation.[9] In contrast with the anthropocentric Christology of Schleiermacher, Kumano considers the kenotic theory as fundamentally refusing metaphysical speculation and seeing solely the descensus from above. The kenosis shows the absolute might of the eternal in the Incarnation. Through it the Incarnation is clearly submitted as not something to eternalize time but to put an end to time.[10]

For Kumano, therefore, Christology is a living reality as the radical basis for man's historical existence. This Christology however becomes a living reality within a historical and social reality, which is the church as the Body of Christ. But the church is the place where man's inability is revealed and promise is given for a new life on the basis of this human failure. The church with its radical eschatological nature stands counter to the movement of society and as such is a call for repentance. She is an organ that makes the death of Christ Son of God meaningful in history.

1. *Kirisutoron no konppon Mondai*, p. 5.
2. *Ibid.*, pp. 8–9.
3. *Ibid.*, p. 50.

4. *Ibid.*, p. 66.
5. *Ibid.*, p. 66.
6. *Ibid.*, pp. 102f.
7. *Ibid.*, p. 152.
8. *Ibid.*, p. 158.
9. *Ibid.*, p. 180.
10. *Ibid.*, pp. 230ff.

Appendix 3
Nobuo Odagiri's Challenge to Traditional Christology

Odagiri's controversial book has the subtitle, "Against the Ancient Faith of the Confession." As the result of his many years' struggle with the Bible and ceaseless search for the center of Christianity, Odagiri has gradually come to the conclusion that Christology is really the central concern for him, but this discovery of Christology by him has some special nuance; he remarks, he read the Scripture again from the viewpoint of the Gospel of the Cross and came to distinguish the center from the peripheries of the scripture.[1] Thus he discovered that there exists no identity between the God of the Bible and the Christ of the Bible on the one hand, and the God of the *credo* taught by the Christian church and the Christ of the confession on the other. Odagiri observes that Christological issues divided Christians bitterly in the history of Christianity. Christology was already an issue for the Christians during the period of Roman persecution. He summarizes the historical circumstances of the Christologically important Councils of Nicaea and Chalcedon, which had then political and social consequences.[2] In a sense Odagiri sees with remarkable accuracy the heart of the tension that makes Christology or theology in general a most dynamic investigation. The Council of Chalcedon according to him is the consummation of the previous tendency towards the Trinity, and Christology was, as it were, demonstrated with the massive help of the Trinitarian doctrine. Odagiri maintains that the Trinitarian expression is a far-fetched one; it is the product of the church, and however strenous its work may be, it is the product of the church's great writhing with the problem. And this agony of the church has continued even till today. There are in the New Testament only the Father, the Son and the Holy Spirit, but no remark about their substantial unity.

While admitting that Christology was already the central issue in the New Testament, Odagiri ascribes to the formulation of the Trinitarian doctrine by the church all the bitter struggles and acts of intolerance that happened later when Christianity became the official religion of the Roman Empire. Based on the non-Christian milieu of Japan, he objects to the acceptance of the traditional view that Christ is God according to the Scriptures. Here he refers briefly to the concept of god in Japanese.[3] God as the Only One and the Creator in the Bible is not Christ Himself. Odagiri defines Christianity as the religion of redemption. In order to understand the Gospel of the Cross most radically, Christ must not be God. To identify the Christ who died on the cross (for us) with God Himself is therefore a threat to the Gospel. In order to know Christ truly one must return to the only document, the New Testament. Consequently the New Testament Christology assumes an immeasurable importance. Since its central event is the message of the cross, Christology must be developed from this event. Since Christology is the problem for Christianity it must not be hampered by Trinitarian considerations and philosophical speculations, which inevitably follow from the former. The Christology proclaimed by the Gospel, unalloyed and original, has the exclusive right to be called such.

Odagiri understands his position as the radicalization of the nonchurch thought initiated by Uchimura.[4] He interprets its chief message as the Gospel of the Cross and this insistence is something unique and proper to Japanese Christianity. He claims this against the ancient faith of the credo of the West. For Uchimura, he remarks, Jesus Christ's Redemption of the Cross is God's absolute grace, which is truly the Christian Gospel. Jesus' death on the cross should be strictly taken to be the death to redeem humanity before God and is essentially different from our death and that of martyrs in history. The last words of Jesus on the cross reflect the existentialist sentiment of the redeemer and the relationship between God who admits the act of the Redemption and Jesus Christ who accomplished it. For Odagiri the two are entirely different, and he considers that the Chalcedonian definition, "Christ is God," does not adequately express the radical realism of the Redemption. To make Jesus Christ truly God deprives realism of the death on the cross. As its consequence the Christian kerygma

would be destroyed. Odagiri refers to the fact that Jesus is vividly
described as a true man in the Gospel accounts, and further they
recount how this typically historical man lead the Apostles and
the early church as the divine being after the resurrection from
the dead. The New Testament never testifies that the Jesus of
history became God after his resurrection. Even after his resurrection he is thoroughly a man and acts as the first fruit. Emphasis must be put on the fact that this living Lord has once been
called the dead one and then risen out of the dead. The secret of
Jesus Christ's that never separates from history lies in the proclamation of the risen Lord who is inseparable from the redemptive death. The incarnation is for Odagiri the decisive historical
event, and he takes the Preexistence seriously also. But the Incarnated was not Jesus Christ before the Incarnation; he is the
Logos, the Son and the Only Son of God. Preexistence, incarnation, death, resurrection, ascension and second coming constitute the wonderful process of time; the Incarnation and the
death exclude eminently the possibility of docetism. Christian
faith proclaims that this is the Incarnated, not God. The God of
the Bible can never incarnate himself, for God cannot die. Thus
for Odagiri God is the invisible, transcendent one. The Redemption is an event inside history, and in the Bible the unique person
of Intercessor between God and His Creation is mentioned, according to Odagiri.[5] God's words are not to be heard directly, and
unless He is revealed, He does not come to be understood and
believed. Here lies the mission of Jesus Christ as Revealer of God,
God's Son and His Intercessor from the time of Creation till the
end of the world. He came to men, incarnated, as Jesus Christ,
appeared in history, seen by men, heard and believed, and thus
revealed God. Thus the Incarnation opens the mystery of Salvation. The person, incarnated and called Jesus Christ, is the exhaustion of the Revelation of God Himself. It is significant that the
New Testament did not come to name Jesus God in the biblical
sense, although the later tendency was to elevate him to God, because he was a historical person who had contacts with many
people, and who died. For primitive Christianity, Odagiri insists,
the kerygmatic truth is most important. Later Christianity has

accepted for about two thousand years the dogma of God the Son, which had no foundation in the New Testament. Thus Odagiri emphasizes *time* in the Son of God.

According to Odagiri, God in flesh does not exist in the Judeo-Christian theology. If Judeo-Christian God is such a god, He must have his fate to end by death, and Odagiri observes that such a dying god is a pagan god but no Christian God. The Greco-Roman world was filled with miraculous stories about God who took human shape. Jesus' Disciples had to answer on the one hand the claims by the Jews that Jesus was no Messiah, no Christ, for if he were so he would never have suffered such a miserable death (the Jews naturally denied the resurrection), and on the other hand that this Jesus who had risen in three days from among the dead, must not, according to the Gentiles, be simply a human being but God, who had appeared to men. In order to set clear the fundamental difference between God and the Son of God, Paul emphasizes always Jesus' death on the cross. Thus he calls the Only God the Father of our Lord Jesus Christ. Odagiri thinks that here is told the essential relationship between God and Jesus Christ. He said to the Jews that Jesus is Christ (there is an "obvious" [sic] distinction between God the Father and Christ the Lord) and to the Gentiles that Jesus is the true Lord of the Lords and there is only one God who is the Father of Jesus Christ. Thus Odagiri rejects the idea of divinization of humanity as something pagan. A human being remains a human being, even when he is saved. If saved, he participates in divine nature (II Peter 1, 4), is transfigured in divine likeness (II Cor. 3, 18) and comes to possess eternal life. He is therefore according to Odagiri a divinely transfigured person, but not a god, whose original type is Jesus Christ, as the Son of God. Christ as the Son of God is the first one according to Paul, so says Odagiri based on Rom. 8, 29 and 8, 16–17. All those saved become his brothers in God's Kingdom. The eschatological kingdom of God is constituted of the children of God who adore God as the Father. As the First one of them, Christ obeys God the Father (I Cor. 15, 28). This distinction in the hierarchical order Odagiri believes to be contrary to the Trinitarian doctrine. He rejects here the evolutionary view of divinization.[6] Because of the work in time of the Only Begotten Son of God He is no longer the only one, but there are the children of God as brothers. This process is well described by the Gospel according to John. Furthermore the process is described as the second creation by Paul (II Cor. 5, 17; Gal. 6, 15). Odagiri emphasizes the *Einmaligkeit* of the time of the Son of God, in which brief though it may be He became a man. Here Odagiri introduces the idea of *kenosis* and combines it with that of Preexistence. It is no longer that Christ regained His former position of Preexistence after the Ascension, but this position has been eternally lost, and He stands now on the side of humanity, which He saved as the First Son. The dynamics of the Gospel is that through the Incarnation of the Only Begotten Son the formerly lost children become transfigured into the children of God. Odagiri however distinguishes his emphatically biblical position from that of Fundamentalists. All that is important in the Scripture is Christ, His death on the cross and the Resurrection. Without these it is an ancient document and nothing more.

Odagiri's view contains many fascinating insights, some of which can be valid in different contexts. He went to Germany with this view and lectured at several places and interviewed Bultmann. The trip was made at the invitation of the Deutsche Ostasienmission. His book contains also questions and answers after his lectures. They indicate somewhat that his listeners did not come to understand his Christological position. It is Odagiri's wish to take the oneness of God and the fact of Redemption seriously. This is all legitimate and fine, but it seems that he inevitably creates some intermediary being which is neither God nor man, although he keeps insisting that this intercessor is a human being, but he is a very special type of person who cannot quite be called a human being. At any rate his distinction between God and the Son of God, who is fundamentally non-divine, provoked a good deal of resentment among Japanese Protestants.

Odagiri's Christological view had been heard in Germany with politeness, though probably not understood fully. But it met what he himself considered to be a conserted action, especially by Kitamori and Fujiwara Fujio. He answers them rather emotionally in the book.[7] He maintains again the distinction between God and the Son of God and practically repeats his former position. If Christ is God as the Son, the Christians will become gods as children.[8] Odagiri finds a great danger in the interpretation of the Logos in Fujiwara's *Soteriology*, which starts with John's Prologue. He accuses Fujiwara of not thinking on the meaning of the Incarnation radically enough. To make the Incarnated God die on the cross eventually nullifies the seriousness of the event. The passage in the Apocalypse (14, 10) shows the highest degree of the unity between anthropology and Christology. The depth of anthropology inevitiably turns into Christology, which in turn proceeds into the vision of God. Thus it is precisely Christology that mediates between anthropology and *Gottesanschauung*. That is to say, one can know God and at the same time man only through Christology. But according to Odagiri the church has until now preached too much either God or man and asked as to Christ if he is God or man and forgotten that he is the Son of God. Thus the church has neither been able to understand God nor man truly. Jesus Christ as the Son of God is the only key to the understanding of God and man.

It is clear that Odagiri cannot accept the pain of God and its theology by Kitamori. For him God is spiritual and cannot suffer. And he rejects Kitamori's Trinitarianism. He questions which God Kitamori is speaking of when he refers to the pain suffered by God. To say that God suffered pain on the cross is automatically patripassianism. Kitamori's famous book is therefore doomed with its Trinitarianism. Kitamori's attention to the physical pain of Christ as God sets limits to the Infinite God, who is indescribable in physical terms. The physical pain can never become the symbol of God.

Thus Odagiri would like to maintain a rigorously monotheistic or theistic position. One can call his position neo-arianistic, but one must also notice his almost Ebionistic tendency, for he rejects all the Greek, and therefore in his view pagan, elements in Christianity and even in the Bible itself; e.g., Luke's account of Virgin Birth on the ground that Luke, a Greek, liked a fantastic story of miracle birth, which originated in the last analysis from the Hellenistic frame of mind, which made inroads into the church. It is almost ironical that the one who desired to be faithful to the Bible ends up purging it of the elements he does not wish to see in it.

1. *Kirisutoron Doitsu no Tabi*, Tokyo, 1964, p. iii.
2. *Ibid.*, pp. 3–5.
3. *Ibid.*, p. 8.
4. *Ibid.*, p. 121.
5. *Ibid.*, p. 125.
6. *Ibid.*, p. 181.
7. *Ibid.*, pp. 205ff.
8. *Ibid.*, p. 231.

Appendix 4
Fujio Fujiwara's Answer to Odagiri and Comment on the Theology of the Pain of God

Fujiwara had fully developed his soteriology in his previous book on the basis of the Incarnation as Redemption.[1] The book shows Forsyth's enduring impact on Protestant theology in Japan,[2] but Karl Barth is more or less the starting point for Fujiwara's soteriological-Christological thinking. He places Jesus Christ as Redeemer in the center of theology and remarks that the question of Jesus Christ is to be that of His person and work, who He is and what He did.[3] The person and the work in Jesus Christ or Jesus Christ and Redemption are interpenetrated.[4] Jesus Christ is in reality Jesus Christ crucified. Thus we cannot really know the Redemption of the cross without Him, but at the same time we can never know Him without the cross. Thus there exists a strict identity between person and work in Christ. As with modernism in theology, the humanistic rejection of Jesus Christ as God made the development of soteriology impossible.[5]

Significantly enough, Fujiwara declares that the mystery of Jesus Christ's person lies in that of the Incarnation.[6] The Incarnation is for the Redemption of sinners. The God that Jesus Christ through His Incarnation has revealed is the living God the Father. That God is the living personal God means no more than that God is the God speaking the Word. God created the world through the Word and has spoken to his creatures with the Word, but it is not that God first began to speak the Word after the creation. He speaks the Word from all eternity. This relationship within God is an *Urdatum*. It is therefore not that God has become first living, personal God after the creation. The Incarnation, however, does not mean the inner change of the Word. There is no mixture of the *Verbum* and the *caro*. Thus Fujiwara rejects the idea of divinization of human nature. Both are one but not mixed. In order to analyze the soteriological significance of the Incarnation, Fujiwara examines closely the passages in the Letter to the Romans (1, 23; 5, 14; 6, 5; 8, 3). The key word for him is *homoioma* (likeness, figure, image and form). God has sent "his own Son in a form like that of our own sinful flesh." Our human nature is the sinful flesh. The expression "Christ in a form of sinful flesh" indicates that Christ's humanity is genuinely human flesh, but it has difference in one point: sin. Thus Fujiwara utilizes here the concept of identity in difference in the Incarnation in order to explain the Redemption. Christ is no sinner, never takes up the flesh of sin, for He is God, but in the *homoioma* he accepted the weakness and burden of human sin, tried like ourselves (Hebrews 4, 15). Thus the Incarnation points sharply to the Redemption. For the human eyes only the flesh of the Incarnated is perceptible. One cannot perceive—incognito—the Word in the flesh. In order to hear the Word in the flesh of Jesus Christ, one must be moved by the Holy Spirit. It is faith alone that recognizes in Jesus Christ the Son of God, God the Son and the Revelation of God.[7] Fujiwara thinks that emphasis must be put on Jesus Christ as man to have the soteriological function of the Incarnation in mind.[8] Jesus is not only a historical figure but also a human being who lived in history, and thus one cannot remove him from the earth into some supernatural sphere. He lived and suffered like us ordinary men. Without sin in himself He came into the history of sin. His suffering and trial are those of the Son of God and a human being in unity. Thus "since He himself has passed through the test of suffering, he is able to help those who are meeting their test now" (Hebrews 2, 18). Basing himself on Forsyth and Barth Fujiwara defends the Nicaea-Chalcedonian definition; the foundation of soteriology is Christology.[9]

Fujiwara rejects the idea that Christ came to the world as a man even if there were no sin; the Incarnation can never be without sin (1 Tim. 1, 15). The reparation for human sin can be performed through the miracle of grace that is the Incarnation. The Redemption is the only essential end of the Incarnation. This work of Redemption is accomplished by the cross and the Resurrection. The Divine Word is in its ultimate sense Jesus Christ. He is the Incarnated personal Word of God, which encompasses not only His words but also person, life, deeds, suffering, death and Resurrection. Faith as the creation of God hears the Word of God of the cross and the Resurrection through the Holy Spirit. Thus to talk of God without Christ is sheer paganism.[10] The knowledge of the Trinity is also the event of faith in Christ. Fujiwara warns against the possible danger of infiltration of paganism in Christianity. It is not that we apply our preconceived notion of God to the event of faith. Our human image of God contradicts God in Jesus Christ. Revelation destroys all our concepts and notions about God. Jesus Christ as God requires no proof, no raison d'etre. Ultimately Christ is God because He is God. Here we may feel the Barthian distinction between religion and faith. All religious concepts without relation to space and time are paganism. We must always look sharply at the event of Jesus Christ in Incarnation and Redemption. Jesus Christ is the point of contact, where eternity cuts vertically human time; it is the moment, the moment in eternity where time is judged and saved. In Jesus Christ as the Incarnated and the Redeemer, eternity becomes time and time eternity. We encounter here in this moment God's revelation, redeemed from time dead in sin and become living creatures in the eternal time of God.[11]

Against the neo-arianism of Odagiri and others, though he does not specifically mention names, Fujiwara stoutly declares that the cross is genuinely God's tragedy.[12] One ought to abandon human reason to comprehend this tragedy. Fujiwara formulates the neo-arian Christology: God cannot die, but Christ died, and therefore Christ is not God. Thus this rationalistic way of thinking refuses to believe in the God of the Trinity attested in the Bible. Human sin is no evil in nature that it forces God "to die" (on the cross), Fujiwara asserts on the basis of Forsyth's statement, while granting that God never dies. God's death is in a sense made possible by the Incarnation; God the Father can never die, but the Incarnated

God the Son dies the Redemptive death, as God's self-reconciliation. Thus he sees the Redemption as the motion starting from God and returning to God, for it is in its essence grace. Should the death of Jesus Christ on the cross not be the death of God, the cross is neither Redemption nor reconciliation. The last words of Jesus on the cross can never fully be understood in their sharpness unless as God's death. But this death of God is no death on the part of the Father. In this death of the Incarnated we are to see the unity of the Son with the Father. And precisely here the Trinitarian nature of God is revealed, not evaporated as the neo-arians assert.[13] Thus one should not make a distinction between God and the Son of God, as they insist; on the contrary the lack of distinction on the part of the neo-arians between the Son of God and a son of God (or a child of God, or its plural form, children of God) is fatal for Christian faith. Fujiwara considers that ultimately the soil for this neo-arianism had been, prepared by Kitamori's theology of God's pain. When we speak of God's pain, we must begin with Jesus Christ, the person of the Son. The Redemption is strictly the work of the Son. Kitamori speaks of it too much from above. But more than that, it is dangerous according to Fujiwara to find solidarity between God and man in human pain. Pain can be a condition for faith or its occasion, but it is never the meeting place between God and man.[14]

1. *Shokuzairon (Soteriology)*, Tokyo, 1961 .
2. *Ibid.*, p. 4.
3. *Ibid.*, pp. 191ff.
4. *Ibid.*, p. 192.
5. *Ibid.*, p. 194.
6. *Ibid.*, pp. 195ff.
7. *Ibid.*, pp. 199ff.
8. *Ibid.*, pp. 204.
9. *Ibid.*, pp. 209–11.
10. *Ibid.*, p. 242.
11. *Ibid.*, pp. 350ff.
12. *Ibid.*, p. 350.
13. *Ibid.*, pp. 379ff.
14. *Ibid.*, p. 384.

Kinya Tsuruta

An Interpretation of *The Ruined Map* by Kōbō Abe

1. "Rooted in the Room" and Different Levels of Reality in *The Ruined Map*

The hero of *The Ruined Map* is an investigator hired to track down a missing husband. As the investigator, significantly nameless throughout the novel, pursues Nemuro, the missing one, he gradually grows unsure of his own identity. The hero begins to ask "Who am I?" and to confuse himself with Nemuro. As the demarcation between the two becomes obscured, the hunter becomes the hunted.

One may be tempted to see something of a detective story in *The Ruined Map;* in fact one reviewer mentioned Graham Greene and Georges Simenon in reference to the work, but this is obviously not a detective story, at least not a straight one. The investigator's work turns out to be focused not upon the other man but upon his own self. In this respect the investigator-hero is like a Zen archer who shoots an arrow not at the mark but at his own ego. Unlike an old Zen master who, assured of his identity (or nonidentity), works methodically toward satori, the hero of this novel is a modern man in that he is not willing to demolish the workings of his intellect completely. He does feel uneasy, however, with the results of the adult intellect: laws, certificates, calendars and maps. The investigator is clearly an antisociety man in this respect but without being an active social rebel. He is neither like a regressive hero in a traditional kimono, nor like a Western social reformer who charges at the first windmill.

The Ruined Map resembles rather more a picaresque novel than a detective story. It is true that the hero lacks enough rascality to be called an out and out rogue, but he lives definitely outside conventional standards. The hero goes through a series of incidents, but the plot that connects these events is more perfunctory than inevitable. He does not mature after being exposed to different experiences; in fact, if there is any change at all in the hero's character at the end, one may hesitate to call it growth; it is something entirely different. The aim of this chapter is to make an attempt to trace the investigator's journey, to examine the implications of his brushes with several different levels of reality, and finally to map a course in the mapless world to the hero's destination.

There are several people in this novel who represent the order and solidity of the society they live in. The person introduced only as the chief of the investigators is the hero's boss and a die-hard professional. The chief sticks closely to the rules of survival and does not tolerate the slightest deviation on the part of his men. He wants them to remain cool, professional investigators, no more, no less. He tells the hero: "Listen I think you understand. In our work, you don't invade the privacy of the client. You don't stick your nose in business you can't write in your report. If you can't observe the rules you had better wash your hands right now—and change your profession to priest or extortioner." (p. 65)* Anything that suggests a deviation of his framework incurs the chief's scorn: "He thought any enthusiasm, as such, stupid." (p. 150) When the chief detects the detective's more than normal interest in the case, he issues a warning: "You've gotten damn serious about this." (p. 64) The chief knows that an investigator's overly serious interest in his job is not good business, especially when he interprets his job as a search for truth. The chief evokes the hero's memory of one detective who "decided to push things through with no concessions, like a kindergarten teacher who tries to correct a child's unbalanced diet." (p. 78) This man eventually went insane, the hero is told.

---

*Quoted material throughout this chapter is from *The Ruined Map* by Kōbō Abe, translated by E. Dale Saunders (New York: Alfred A. Knopf, 1969). Page numbers refer to this edition.

The chief is described neither as a ruthless capitalist nor as a cold-blooded slave driver; in fact, in the eyes of the hero, the chief is "most considerate and thoughtful of others." (p. 208) The chief is simply interested in living and staying on in this society that supports his profession. The rules are of the utmost importance to him because they are the foundation of any society and community. No rules, no society. He is a society man, a rules man. That is why the chief "demanded the strictness of an ascetic" (p. 208) in matters of the rules of survival. As we will discuss in greater detail later, the hero who distrusts the solidity of society ᴄᴸɪɴᴛ ᴇᴀꜱᴛᴡᴏᴏᴅ ? stands in contrast to the chief who is firmly rooted in the rules of society.

Another contrast to the hero is his wife, from whom he is separated and who runs a dressmaking shop. She is definitely a survival-oriented woman; she ignores her husband's protests, sets up her own successful business, and makes her husband acknowledge that he is, after all, the "loser." She points out to him that he himself is a runaway.

> "From what? You?"
> "Certainly not from me," she said, shaking her head vigorously.
> "From life, from the endless competing and dickering, the tightrope walking, the scramble for a life buoy. It's true, isn't it? In the final analysis, I was merely an excuse." (p. 172)

His wife forces him to realize that he evades the issues of life, problems arising from being an individual in a competitive society. Competition makes one an individual. The hero hates competition and hates to be an individual. By pointing this out, his wife corners him into thinking that the runaway husband he is after may be himself.

> "Ran away?"
> It was obvious, wasn't it? That was my intent. I understood that without being told. Something was definitely wrong if I was surprised at this late date, as if I had made some new discovery. While I thought this, it was also a fact that I experienced a strange confusion at being reminded of the obvious. Suddenly the indignity of it penetrated painfully into my head, as if the contents of the ashtray had been dashed over me. Why? Perhaps because I had the feeling that the husband I was investigating and I were fused. (p. 172)

Thus his wife, unlike Mrs. Nemuro, who "floats like a foetus in the lemon-yellow liquid" (p. 205), functions as a stern reminder that the detective ought to be a participating member of society. In this regard it is significant that the door of his wife's dressmaking shop is a single black acrylic panel, which, acting "like a mirror," mercilessly reflects the image of the detective: "A disreputable character much more suitable to be sought than to be seeking, with his unsteady shoulders in the mirror as if he had risen from a sick bed, and his ruffled hair tousled by the wind." (p. 166) This mirror door insists on its confrontation with the hero and forces him to recognize himself, but Mrs. Nemuro's door is a white one never demanding such recognition.

It would be difficult to dispute that the chief and the detective's wife represent the values of society, but would it be too wild an assertion to say also that Mrs. Nemuro's brother, a smalltime underworld character, stands for society? One can not deny that the man did opt out of the normal society, but in so doing, ironically, he ends up being a relentless organization man. He is much more an intense rules man than the chief, because survival in the underworld requires stricter adherence to rules.

We are not told exactly why he chose the underworld, but we begin to get some glimpse of this man's psyche as we are gradually informed of his aversion to women, his homosexual tendency, and so on. The best clue to understanding him is provided when his sister tells the detective:

> "He says a single map for life is all you need. It's a saying of his. This world is a forest, a woods, full of wild beasts and poisonous insects. You should go only through places where everyone goes, places that are considered absolutely safe, he says." (p. 28)

Two points emerge from the above: his determined hostility, fear of life, and his desperate need for a guide in the hostile environment. The woods of the underworld, like those of the military, can give this kind of man a haven for blind dedication to its law and codes. This, in part, explains his passion to seek out his missing brother-in-law; willful desertion of his sister confirms his world view that life is a lawless jungle. He simply cannot let this happen to his only sister. The rules are the only thing that saves life from being a menacing jungle. He confides his feelings to the detective about this:

"I can't forgive him. I can't stand his self-centeredness. Even a thug, when he wants out, pays for it. Unless he plays by the rules, how can I forgive him? He said something about my sister's not being a complete woman. He's some kind of queer. Let him be, I don't care, but if he doesn't follow the rules— One way or another, I've got to get him back and make him smart for it. My sister's a mess, damn it. Do you understand?" (p. 100)

To Kōbō Abe the idea of a wall is almost an obsession. It is difficult to think of any of his major works that are without some thematic treatment of a wall in one way or another. Images of a wall abound in *The Ruined Map*. As one might expect, it is given negative implications on the most obvious level; a wall partitions, separates, restricts freedom and stops the flow of movement. There is more than one reference to a wall in regard to Mrs. Nemuro's brother: "his broad shoulders were still stiff—like a wall. The only thing missing was the black hole in a picture painted on a wooden panel." (p. 48) "Wearing his jacket, he instantly became a black wall again." (p. 98) There is nothing ambiguous about what a black wall means to a detective: an obstruction of a clear view that a detective must have. That is why the hero detects in the brother something intolerable in their first encounter. What then is the link between the brother being a rules man and being a wall man? A wall is simply a metaphor for the rules: both obstruct a clear view, stop the free flow of movement, divide and then confine people into a hole. The hero, an ad man turned detective, hates what the rules and walls do to a man, in short, hates what society does to a human being. Thus he is here contrasted to his chief, who takes the rules seriously; to his wife, who wants him to be a responsible citizen, a competitive individual; and finally to the client's brother, who seems to represent the ultimate opposition to freedom.

In this novel there are two people who appear to subscribe to social values, but who are actually more ambivalent about the kind of life society prescribes for an individual. Tashiro, one such person, is a company man who worked under Nemuro the runaway. In an interview with an executive of the fuel company where Nemuro once worked, Tashiro is introduced to the detective as a "promising young man." He may look, to the eyes of company executives, like a good organization man, well placed on the ladder of success, but the reader gradually finds out that he nurses a smoldering hostility against society and suffers from a searing alienation. Tashiro sees even in his superior's disappearance another confirmation of an estrangement from his fellow men:

> ———when I considered that Mr. Nemuro had disappeared for no reason, I realized I had been completely abandoned. No, I suppose that's not quite right. Maybe I should call it an inferiority complex—or jealousy. The best things in life are kept from me, only me; I'm the only one who's left out. (p. 237)

Tashiro first approaches the investigator with plausible stories about the missing Nemuro, but the investigator abandons Tashiro after discovering him full of fantasies and fabrications. It is as if Tashiro becomes jealous of the identity Nemuro has acquired by having disappeared. Tashiro seems to want the same attention that his superior is getting, and the only way he can get it is through fabrication of likely stories such as Nemuro's hidden passion for nude photography. Failing in this, he has to go a step further. He makes a 5:30 A.M. phone call to tell the investigator that he is about to hang himself in a public phone booth. Told that he is not being taken seriously, Tashiro angrily abuses the detective:

> You unfeeling bastard. You're a pig, not a man. How can you say such a thing to somebody who's on the brink of death? You're ridiculous. I don't give a damn about his disappearance. It's pretty sneaky—something a coward'd do. What's the point of putting up such a great fuss about somebody like him? I'd never do that. There—I've put the rope around my neck. The position is right, it'll bite right in. Pretty soon I'm going to feel the blood coming out of my nose. I'll be gone further than anyone who's disappeared— much much further. (p. 258)

Here is a terrifying picture of a man completely incapacitated by loneliness. Having failed in everything, he is now ready to commit suicide in order to yank out some form of recognition of his existence. Nemuro has never been the object of Tashiro's interest. Nemuro's disappearance simply shocked him into realizing the irony of the identity gained through the loss of identity. Tashiro follows Nemuro's example; the only difference is that he takes a perverse pride in going much farther.

While Tashiro does not furnish the investigator with any significant clues to finding Nemuro or, for that matter, valuable information on Nemuro's character, Tashiro does function in a curious way as somewhat of a shadow of Nemuro. The reason is that Tashiro and Nemuro have something in common; they appear anchored in society, but they leap out of it with undetermined motives.

Let us look at Nemuro a little more closely. He never surfaces in this story from the beginning to the end, so we must rely on the testimony of others who knew him. How good a society man he had been is related eloquently to the investigator by an executive of the company for which Nemuro had worked.

—Anyway, Nemuro—how shall I put it?—is really a hard worker, a serious type, straightforward, you know. A golden tongue is capital in this kind of cutthroat business. So you've got to be a clever fellow with a lot of grit and stamina along with his gift of gab. And he is absolutely honest. You don't get that everyday; you can use his wallet as a safe deposit box. (p. 51)

His wife reveals a fascinating aspect of this model salaried man. She tells the investigator her husband had one obsession, that of acquiring all kinds of licenses, such as mechanic, radio operator, electric welder, a handler of explosives. The investigator's initial reaction is that Nemuro is "a very practical type," but as he finds that Nemuro has even acquired a movie projectionist's license and a secondary school teacher's certificate, it changes to an impression of "a strange character."

What is the meaning of Nemuro's "license mania"? Mrs. Nemuro reports that he used to say "licenses are the anchor of human life." We recall that his brother-in-law thought life a jungle and felt the need of a good reliable map. Nemuro's anchor and the brother's maps and rules have a strange overlapping area; both are frightened of the fluid, flowing state of life, and they want to do something about it. But the difference lies in their methods of allaying their uneasiness with life; while the brother opts out for the more "ruled" and consequently less fluid society of the underworld, Nemuro attempts to solidify himself by casting as many anchors as possible into the flowing life. Their common ground widens further when both fail in their attempts: the underworld turns out to be more of a lethal jungle for the brother, and Nemuro's anchors can not firmly hold him in this slippery world. The final difference between them is that while the brother is convinced that life is a jungle, Nemuro appears to feel ambivalent about it.

We are told by Mrs. Nemuro that her husband is a "very matter-of-fact man" and that when he became section chief he was very happy because this promotion would work as a "skid-stopper on the slope of life." The missing husband did leave plenty of proof for his being a "matter-of-fact" man, a man whose wallet one could use "as a safe deposit box." But his need for licenses and "skid-stoppers" betrays his wife's and the company executive's view. The investigator, for instance, feels that Nemuro is actually a dreamer. "Using so many anchors for such a small boat certainly puts him in the category of dreamers doesn't it? If he didn't use them, he'd float away." (p. 136) His own name provides an important clue. Nemuro (根室) consists of two characters; the first one *ne* (根) means a root and the second *muro* (室), a room. Therefore one may derive a meaning "rooted in the room" from the combination. Like some of the Theater of the Absurd playwrights, Abe has been interested in the theme of a room, and Abe's room like his wall frequently symbolizes restriction of freedom and something that checks the flow of things. The meaning of this missing person takes on a fascinating duplicity when we examine the character for his first name. The first name, Hiroshi, is given the character 洋, signifying a river and an ocean. Nemuro's name thus suggests two contradictory attributes, the settled state and confinement of solidity on the one hand and the flow and expansiveness of freedom on the other. That Nemuro hankered for a second-class radio operator's license to enable him to get on a large ship is more than a coincidence. The investigator pursues Nemuro's path, and he finds traces of the struggle of two opposing forces that remind him of his own struggles. In tracking down

Nemuro, the investigator had only two of what he calls "maps," a photograph of the man and a matchbox left in a pocket of the man's raincoat. The matchbox leads the investigator to a coffee house called "Camellia."

Report

12 February: 9:40 A.M.—I investigated the origin of the matchbox. About twenty minutes by foot from the client's house, I faced in the direction of S——station on the main road, and looking to the right at the subway station at the bottom of the hill below the housing project, I saw on the left an open-air parking lot. Immediately diagonally in front, I could see a sign bearing the word "Camellia," just like the name on the matchbox. A very ordinary coffee house: capacity about eighteen seats. Besides the owner, there was one waitress . . . about twenty-two, more or less . . . fattish, with a round face and small eyes . . . traces of pimples on her forehead. She had a liking for showy things and wore patterned stockings, but she was an unattractive girl. She is doubtless outside the scope of this investigation. On the door there was a sign "Girl Wanted," and I imagined that someone must have quit recently. I inquired directly of the proprietor, but it was not that. They simply needed a new girl. They had no reaction to the picture of the missing man, no special comment; at least both agreed in testifying that he had not been a regular customer. (N. B. eighty yen for coffee.) (p. 35)

The moment the investigator steps inside the Camellia, what confronts him is the "tired old wall." Everything the investigator sees in the coffee house disgusts him: a color print of a coffee plantation on the wall, a sour looking waitress and the proprietor. The investigator feels:

If I must add something else, I suppose it would be the remark: Dead End. Anything more would be as ridiculous as searching the print of the coffee plantation with a magnifying glass. Not only Nemuro but also anyone else walking into this place would at once be struck with the thought of how fortunate he was to have a home to go back to. (p. 37)

2. Color Symbolism and Understanding of Reality

The predominant feeling this coffee house generates is one of a definite termination, a feeling that one can not go any further.

This is further strengthened by the black color that dominates this place: "With every step a black oil oozed up between the floorboard" (p. 37) and "when I looked back, the curtain, what had seemed to be mesh when I was inside, was blocking the window of the Camellia coffee house like black paint . . ." (p. 39) "There were almost no passers-by yet, but the window of the Camellia had already become a black mirror, and the surroundings had taken on color with the onset of morning." (p. 265) As in the case of the brother the black color signifies something ominously impenetrable, something that blocks clear vision and free movement. A window should function as something opposite to a wall in that it should allow vision, but the window in the Camellia not only blocks but repulses one's attempt to see through, in the manner of a mirror. The investigator learns that the Camellia operates an illegal taxi driver agency for social dropouts. The Camellia is "Dead End." (One is tempted to read a hidden meaning in Camellia because it is a flower known for its sudden "dropping.")

The Camellia may be the Dead End sign for those who are anchored in society, but is definitely a new start for those who refuse to play a citizen's responsibility game. The investigator discovers something about these illegal taxi drivers through his interview with the man to whom Nemuro sold his car.

> Of course, there are all kinds of off-beat types among the drivers: men who used to be school teachers, priests, painters. It's hard work physically, but it's different from other work; the relationship between the men is not troublesome. It's a good job for someone who finds it congenial always to be his own master—to matter what crowd he may be in. (pp. 160–61)

What is stressed in the above are both freedom of movement and freedom from troublesome human relationships. There are vague hints that Nemuro dropped out of society through the door of the Camellia. Furthermore, toward the end of the novel the investigator, who has been blocked by the black window of the Camellia, is able to see through it to the inside of the coffee house: "—through the loose weave of the Camellia's black curtains I could clearly make out the interior." (p. 263) In fact it is in this Camellia that the investigator is severely beaten up and goes into amnesia, marking the beginning of his entirely new relationship with his environment.

Mrs. Nemuro is perhaps the most important person next to the hero for an understanding of the theme of this novel. As the investigator approaches the apartment district where Mrs. Nemuro lives, we notice that her world is strangely dominated by white: "a straight, white line of road stretched to a sky daubed with white" leads him to her apartment complex whose fronts were painted white, and these "buildings were laid out in staggered lines, on both sides one's view met only white walls supporting a milk-white dome of sky." (p. 7) As he goes up the stairs, he notes the name Nemuro underneath number 12 "written in white paint." (p. 7) Then he is confronted by a "white steel door" and a "white buzzer." (p. 9) Toward the end of the novel the hero, worked over by cab drivers in the coffee house, returns to Mrs. Nemuro's apartment, and "the white sky—to which the white road seemed directly connected," "the white bell" and "the white steel door" (p. 266) greet him again.

The significance of white can perhaps be best ascertained by reflecting upon the function of black. We recall that it is associated centrally with Mrs. Nemuro's brother, the Camellia coffee house and with the idea of a wall. Therefore black in this work, as stated earlier, connotes some force hindering vision and movement. The white that surrounds Mrs. Nemuro seems to imply the opposite. The investigator has unusual difficulty in remembering Mrs. Nemuro, whom he has just seen:

> With the girl's disappearance beyond the curtain even my impression of her suddenly became faint and indistinct. I was annoyed . . . yet it was a strange business. The window was beginning to grow dark in the early winter evening, but it was not yet time to turn on the lights. If I concentrated I could just make out the black pen cap that had rolled under the telephone shelf. I had really seen her clearly. She had advanced a chair for me on the other side of the table and we had faced each other scarcely six feet apart. I was quite unable to understand why my impression had suddenly blurred . . . A woman I could not recall . . . a woman whose face vanished with a ripple of the curtain as if by sleight of hand. Was her face so impersonal? I wondered. Yet I could describe in detail over a hundred items of her clothing. (pp. 11–13)

The vagueness Mrs. Nemuro generates derives from the lack of her solid existence and of her individuality. In this respect she forms a sharp contrast to the investigator's wife, who exerts her individuality in a competitive society. When the investigator is with his wife in her dressmaking shop, we sense through their dialogues that he is confronted by a definite, mature individual. But in her apartment, unable to get Mrs. Nemuro into a dialogue, the investigator is constantly frustrated because he is denied, he feels, access to the information he suspects Mrs. Nemuro has. Mrs. Nemuro is perpetually vague and transparent. We are made to feel as if we can walk through her as through a thin white fog. If the investigator's wife is like that mirrorlike black acrylic door of her shop, which reflects the hero's person and forces the recognition of himself, Mrs. Nemuro is like a white fog that rejects a sense of individuality by blurring the demarcation between individuals.

The solidity of the existence of black in the investigator's wife comes from her maturity or willingness to assume her own responsibility in a survival game. The transparency (white) in Mrs. Nemuro derives from her being in a childlike state. There are repeated references to her "childlikeness," for instance when the investigator sees her for the first time he "could have mistaken her for a child," "had it been a little darker" (p. 9), and a little later he notices "her somehow childish body harmonized with the breasts that were neither too big nor too small" (p. 11) and "a lip like that of a still-nursing child." (p. 26) Her transparency receives emphasis both in reference to her physical body and in the atmosphere she exudes. For example, she has "fingers so transparent that you can see her blood veins" (p. 100), and the hero thinks that "this woman became more transparent by using cosmetics and she could easily be seen through." (p. 126) One evening the hero is in her apartment, then the phone begins to ring "breaking the impression that the lemon-yellow room was some solitary island; the outside world bored in through a black hole." (p. 207) He, suspicious of a secret liaison with her husband, asks if he can take the telephone. Permission is nonchalantly granted. Then he feels "the degree of transparency in her situation was greatly increased . . ." (p. 207)

If the environment outside her apartment is characterized by

its whiteness and her existence inside the apartment by her transparency, all hostile to maintaining one's demarcated self, her
apartment is characterized by the lemon-yellow color.

With the light on, it was already evening outside. The Picasso print was
reflected in the panes. As if threatened by something, she roughly pulled
the curtains that covered half the wall, and their lemon-yellow color transformed the room. Lemon-yellow it was, but it was not very fresh. A rather
withered and shop-worn lemon. The masterless room, which had been like
a cast-off cicada skin, suddenly came alive again, thanks to the color. One
could say that it was not the lost man that had been missing but simply the
lemon color. Suddenly a stuffed cat appeared above the bookcases. Below
the cutaway view, Formula I, was a small sconce and on it a lace-net glove.
A room well suited to lemon-yellow. A woman well suited to lemon-yellow.
Her room. A room for her, adjusted to her life. (p. 22)

This lemon-yellow fascinates the hero, and he can not get away
from it. One day he is writing a report at a library, and he closes
his eyes. Then behind his closed eyes, all turns lemon-yellow: "I
could imagine the contours of her ear, bright with lemon-yellow,
luminous with the light reflected from the lemon-yellow curtains.
Lemon-yellow fragrance. Lemon-yellow—" (p. 138) When the
hero finds the lemon-yellow curtains replaced by different curtains, he experiences a deep shock: "It wasn't there! The lemon-
yellow window was gone! Curtains of white and brown vertical
stripes, completely different, were hanging in the place where the
lemon-yellow window should have been. What in the name of God
had happened?" (p. 248)

Why such a fascination with this particular color? A clue is
provided in the scene when the hero, after his first encounter with
his client, leaves her apartment and, suspicious of her relationship
with her "brother," watches her through the lemon-yellow
window.

Something I wanted to see was already visible. I would continue to concentrate on the single point I would see. That faint rectangle of light—the
lemon-yellow window—the window of the room I had taken leave of only a
moment ago. The lemon-yellow curtains resolutely held in check the invasion
of darkness and mocked me derisively—I who was frozen in the dark. (p.
31)

The novel is set in winter, and there are numerous references to the hero's feeling "frozen" throughout the work; "I seemed to be wearing frozen fish bladders" (p. 32), and so on. As will be discussed in more detail later, being "frozen" seems to go beyond a mere physical implication. What is useful, however, at this point in determining the meaning of the lemon-yellow curtains is to see that the curtains and the word *frozen* are placed in diametrical opposition. Their tension-relationship implies that the curtains do something contrary to the frozen state of the hero, in other words the lemon-yellow curtains represent warmth and function to thaw the frozen hero. A further question is why the hero is attracted to this aspect of the curtains. The question addresses itself to one of the basic points of the novel in that it illuminates the hero regressing. The hero sees Mrs. Nemuro "float like a foetus in the lemon-yellow liquid." (p. 205) Taken together with Mrs. Nemuro's transparency and child-quality, her apartment can very well symbolize a womb. It is this lemon-yellow warmth that keeps her from developing her individuality, and that entices the hero from his individualized wife. Thus we see the hero suspended between the two polarities of Mrs. Nemuro and his wife, although he leans far more toward the warmth of the womb. But this is not without some perils.

As the hero-investigator approaches the apartment, a large signboard with a yellow background, "UNAUTHORIZED VEHICLES FORBIDDEN WITHIN THESE PRECINCTS," leaps into his sight. He ignores the threat and drives up the slope, but he encounters some more signs, "NO ENTRY" followed by "NO PARKING." One may very well argue that there can be no special meaning in these signs other than what they state. But when a novelist like Kōbō Abe takes pains to place as many as three warning signs in the space of slightly more than one page, one can not just dismiss them as a coincidence. The point is that the hero not only recognizes each sign but reacts sharply each time. The signs do contribute toward creating an unsettling feeling that the hero is stepping into a place where he should not. We have already suggested that the apartment is a kind of womb. In the Japanese language a womb is *shikyū* (子宮), literally meaning a "child palace." It is a sanctuary, a place to be guarded from outside elements; we recall that this is where Mrs. Nemuro floats, still not thoroughly differentiated, like a foetus in a lemon-yellow juice.

These signs seem to function as more than just a warning against disturbing the "child palace." They may be for the protection of the hero, saying that the apartment is a dangerous place for him and that he is well advised to stay out for his own safety. Once inside the apartment, the hero finds Mrs. Nemuro dressed in black against the lemon-yellow curtains and thinks to himself: "—black and yellow were signs of 'Danger, beware.' " (p. 30) Mrs. Nemuro consistently wears black clothes, and the hero admits: "They suit you. I suppose it's curious to say so, but black becomes you." (p. 178) The black has always been implicated with something negative in this novel; it ranged from blockage of clear vision to restriction of the free flow movement. The black here appears to embrace these implications and also to suggest a little more. To help to clarify this we may do well to examine the meaning of Mrs. Nemuro's name. Her first name is Haru. The first association is one of "spring," and this coincides with the peculiar warmth of her apartment in contrast to the cold outside, and possibly with her ever-present lukewarmness. However the meanings of the characters used for Haru are quite interesting. The first one, *ha* (波), indicates "waves," and the second one, *ru* (瑠), which is meaningless unless combined, has on its right side a character signifying "to stay," "to stop," "to wait" and also "to stagnate." She does all of these in fact, but combined with the preceeding character "waves," the choice of "to stop" begins to take on an intriguing meaning: "wave-stopping." Significantly, her husband's name, we may recall, is an "ocean" or a "river." If we stayed within a framework of the probable implications of these two names, it would seem to suggest a basic pattern; the husband represents a free-moving force while the wife stands for a force that stops it.

If the apartment symbolizes a womb, and if Mrs. Nemuro represents the cessation of movement, it would seem that the apartment–Mrs. Nemuro complex indicates the terminal point of regression, the point from which one can not go any further. This is the complete ego-dissipation point. If it is the death-point, this would be the ultimate of the black wall. But the paradox is that the apartment is where the hero, repelled by the pressure of a competitive society, feels warm, attracted and liberated. The black wall should be outside, not inside the apartment. This kind of a paradox is typical of Abe: flowing sand turns out to be a solid wall, and conversely a sand pit liberates you from urban pits.

In the same way Mrs. Nemuro is a paradox. You can walk through her like a thin fog, but she is a "vessel for my sleep" (p. 269), the dark "depression" (p. 269) from which you can not crawl back. She is the coveted warmth of the lemon-yellow that thaws you from the frozen rigidity of social reflex, but Mrs. Nemuro is the "sharp pin sticking out from the opening in the lemon-yellow curtains" that nails you "to an invisible wall like an insect specimen" (p. 48) She is white and she is black: "—when she crossed in front of the lemon-yellow curtains, her face became black, her hair white, and her lips white too, the irises of her eyes became white and the whites black, her freckles became white like dust that has gathered on the cheek bones of a stone image." (pp. 271–2) She is a woman and also a child. She tells the hero that she loves a kind of "talk that reverses itself, where top becomes bottom, as you're listening to it." (p. 211) This "top becoming bottom" relativity in Mrs. Nemuro is an important key for understanding the hero.

The Ruined Map is about the investigator; it is about his journey in search of his real identity. He encounters a number of people as a traveler would, passing through several different countries. He does not feel completely comfortable in any of these worlds. The world that frustrates him most is the world of competitive survival. Such a world, by the very nature of the competition, demands rigid laws and rules. A person living in this world must have a honed awareness of time and space; in other words he is perpetually conscious of his own territory versus others' territories (space) and of his promissory notes (time). It is a world of rational, responsible grownups whose behavior must be predictable in accordance with their agreed-upon codes. Most important, he must be a thoroughly differentiated individual—as opposed to an undifferentiated foetus—who has a capacity and willingness to honor a contract. A contract separates people by connecting them, or if you like, it connects them by separating. A contract demands that a participant be a separated (from the womb?) individual. The investigator's wife and his chief are the contractual, responsible and rational grownups in this novel. His wife regards marriage strictly as a contract, refusing to play a "womb-game" for her husband. She is a distinct individual, successful in her survival game (her dressmaking shop). The investigator's chief is a real "pro," a strict boss, but fair and reasonable as long as his men stay within the framework of his professional rules.

When the hero changed his job to private investigator, he might have thought that the new work would allow him more freedom. The result is that he is not completely happy with his new work. His unhappiness takes an interesting metaphor, his being "frozen." We have touched upon this earlier in connection with the lemon-yellow curtains, but now let us examine the implication of the "frozen" image a little further. Mrs. Nemuro looks out of the window and points at the place where her husband has disappeared. As he watches the area that Mrs. Nemuro is pointing at, the investigator is severely affected by the desolate winter scenery of metropolitan Tokyo:

> The wind blew, threading its way between the dwellings. Freezing blasts of air, striking the sharp corners of the buildings, howled in a bass that the ear could barely catch. Even so, the moanings of this great pipe organ penetrated to the very quick of me. My whole body became gooseflesh, my blood congealed, my heart was transformed into a red, heart-shaped ice bag. A trampled asphalt walkway. The broken, abandoned rubber ball visible as a white speck on the lawn. The cracked corpse of the street, illuminated by the street lights that gilded even my dust-speckled shoes. One could scarcely hope to arrive at any place worth mentioning along such a street. (pp. 19–20)

We see in the quotation above a juxtaposition of a human heart that has ceased to function and a street that is dead. The heart has stopped its blood flow and has just been frozen into a "red, heart-shaped ice bag," and the street is a "cracked corpse," having stopped its flow of really alive people who want to "arive at

any place worth mentioning." In the world of Kōbō Abe any
force that solidifies, freezes, stops flowing is treated as a villain. In
this respect Abe is antisociety, because society freezes man's free
flow instinct by passing laws, issuing licences and certificates,
erecting boundaries and walls, creating labels and names and
printing maps as if streets and township boundaries were real.
Thus his "freezing" metaphor, e.g. a "frozen fish" (p. 67), is an
expression of a man, who totally immobilized by walls, fences,
identification cards and maps, has lost the blood-flow in his heart.
He has earned his solid individuality but has been robbed of his
human warmth. That is why the lemon-yellow curtains of Mrs.
Nemuro's apartment spellbind the hero so much:

> Whatever happened I could not give up—there was some hope albeit slight.
> I had been numbed to the bone like a frozen fish by that rigid wind, but
> the faint light of the lemon-yellow window had transfixed me. I could not
> help but feel I was being beckoned in, that she wanted me to ignore the
> fence and come in. There was no basis for such a thought. Yet my heart
> throbbed. I had a nagging suspicion that my client's fence was not necessari-
> ly one and the same as that of her self-styled brother. (p. 67)

It is interesting to note that Mrs. Nemuro functions as one who
revives the hero's heart and that she demands him to "ignore the
fence." The womb is warm, and there is no artificial demarcation
in there. Everything is afloat in the womb.

The hero wants to be perpetually afloat, as Mr. Nemuro wanted
to get on a commercial steamer. Perhaps this is the reason why
he chose the investigator's job. A person afloat is not a very good,
responsible citizen; he has little sense of time and space. The hero
gets on a freeway, forgets about his appointment with his boss and
enjoys his ride without a destination.

> The hour when I was supposed to go back to the office and see the chief had
> long since passed. I had quite neglected contacting my client too. I had no
> need to be here; there was no necessity of getting any place, I suppose. Pure
> time—time spent to no purpose. What a luxury. I pressed down on the ac-
> celerator. The speedometer steadily mounted—seventy-five. The wind began
> to affect the steering. I was a point of tenseness. I had the sensation of sud-
> denly awakening on a calendarless day at a place that appeared on no map.
> You are free to call this sufficiency flight if you wish. When a pirate becomes

a pirate and sets sail for unknown seas or when a brigand becomes a brigand
and conceals himself in the depths of a city or a forest or an uninhabited
desert, both—surely some place, some time—feel like this. (p. 175)

The investigator, through floating (moving without a set goal),
achieves pure time free from a calendar and pure space free from
a map. A calendar and a map were invented to further man's
practical conveniences. A practical man divided time and space
so he might have control over them. In so doing a practical man
froze the flow of time and space. After all, controls are more effective when things are frozen, still and dead. The investigator wants
to restore life to time and space by removing the man-made divi-
sions. He aspires to be a pirate and a brigand because they do not
live in a divided time and space; they live on an ocean or in a desert where no certificates, no license, no name card are of any
help. Water and sand are in perpetual motion and no dividing
walls—a calendar, a map, a table—can affect them.

Does the hero really want to stay in pure time and pure space?
One can rephrase the question: does he want to stay on an ocean
or in a desert? One can push it still further and ask: does he want
to regress into and stay in the womb where there is no awareness
of divided time and space, where there is little division between
life and death? The hero recounts his pure time experience to
Mrs. Nemuro:

> "As I went along I thought how wonderful it would be if I could go on like
> that forever. And then I felt I really could. But I shudder now when I think
> of my psychological state at the time. Supposing everything had come out
> as I wished, supposing I had gone on and on and no matter how far I went,
> never, never came to the toll gate—" (p. 190)

Thus we see a distinct conflict in the hero's mind: a desire for the
fluid state of non-time and another hankering for a solid termination. The conflict is between cyclic time that has no end, like the
Tokyo loop expressway, and linear time that must begin somewhere and end somewhere else. In other words this reveals the
hero has accepted neither his fantasy world of a pirate nor his
work-a-day where a map and a calendar are reality.

3. Toward Pure Time or Out of the Womb?

The question, then, is: where is the hero heading? The investgator leaves his competitive advertising job for freer wheeling work; he leaves his wife, a successful business woman who is a constant reminder of the name card—social reality. He then encounters his enigmatic client, Mrs. Nemuro, who dissolves and frustrates all of his social reflexes, no dialogue, no linear time but a lot of beer and the lemon-yellow curtains. In the meantime a man who calls himself her brother appears and stands between them like a black wall, but the brother gets eliminated in an underworld skirmish. So it does look as if the hero is heading straight for Mrs. Nemuro. However there is a definite counterbalancing force in the course of the hero's fantasied regression toward "pure" time. The author achieves this counter force through his ingenious device of the hero's toothache, to which the author repeatedly refers in strategic situations. The first mention of the toothache is made when the investigator is vigorously quizzing Tashiro, who seems to hold back some information. The second one appears when the investigator, having failed to make any progress in pursuing Nemuro, takes a direct flight into a world of fantasy.

> Moreover, at the time when the possiblities were collapsing one after the other, the vexatious quiverings of huge, flesh-colored moth larvae nestling in my breast were growing in intensity, as if they were on the point of bursting forth from the cocoon and flying away. As soon as they were liberated, these gory moths would make a dash straight for that lemon-yellow window. (p. 87)

He goes on fantasying the moths' attack on the brother, and through the association of their fangs, he is reminded: "I would have to go right to the dentist's myself. When I put the tip of my tongue in the hole left by my molar, more and more I got the metallic taste of blood." (p. 88) The third occurs when the hero visits his estranged wife. She reminds him that he did not run away from her but from life and that she was merely an excuse. "Suddenly a flaming, white pain shot through my left eye as if I had been struck with a bent nail. My broken molar, of course. I would have to have it looked after before the decay spread to the jaw."

(p. 172) A basic pattern emerges out of these toothaches; it happens when the hero's movement toward Mrs. Nemuro is deterred. The third one may need a little explanation. The analysis of the hero's wife works as an injector of reality into the hero's regressive process, because it reminds him, "your life was such that there would never be a solution unless you won out over the competition in the office" (p. 173), as she adds immediately. This in turn acts as a deterrent from his course toward Mrs. Nemuro. One also notices that the toothache seems to gain intensity as the story progresses and as the hero gains proximity to "the depression she had left in the bed—the vessel for my sleep." (p. 271) It should also be noted that the hero worries about the decay spreading to the jaw.

This black cavity in the hero does seem to be alive, to grow and to spread. The cavity grows so large, at the end of the novel, that it can hide the hero from the woman who may be Mrs. Nemuro. The investigator, in a state of amnesia, dials a phone number found in his pocket. A woman answers the phone and recognizes his voice. He asks her to come and help him. He hides himself in a "black opening like some decayed tooth—a narrow alleyway between a small shoe store and a liquor store that doubled as a tobacconist's" (p. 298), and waits for the woman. She turns out to be the woman who served him in a coffee shop. To the hero who suffers from amnesia it is not clear, but to the reader it is sufficiently clear that she is Mrs. Nemuro with all of her characteristics. Mrs. Nemuro stops at the phone booth where the hero said he would wait for her. She looks around uneasily but is unable to discover him because the "narrow, dark crevice" protects him from her. It is relevant to mention at this point that the missing Nemuro has already been referred to as "black holes."

Perhaps the husband's silhouette had come into view. In some corner of the superimposed town landscapes there were empty black holes. Shadows of the nonexistent husband, he was not alone; there was a limitless number of different hims. Mine, hers, his. Apparently in my mind some great change was taking place. (p. 177)

The black holes left by a missing person and the black cavity left by a missing molar. What is the link? It seems that the hero had inside him a little of Mrs. Nemuro's missing husband in the form of a hole vacated by a tooth. Nemuro, we may recall, was the one who needed many anchors to keep him firm in society, and who eventually left his apartment-womb. If the hero is heading for Mrs. Nemuro, her husband is getting away from her. While they are heading, at least so it seems, in opposite directions, they do cross each other at some point, and the hero begins to question the solidity of his own identity. The erosion of his identity, which becomes complete later with the loss of his memory, appears to have already been seeded in the crevice of his decayed tooth from the very beginning. Thus as the hero progresses in his regression, the antiwomb force begins to make itself felt. This is the very force that prevents him from his final union with Mrs. Nemuro in the last scene of the novel.

> Once she glanced over toward me, but she could probably make out nothing in this narrow, dark crevice. I continued to wait intently, choking back my screams behind clenched teeth. Nothing would be served by being found. What I needed now was a world I myself had chosen. It had to be my own world, which I had chosen by my own free will. She searched; I hid. At length she began walking slowly away as if she had given up; suddenly she was cut off from view by a car and was already gone. (pp. 298-9)

One notices that the hero's regression abruptly ends here and that it marks his turning point. One may also note that the metaphor of the "toothache" and the "black cavity" are significantly associated with loneliness. The end result of the antiregressive force in the hero is individuation, honed awareness of time and space, hence loneliness. The hero could have gone back to the lemon juice-filled womb and allowed the lemon acid to corrode what was left of his individuality, but he clenched his teeth and held out, fighting his loneliness, the amnesia loneliness where his past has been wiped out.

Why loneliness in the antiregressive force, a force which drives one toward the matrix of society? Abe has consistently distrusted what seems to an ordinary man the solid, tangible phenomena of society. To Abe's eyes, social structures, institutions, laws and what even looks like a rock-hard human relationship are extremely fragile and fluid, like an ill-founded shack that can be blown off by a sudden gust. Abe himself closely witnessed a dramatic distintegration of a society in Manchuria when World War II ended. Certificates, name cards, maps were suddenly reduced to pieces of scrap paper, but Abe learned how to survive in the mapless, licenseless, fluid state by floating and came to accept it as more real than what once seemed a solid reality backed by certificates. As mentioned before, Abe often uses a wall metaphor to describe these solidifying devices; for instance the hero, looking out of the window of Mrs. Nemuro's apartment, sees commuting workers returning home and thinks to himself: "Some are returning, going back to the place they had left—leaving in order to return. They go out to obtain walling material to make the thick walls of their houses thicker, stronger than ever to return to." (p. 14) Walls create cracks and holes in the flowing reality of Abe, and that is why he uses these images to symbolize loneliness. At the end of this novel the hero, completely lost in his amnesiac isolation, dials a phone number found in his pocket, then he finds in the phone booth:

A rolled-up newspaper lay in the corner: the dried black tip of a turd of human excrement peeped out from underneath. The tip was tapered and there were ropelike depressions in it. In the depressions some vegetable fibers, like the tufts of a rough painter's brush, stood out. There was no particular smell, but without thinking I rose. The cracks, like those of the shell of a broken boiled egg, which covered the tapering head end, frightened me. This was excrement that had stood for a long time. The man must have held it back until he had had to go in the telephone booth—it was probably a man—it might have been a woman—but it was probably a man. Some lonely man denied the use even of one of the innumerable toilets in the limitless labyrinth of the city. When I imagined the figure of the man crouching over in the telephone booth, I was stricken with a feeling of dread. (p. 196)

Cracks are the markers of time and space. They appear after the flow has stopped and things have gotten hard and dry. With markers, calendars and maps, you can be sure that you do not get lost in the labyrinth of city life and that you are a model productive member of post-Industrial Revolution society. The markers, like cracks, isolate you from other people. Society, which relies on markers (laws and certificates) for its survival, has to be a lonely place despite or rather because of the crowds of people in it. The more crowded, the more cracks and rules. The more cracks, the lonelier. Therefore in Abe's works any force which drives one toward the center of society is associated with loneliness.

The hero of the novel is willing neither to accept the society reality, as most people are, nor to embrace the foetus reality. The hero, then, must be somewhere in between the adult world of differentiation and the foetus world of nondifferentiation. When we examine the entire course that the hero has walked, we find a zigzag pattern he has traced between Mrs. Nemuro and his chief, resembling the figure of a young boy. The kind of enthusiasm that he displays for his detective work is more akin to that of a boy absorbed in his favorite project than to that of a cool professional like his chief. The very fact that he suffers from amnesia at the end seems to complete what he sets out to become, because a boy by his very nature has little of an adult's past. What is perhaps more significant than the erasure of the past is the appearance of several boys in this novel. The most important of all is a boy who appears in the very beginning and the end. At the outset of the novel the hero is heading in his car for Mrs. Nemuro's apartment, when all of a sudden a young boy perched on one roller skate sails around the curve and comes sliding down toward him. He slams on the brake and barely misses the boy, who skids into the guard rail. At the end of the novel, after the attack of amnesia, the hero encounters a similar scene, but this time he is not in a car but walking, and he yields when the boy on a roller skate comes sliding down the grade. The meaning of this will become clear when we examine identical paragraphs of about one hundred and twenty words that precede these scenes:

> The surface of the street was not asphalt but a rough-textured concrete with narrow grooves about five inches apart, apparently to prevent slipping. But they did not look as though they would be much help to pedestrians. The purposely rough concrete surface was covered with dust and tire shavings, and on rainy days, even if one wore rubber-soled shoes, it would surely make difficult walking. No doubt the pavement was made in this way for cars. If so, the grooves every five inches would be very effective. When the drainage of the street was obstructed by melting snow and sleet, they looked as though they would be useful in channeling the water into the gutters. (p. 5 and p. 272)

The whole paragraph is concerned with the issue of slipping and
stop-slipping. It is highly significant that the passage that deals
with this theme opens and closes the novel. We come to realize the
importance of the theme in this work, if we change *slipping* into
flowing. Abe's reality is not a walled reality propped up by certificates but the one where everything should be in a state of flux and
be flowing and moving. The paragraph above says that the surface of the street is designed to stop slipping, but this design does
not work for pedestrians; is effective only for cars. As the hero is
in his car at the outset, it means that this stop-slipping is working
for the hero, suggesting nonflow in the beginning. Furthermore,
at the start, he also *stops* the young boy on a roller skate who
crashes into the guard rail. But at the end the hero is now walking,
and the boy swishes by him on a roller skate, suggesting a flowing
state at the end of the work because the stop-slip mechanism does
nothing when walking. The hero with his amnesia is indeed in
a state of flow, liberated from the anchors of his past memories.
He is very much like the boy on a roller skate. Another difference
is that while in the beginning the hero reacts sharply to surrounding phenomena as a detective should, at the end he is no longer
sure about these surrounding things. They are not clearly defined
but fuzzy, blurred as though looking through a white fog. His own
identity has been obscured because all the external things that
affirm it have become ambiguous. The last difference is that at the
beginning the hero is heading for Mrs. Nemuro, but at the end he
has just left her apartment. He is out of the womb but not quite in
the "mapped" world; he is a "slip" of a boy, forever floating on a
roller skate.

Kazuko Tsurumi

Student Movements in 1960 and 1969
Continuity and Change

1. Dissatisfaction and Politics: Convergence

There are now about 379 four-year and 400 junior colleges in Japan, the students in which total 1,525,000, or 19.4 percent of the total population of their peers (male 24.2 percent; female 14.5 percent).[1] Since only 2.45 percent of the Japanese population between eighteen and twenty-one years of age received higher education in 1936, these figures indicate a conspicuous increase during the postwar period. According to an estimate made by police headquarters in July, 1969, only 26,600 out of the total Japanese college student population of 1,525,000 can be called activists, more than 14,000 of whom belong to the Democratic Youth League, which is affiliated with the Communist party, and the rest of whom belong to factions opposing the Communist party. According to the police estimate, the leaders of the anti-Communist factions are capable of mobilizing only 42,550 fellow students in their support.[2] If, however, the leaders of unaffiliated factions are added to that police estimate, the number of anti-Communist radical activists is really much higher, and the number of student mobilization may be judged partly by the turnout for a demonstration staged on June 15, 1969, under the auspices of Zengakuren ("The National Federation of Student Self-Government ment Associations"), Hansen Seinen Iinkai ("Anti-War Youth Committee"), Beheiren ("The Citizens' League for Peace in Vietnam"), and various other leftist organizations, from whose combined sponsorship the Socialist and Communist parties and Sohyo

195

("The National Council of Labor Unions") were conspicuously absent. With alleged aims that were "antiwar, anti-Japan-United States security treaty, pro-reversion of Okinawa," and commemorative of the death of Miss Michiko Kanba (the event that precipitated the government's decision to postpone President Dwight D. Eisenhower's 1960 visit to Japan), about 70,000 persons participated throughout the country. Since it indicates the mobilization now apparently possible to this grouping of New Left organizations acting as a united front independent of other, Old Left organizations, this number is especially significant, although it may also incidentally reflect the fact that Zengakuren's agreement to forego the use of *Gewalt* staves (*geba bo*) helped raise the level of participation among those persons opposed to measures of violence. The figure also indicates the rather high level of rank and file student participation in political activities that exists in Japan in comparsion to the relatively small number of student leaders.

Japanese students can be divided into three categories: first, the genuine activists, who are vitally interested in student movements and hold office either in the student self-governments of their own universities or in interuniversity student organizations or both; second, the merely interested, who support student movements but do not hold offce in any pertinent student organizations; and third, the apathetic, who neither support nor hold office in any such organizations. Although no available statistics show the exact ratios of membership in these groups, it is reasonable to assume that the majority of students in Japan, like the majority of students elsewhere, belongs to the third group, whereas the minority belongs to the first, with a variant number falling somewhere in between. According to a survey I made in 1962, 47.8 percent of the Japanese students classifiable as "apathetic" said that they joined the antisecurity treaty demonstrations of 1960, whereas 80 percent of the "interested" and 100 percent of the "activists" did so.[3] Although their percentage of participation in 1960 was the smallest, it is significant that the apathetic took part at all in those demonstrations. Meanwhile, although no similar survey has since been made, there were some indications that their participation had been rising.

One of the major reasons for even apathetic Japanese students to take part in political activities derives from widespread student dissatisfaction with university life during the postwar period. Only one out of a hundred students interviewed in my 1962 survey expressed complete satisfaction with his classroom lectures, whereas seventy-six out of a hundred expressed only minimal satisfaction or none at all. As for the sources of their reactions, forty-seven students out of a hundred stated that the content of lectures was poor; fourteen, that the teaching methods to which they were subjected were poor; eleven, that school facilities themselves were poor; and three, that the attitudes of their teachers were bad. Fifty-three students said that they found communication with their professors impossible even with respect to issues of their study.[4] Have academic conditions improved since 1962? Far from it. Not only have they deteriorated, but also the students' sense of relative deprivation has increased, so that what is so euphemistically called "campus unrest" has sharply intensified in recent years.

Let me cite two episodes to show how Japanese university students at large feel about their education. In 1968, at a private university where I was then teaching, a class of students protesting in an open letter against a certain professor who had not come to his scheduled classes two-thirds of the time, as well as against the administration that had permitted him to do so with impunity, raised the thoroughly just question of how they could possibly be adequately trained in a presumably organized field by receiving only one-third of the lectures. To this protest the professor orally replied that since he was then only a part-time teacher at the institution concerned, his primary obligation was to the institution in which he was a full-time teacher; accordingly, he thought it perfectly legitimate to not come to classes in the one institution when the other required priority. This professor's logic arose directly out of an unfortunate peculiarity of the Japanese system of faculty recruitment, which depends very heavily upon the hiring of part-time, moonlighting teachers. Since private universities in Japan are especially short of funds, chiefly because the government helps them very little, they notoriously resort to the hiring of part-time teachers from other institutions at such incredibly low salaries as about two dollars an hour. According to Professor Michio Nagai, "The ratio of part-time and full-time teachers at the present time in most private universities in Japan is about 50 to 50."[5] Although the employment of part-time teachers is a money-saving device for Japanese private universities, it is one of the foremost causes of Japanese student complaint.

In the university in which that open letter was written, I had three hundred students in an introductory sociology class; most of them came from relatively well-to-do families. At any rate, I set the final examination of my introductory sociology class as a choice between two books, one of which was Professor Nagai's *Japanese University*. Overwhelmingly, the majority of my students chose to write on this book, specifically with respect to two questions: (1) What does the author consider the shortcomings of the Japanese university system? And (2) What do you consider the shortcomings of the Japanese university system? Out of that total of three hundred students, only one wrote that he was so completely happy with his own university that he could not think of any shortcomings in the system. The rest of the students, however, listed specific complaint after specific complaint against the system. Particularly noteworthy was the fact that even those students who severely criticized the radical student movements rampant on various campuses also expressed strong complaints about the university system.

These recent personal experiences would indicate in a limited manner that Japanese students, whether politically conscious or politically indifferent, are deeply dissatisfied with their universities. The fact has been publicly confirmed, as well, by nationwide surveys of university students conducted by the Yomiuri newspaper twice: in August, 1968, and February, 1969. In answer to the question, "Are you satisfied with the present university education?", the ratio of those satisfied to those dissatisfied was 50:50 among 1,530 students of twenty-one universities interviewed in the 1968 survey. In contrast, 75.8 percent of the students interviewed in the 1969 survey were dissatisfied. Nevertheless, only 13.9 percent of the dissatisfied students supported the violent tactics of student activitists, whereas 62.9 percent opposed them.[6] Thus, although a majority of students are critical of the use of violence in student political affairs, a majority of them are at the same time dissatisfied with their education.

It is, of course, the prevalence of such student dissatisfaction that makes it relatively easy for the politically conscious activists to solicit sympathy and support from politically indifferent students for various kinds of protest, on campus or off campus. If the trend was merely latent during the antisecurity treaty demonstrations in 1960, it has now become clearly manifest, especially since the launching of two major campus struggles: one at the University of Tokyo in January, 1968, and the other at Nihon University in May, 1968.[7]

Against this overall background, an examination of the goals, methods, and ideo-affective postures of the leaders of the Japanese student movements in 1960 and 1969 may be more concretely revealing.

2. The New Look of 1960: Departure from the Prewar Communist Pattern of the 1930s

Traumata

The Bund, the major organization of students that led the antisecurity treaty campaign of 1960, was born out of three traumatic experiences: (1) Japan's defeat in 1945; (2) a sense of having been betrayed by the older generation, most of whom suddenly switched with Japan's defeat from the extreme of supporting Japanese militarism and hatred of the Americans and British to the totally contradictory extreme of supporting democracy and love of yesterday's enemies; and (3) disillusionment with the Japanese Communist Party, especially after its sixth party conference of 1955, which denounced and reversed the violent policies the party had advocated in 1952 and adopted new policies of peaceful gradualism. To most student members of the party, these changes were bolts from the blue, for they had never been discussed among rank and file members. In fact, the students began to suspect that, although the party since its inception in the 1920s had been the staunchest opponent of the emperor system, it in fact shared some basic attitudes with the very system against which the students themselves were fighting. In any case, the student leaders came to realize that the party had become corrupted by authoritarianism and absolutism; it had obviously taken the critiques of Stalinism very lightly and was flatly disregarding the individual opinions of its members. Of course, those students who voiced their criticisms most vigorously were expelled from the party.

Accordingly, when the Bund emerged in 1956 as the first effective organization of radical students independent of the Communists, the fact that most of its leaders were purgees from the party gave the group its basic orientation, for its leaders attempted to form an organization on principles different from those of the Communists and at the same time distinguish their own personalities from those of the Communist leaders who had ostracized them.[8]

Search for New Selfhood

Satoshi Kitakōji, the Zengakuren secretary general in 1960 and chairman in 1961, once stated the basic orientation of the student movement in this way:

> Both as youth and as nascent intelligentsia we are strongly inclined to search for ways in which to connect personal ways of life with social modes of existence. It is therefore extremely important to recognize the student movement as a process of that formation of selfhood which might solve this universal problem of intelligentsia, at the same time that it exists as a political movement.[9]

That the search for new selfhood (*shutai -sei*) was a vogue among both leaders and the rank and file of Japanese students has been pointed out by Robert Lifton, who interviewed some of them in Japan in 1962.[10] The significant part of Kitakōji's statement is that he emphasized the dual orientation of the student movement: one aspect intellectual and the other political. In other words, the movement was directed not only toward producing changes in extrapersonal social structures but also toward producing changes in the characters of those very same individuals who were struggling for external changes.

Although the unity of changing oneself and changing one's environment was stressed as an ideal, emphasis has actually had to alternate between one or the other aspect of change at different periods of the student movement. At the time of a great political campaign, as during the antisecurity treaty demonstrations, external change was stressed, while before and after such a political upheaval, internal change was stressed.

Democracy and Antiwar Sentiment

After the Diet passed the revised Japanese-American security treaty by snap vote on May 19, 1960, Yoshimi Takeuchi, then professor of Chinese literature at Tokyo Metropolitan University, defined the event as "a crossroads of democracy and despotism",[11] and Masao Maruyama, professor of political science at the University of Tokyo, concurred in that view at a meeting of scholars and writers on May 24.[12] For Japanese students educated in postwar democratic principles the term "crossroads" had such effective emotive appeal that it contributed tremendously to their upsurge of demonstrations during the months of May and June.

In answer to the question, "What do you think was the meaning of the antisecurity treaty demonstrations?" forty-nine students out of a hundred in my 1962 survey checked "Opposition to the security treaty," and forty-four checked "Expression of antiwar sentiments," the second most important issue for them. In answer to the question, "What ends do you think the demonstrations should have achieved?" the top-ranking answer was "To make the security treaty noneffective," followed by the replies, "T dissolve parliament" and "To defend the constitution." Thus it appears that in 1960 Japanese students were motivated not only by an enthusiasm for the defense of parliamentary democracy but also by a strong belief in the efficacy of the constitution, for their antiwar sentiments were directly associated with Article Nine of the constitution, which stipulates abolition of the armed forces and renounces war as a means of settling international disputes.

Hedonistic Revolutionaries

In the 1930s the revolutionary commitment of Japanese Communists was invariably associated with predominantly negative affects of self-sacrifice, the miseries of imprisonment and torture, and the fear of death. By contrast, among the student leaders of the 1960s, political activities were predominantly associated with positive affects of joy, excitement, and happiness. For example, in 1960 Shigerō Shima, a central figure in the formation of the Bund, described himself and his fellow students as follows:

> At the time of the antisecurity treaty campaign, the situation in Japan on the whole was not dark and oppressive as it was at the time of the red-purge in 1950. The general atmosphere surrounding us was full of light, and we also felt full of light within ourselves. Our primary motivation was to revive our own humanity. We had been reading Marx's earlier writings, for we had been alienated to such an extent under the capitalist system as to become part of the machine, completely losing our humanity.

> We feel there is a clear line of demarcation between ourselves and the Communists of the prewar days. Their primary motivation was the spirit of martyrdom. In contrast, emancipation of ourselves as human beings has become our primary concern since the time of the antisecurity treaty campaign.[13]

If Feuer's classification of basic ethical attitudes were applied, the postwar generation of student activists might be characterized as hedonistic revolutionaries, whereas the leftist intellectuals of the 1930s might be characterized as ascetic revolutionaries.[14]

Eclectic Approaches to Marxism

According to my 1962 survey, 78.7 percent of Japanese student activists, 76.7 percent of the interested, and 13 percent of the apathetic said that they were "very much interested in Marxism," showing a quite high percentage of Marxist interest that may not be surprising among radical students, especially in Japan. But a significant change seems to have been occurring in their view of Marxism, for easily one-half of those respondents sympathetic to Marxism also supported another ideology or other ideologies—most frequently, for example, Humanism, Existentialism, or Nihilism. Such an eclectic attitude toward Marxism very sharply contrasts with that monolithic and absolutistic approach that prevailed among prewar Japanese Communists.[15]

Toward the Rediscovery of Indigenous Patterns

Meanwhile, on Christmas Eve of 1961, the secretariat of the Socialist Student League issued a leaflet urging Japanese students to join a study group on the constitution and justifying the establishment of such a group. Among other things, it expressed the following views:

> We believe that people, through studying the constitution, will eventually formulate their own theory of a revolution in a "Japanese style." In the process of formulating our own theory we can learn from Ikki Kita, the only true revolutionary in Japan and a Japanese-style fascist, who was executed on account of his involvement in the February 26th Incident. It was through the rigorous examination of the essence of the Meiji constitution [of 1889] that he managed to build up his original theory of revolution. A formulation of our own theory of revolution, through studying the constitution of 1946, as Kita formulated his theory by examining the constitution of 1889, will provide the only theory of revolution that can serve as an effective and practical guide to our political movement.[16]

The leaders of the Socialist Student League were thus unique among the leaders of different factions of the student movement in recognizing the importance of learning from the past experiences of revolutionary movements in Japan. The failure of the Communist intellectuals of the 1930s was due partly to their insistence upon applying to the Japanese situation an exogenous ideology that they regarded as absolute, without paying sufficient attention to indigenous Japanese patterns of thought and feeling. In this way they alienated themselves from the very people for whom they had allegedly been working.[17] Addressing themselves vigorously to the avoidance of a similar mistake, the leaders of the Socialist Student League turned to the study of the work of Ikki Kita, who had attempted to combine the theory of revolution with the cult of the emperor. Some leaders of the league also proposed a reassessment of the works of Yanagita Kunio, the pioneering scholar who established the science of folklore in Japan. Thus at least some of the 1960 leaders tried to learn from non-Marxist, indigenous Japanese thinkers.

3. The Styles of 1969: Continuity and Change since 1962

Traumata

Just as the postwar generation of the leaders of the student movement emerged out of the trauma of Japan's defeat in the Pacific
War, the post-*ampo* (antisecurity treaty campaign) generation of
student leaders emerged out of the trauma of their movement's
defeat in the 1960 struggle. Having clearly failed in their professed
aim of nullifying the revised security treaty, for some time after
the struggle they felt oppressed, and depressed, by an overwhelming sense of frustration. Specifically, they attributed their failure
to their primary use of nonviolent democratic methods; garnering
signatures on petitions, the holding of assemblies, and the marshal-
ling of peaceful demonstrations.

In the meantime, student disillusionment with the Communist
party was severely exacerbated through their experience with it
on the evening of June 15, 1960. At a time when one group of
students had broken through the gates of the Diet grounds to hold
a meeting and were confronted by the mechanized Japanese police
force at the eventual cost of one student dead and many others
seriously injured, there were altogether more than one hundred
thousand demonstrators outside the gates—students, labor union-
ists, and ordinary citizens—who might have come to the aid of
the beleaguered students inside. But the leaders of the Communist party intervened by ordering the demonstrators to get out
and go home, thus circumventing any massive resistance to police violence.[18] The behavior of the Communists that night, and
increasingly thereafter, immeasurably deepened the schism with
the student activists.

Ryūmei Yoshimoto, a poet who is one of the most popular
writers among radical students, has said:

It was after the *ampo* struggle and the Miike Coal Miners' strike [January to
July, 1960] that I determined to part with the classical Marxism of the postwar period and its satellites of progressivism. There was only one hundred
meters' distance between the masses of demonstrators and the students struggling with the police, who were causing tremendous bloodshed. I witnessed
the leaders of the Communist party and its satellite progressive organizations

intervening among the masses of people to prevent them from joining the students, driving them away into what they called "an orderly" demonstration.[19]

This experience, Yoshimoto maintains, was the turning point in his intellectual life, setting him out upon the development of his own idea: "to stand on his own feet."[20]

Enter New Actors

Although the number and names of Japanese student groups not affiliated with the Communist party are in constant flux and difficult to keep track of, some noteworthy changes have occurred among them both in the distribution of power among factions and in new types of activism among leaders.

In *The Dictionary of Student Movements*, published in July, 1969, about forty factions of Zengakuren are listed. According to this source, at that time the Democratic Youth League controlled 339 student self-governments with a total membership of 460,000, directed by some 12,000 leaders, and thus represented a larger number of student self-governments than those under the control of all the anti-Communist party factions combined. The Marxist Student League-Nucleus Faction (Chūkaku) controlled 36 student self-governments with about 2,000 activists, and the Socialist Student League-Unity Faction (the Second Bund) controlled 41 self-governments with about 1,500 activists. These two factions and the Student Liberation Front (the Marxist-Leninist League), then the most active groups, formed themselves into the Three Faction Alliance or Sanpa. The Socialist Student Front, controlling 23 self-governments with 600 activists, and the Proletarian Student League, controlling 15 self-governments with 400 activists, also joined together to form the Structural Reformists. The Marxist Student League-Revolutionary Marxist Faction, a relatively large unit controlling 30 self-governments with 1,800 activists, remained independent of any larger alliance.[21] Judged by these numbers, the relative influences of pro-Communist party and anti-Communist radical factions seem to have been reversed from what they were from 1960 to 1962.[22]

A second, perhaps more important change among Japanese student groups since the early 1960s is the rise of new types of leaders who do not belong to any factions, either pro- or anti-Communist party. Calling themselves "nonsect radicals," they emerged out of the All Campus Struggle Congress (Zenkyōtō) initiated by the students of Nihon University and of the University of Tokyo in their protests against their respective administrations. Since then, wherever a campus protest broke out, this new type of group, Zenkyōtō, led by nonsect radicals, came to be formed. Although the Democratic Youth League has opposed it, members of anti-Communist radical factions have joined it. So a remarkable characteristic of this new group lies in the fact that it includes at the same time both nonsect radicals and students from anti-Communist party factions.

Whereas in 1960 the student movement was limited to undergraduates, now graduate students, teaching assistants, and some young members of faculties take part in Zenkyōtō organizations. Moreover, whereas previously most activists came from the faculties of letters, humanities, and social sciences, now others have come from medical schools, city engineering, and other science departments. Yamamoto Yoshitaka, the representative of Zenkyōtō at the University of Tokyo, was a graduate student in theoretical physics, while Satoru Saishu, another leader of the same group, was an assistant in biology, and both are nonsect radicals.

According to a survey conducted among 1,800 students of the University of Tokyo in February, 1969, it was found that 34 percent had supported Zenkyōtō in November, 1968, and 17 percent the Democratic Action Committee. But at the time of the survey, only three months later, 13.5 percent supported the Democratic Youth League, 19 percent an anti-Communist extremist faction, whereas 68.1 percent supported no sect at all. On the basis of these results, the survey analysts concluded that the percentages of those students who supported the Democratic Action Committee in November, 1968, and the percentages of those who supported the Democratic Youth League in January, 1969, more or less coincided, whereas many more students support Zenkyōtō than one or the other anti-Communist extremist faction. In other words, according to the analysts, many more nonsectarian students supported Zenkyōtō than the Democratic Action Committee.[23]

Although factions affiliated with the Communist party seemed to control the largest number of student self-governments all over Japan, the emergence of Zenkyōtō on various campuses under the leadership of nonsect radicals indicated that the influence of the Communist party was not as great as it looked. But there are still other factors to be considered. While Zenkyōtō organizations had been losing their leaders and members through injury, arrest, or imprisonment in each campaign they had staged, the Democratic Youth League had suffered no such casualties and thus maintains an advantageous position. Still, owing to the recent expansion of protest movements onto previously quiet campuses, Zenkyōtō membership was on the increase, a trend that may have counterbalanced its earlier losses. As a matter of fact, the report of July 31, 1969, shows that a considerable increase in activists and self-governments in the Three Faction Alliance and a significantly commensurate decrease in those in the Democratic Youth League resulted in almost a 50:50 balance of power between the two organizations.[24]

Disillusionment with Formal Democracy and Demand for Participatory Democracy

As indicated before, Japanese radical students resorted to violence as a direct consequence of the failure of their 1960 campaign, which they fought basically by nonviolent means. But their resort to violence was also a direct consequence of their disillusionment with formal democracy, a disillusionment caused in part by Japan's support of and de facto involvement in the Vietnam War and in part by the adaptation of Japan's self-defense units into full-fledged armed forces, both of which developments seemed to the students to be clear indications that constitutional stipulations can be nullified at will by the authorities of government. As a countermeasure to this situation, Japanese students had, like American students, increasingly entertained the possibility of recourse to what they call "participatory democracy." Although no commonly understood definition of the term has yet been devised, several conceivable attitudes seem to illuminate it. For example, having read that a demonstrating high school student was admonished by his teacher for wearing an antiwar badge, a relatively conservative student confessed to great shock that such a thing could happen in a nation whose constitution guaranteed freedom of speech and to a feeling of deep shame with respect to her own indifference to the Vietnam War. She concluded with this statement: "If there is a single person indifferent to what's going on in his society, that society falls short of the ideal of democracy, which in its original Greek meaning was *demos kratia*, or rule by the people."[25] For such a student participatory democracy obviously meant sensitivity to public issues and the courage to form independent judgments about them. For other students it meant active participation in university affairs, such as designing curricula, formulating extracurricular rules, managing student halls, appointing faculty members, electing presidents, and having a voice in other personnel and financial matters.[26] For still other students it meant commitment to some political action that might influence the course of historical events. One participant in the demonstration of June 15, 1968, states, for instance:

> We go to the American embassy to stop with our own hands the war that America is continuing to wage in Vietman. . . . The Diet does not reflect Japanese public opinion about the Vietnam War. With its foothold in that Diet, the government continues to support the war in Vietnam, flaunting its disregard for public opinion. It is in order to prevent with our own hands their wayward disrespect for public opinion that we go demonstrating to the Diet and to the prime minister's residence.
>
> At the time of the 1960 antisecurity treaty campaign, our slogan was "Defend parliamentary democracy". . . . But now the Diet is functioning "normally," and no snap vote was taken to support the Vietnam War. But despite these facts, the Japanese government ignores public opinion and a Japanese ambassador is allowed to state publicly that "the Japanese people support the Vietnam War."
>
> Under these circumstances, we should debunk the Diet's fake democracy and, if need be, determine by ourselves which way we should go, refusing to accept the Diet's decisions.

Here, of course, participatory democracy is equated with direct action as the expression of political will, but the statement neither condemns nor advocates the use of violence. Among those who subscribed to direct action, however, two different stands should be clearly distinguished, the one that condemned the use of violence and the one that advocated it.

The Use of Violence

In the demonstrations of 1960 the students neither wore helmets nor carried staves; even at the peak of their activity they refrained from violence. While politicians and policemen alike, the targets of the demonstrations, escaped even minor injury, events cost the life of one female student. Up until 1960, the students had used helmets and staves secretively, it is true, but only in intersect conflicts, not in open defiance of the police. In fact, not until 1967, on October 8 and November 12, near Haneda international airport, when they were trying to prevent Prime Minister Eisaku Sato's visit to South Vietnam, which they took to be a gesture of Japan's open commitment to the American side of the war, did the students use helmets and staves openly against the mechanized police forces marshalled to obstruct them.

In that confrontation a Kyoto University student died, marking the second death among students since 1960. Then later, in a demonstration staged jointly by citizens and students against the establishment of a United States Army field hospital in Oji in April, 1968, there was a third victim, this time not an activist student but an ordinary Japanese citizen. Meanwhile, since their resort to violence, casualties short of death had been rising among students. On January 18 and 19, 1969, while 8,500 mechanized policemen surrounded 729 students on the campus of the University of Tokyo, the policemen used gas shells, tear gas, and water cannons against the students, and the students used stones and Molotov cocktails against the policemen. During those two days alone, one student lost his eyesight completely, 76 persons were seriously wounded, and more than 428 injured.[27] As for the policemen, two of them have been killed since the students resorted to violence; they were hit by stones thrown by student demonstrators.

From the student point of view there are various justifications for the resort to violence, three of which are especially revealing. First, whereas in 1960 the goal of demonstrations was "defending parliamentary democracy," it significantly shifted to "de-bunking fake democracy." Because, needless to say, the effec-tiveness of a stave or a stone is considerably less than the effec-tiveness of a gas shell or tear gas those students who use staves and stones are not so much concerned with military victory over police opposition as with the political aim of publicly exposing the brute force upon which the power of the state is based. Taking for granted Max Weber's assertion that the state is the only source for the legitimate use of physical coercion, or violence,[28] student activists seem to consider that the more violence they can evoke the greater their political success will be, notwithstanding military defeat.

A second justification for the student use of violence was once most effectively expressed by a radical female student who main-tained that students used staves not only as instruments of self-defense in close combat with the mechanized police but, even more importantly, as instruments of overcoming their own fear in their first confrontations with overwhelmingly superior forces. Without staves they had been afraid and had wished to run away, but with staves they surged forward into direct contact with the opposing policemen. As though suggesting the ceremonies of ordeal by which some primitive peoples initiate their youth into adult society, she said that the use of staves helped the students to estab-lish within themselves a new and unflinching "revolutionary selfhood" (*kakumei shutai*)—perhaps the modern counterpart of an initiation ceremony, in this case for a fullfledged revolutionary.

Other justifications of the use of violence vary among the leaders of various factions. In a symposium on how to fight the 1970 campaign, the secretary general of the Nucleus Faction stated:

At present our slogan for campus struggle is "Make the universities citadels of the abolition of the security treaty and annihilation of Japanese imperial-ism." We are trying to orient the university struggle positively toward the fight for recovery of Okinawa and the abolition of the security treaty. At the same time we are attempting the escalation of campus struggles all over the country to the level of what we have attained at the University of Tokyo and Nihon University.[29]

As the same time, the secretary general of the Marxist-Leninist

Faction of the Socialist Student League advocated simultaneous uprisings at all the universities in Tokyo where campus struggles were going on, to disperse the mechanized police forces into many places rather than letting them concentrate on one campus only. The Socialist chairman of the Communist League (the organization overseeing Student League-Unity Faction) proposed to integrate the Zenkyōtō organizations now existing separately on different campuses into one unified organization so that fighting schedules may be coordinated in order eventually to achieve the simultaneous uprisings advocated by the Marxist-Leninist Faction.[30]

Although factional leaders disagreed about whether the Japan self-defense forces might have appeared on the front line against student demonstrations in 1970, they nevertheless agreed that the student use of weapons was likely to increase in the future, at least commensurately with the use of weapons by the police and/or the self-defense forces.[31] Even so, Akio Ōno, an ex-Zengakuren leader and now a free-lance writer on student movements, denied the likelihood of an increase in the student use of weapons beyond a certain crucial limit. Contrasting Zengakuren's modern fighting style with that of the Communist party in 1952, whose secret methods carried out by small guerrilla troops isolated them from the masses and escalated into the use of Japanese swords and rifles that could take many lives, Ōno maintains:

> The *Gewalt* struggle employed by the students since 1967 was planned above all else as a public campaign catering to the maximum mobilization of the masses. That was why the students then limited themselves to the use of stones and staves easily accessible . . .
>
> There has been some escalation of weapons [used by the students] from "square timbers soft and fragile". . . to iron pipes. Molotov cocktails have also entered the pictures. But for my part, I predict that as long as this basic character of the students' fight [planned as "a public struggle catering to the maximum mobilization of the masses"] is maintained, "new weapons" or "new tactics" of *Gewalt*, whatever they may be, will not depart radically from their present form.[32]

Emphasis on Change Within—from a Sense of Victimization to a Sense of Victimizing

In their year-long struggle at the University of Tokyo, Zenkyōtō most conspicuously represented the search for new selfhood that is one of the characteristic aspects of the student movement among anti-Communist radical factions. Essentially, of course, this search emphasizes the importance of change within individual members. According to a survey conducted by *Sekai* in February, 1969, the major goals of Zenkyōtō's struggle at the University of Tokyo, which was supported by 1,800 students, were as follows:

1. Democratization of the University	46.2
2. Formation of revolutionary selfhood	10.2
3. Dissolution of the present university system	27.2
4. Expulsion of the students who use violence	19.1
5. Rehabilitation of rationality	20.1
6. Rationalization of the system	17.9
7. Expression of anti-establishment sentiments	25.0
8. Quest for fundamental ideas	25.6
9. Change of oneself	31.7
10. Sensual emancipation	5.5
11. Establishment of selfhood	41.7
12. Don't care	1.0
13. None	1.5[33]

The analysts classified these items into two categories, the first according to political and institutional orientations (1 to 6) and the second according to existential orientations (7 to 11). Then they applied cross-tabulations in order to discover whether there was any correlation between a subject's motivation by specific goal and his support of a specific group. As a consequence, it was discovered that the goal 1 motivated 92.4 percent of those who supported the Democratic Action Committee (Democratic Youth League) and only 15 percent of those who supported Zenkyō-tō. By contrast, goals 9 and 11 each motivated 51 percent of those who supported the Democratic Action Committee.[34] Obviously, the result of the survey confirmed a proclivity in Zenkyōtō and its sympathizers to emphasize internal individual change in marked contrast to a proclivity in factions affiliated with the Communist party and its sympathizers to emphasize external social change.

As already noted, the search for new selfhood was much discussed in 1960 among the students of anti-Commuinst party factions, but during the year of strikes and barricades on the University of Tokyo campus, the members of Zenkyōtō began to delineate the content of new selfhood more clearly.

First, the expression "the University of Tokyo within ourselves" (*uchi naru tōdai*) circulated among the students as a kind of shibboleth, by which they meant that the target of their attack existed not only outside of themselves but also inside of themselves. In other words, if the institution and its administration were corrupt, they themselves, having done nothing to rectify the corruption, were also corrupt. Since its inception the University of Tokyo has always held the most privileged position of all universities in Japan, and its graduates have always been assured of elitist careers in the nation's government, politics, business firms, and academies, if they kept quiet and cooperated with the establishment. Even realizing that protest against the university authorities could mean nullification of their own fairly well guaranteed futures of privilege, the Zenkyōtō students at the University of Tokyo nevertheless identified themselves with the search for new selfhood, which was in itself a denial of the old selfhood that merely sought its own advantage while ignoring the fate of the underprivileged masses.

Second, the students demanded a unifying closure of the gap that so blatantly existed between the ideal and the actual in the patterns of conduct of their professors as well as of themselves. Perhaps this demand was a corollary of their dissillusionment with formal democracy, which seemed to permit a government, or a ruling party, to override in the crude expediency of the actual the fine pattern of the ideal, to say nothing of the norms of society at large. Indeed, the greater the gap the students recognized between the ideals and the actualities of their environment, the stronger their demand for the closure of that gap became. Marion Levy has pointed out that "for no society . . . do the ideal and actual structure of the members coincide exactly. In individual cases they may coincide. . . . Actually, however, there is no organization whose members live up to all of the ideal structures that as members of the organization they actually hold, let alone those they merely profess."[35] If, even so, the students were asking something impossible, they were at least also raising many questions vitally important to themselves and others. As a matter of fact, the demand for unification of the ideal and the actual was directed most vehemently toward the professors they had erroneously considered to be closest to their own ideological position, the saddest case in point being that of Professor Masao Maruyama, who had been one of the leaders they most respected during the 1960 antisecurity treaty campaign. In any case, the Struggle Congress of Social Science Graduate Students declared in October, 1968:

> The struggle now going on at the University of Tokyo has exposed the fact that [such] seemingly progressive and democratic teachers have in fact been conservative egoists. In their desperate effort to maintain the present status they have earned, they dared to concur in the unjust punishment of those students who had been risking their own existence completely in order to challenge the imperialistic system of suppression operated by the state power. We graduate students refuse to become such hypocritical scholars.[36]

Regardless of their ideological stand, hypocrisy, then, was what the students most detested. That was why, strange as it seems on the surface, they respected those professors who violently opposed them but were consistent in their expressed views and visible actions more than they respected so-called progressive professors who were not consistent in their expressed views and visible actions. Incidentally also, as the demand for the unity of the ideal and the actual attests (as though it were reverberating from the teaching of Yang Ming, who advocated the unity of theory and practice and whose teaching became one of the philosophical sources for the Way of Warriors [bushidō] during the Tokugawa fedual period), there is some resonance in Zenkyōtō of the University of Tokyo from the classical samurai tradition.

The third aspect of the search for new selfhood, and, perhaps, most important of all in its political implications, was the students' recognition that they were not so much victims of the present system as they were themselves victimizers. This recognition perhaps had its inception in the protest of medical students against Japanese medical education, for as early as 1954 they criticized the system under which young medical graduates were forced into some years of unpaid internship in their respective university hospitals before they were permitted to practice as bona fide doctors with regular salaries. Although at first they considered themselves victims of the system, eventually they decided that they had been mistaken:

> . . . the working people who came to visit us as patients at the hospital were suffering just as much as we were as victims of the present system of medicine in Japan. Then it occurred to us, medical students and young doctors alike, that we had been victimizers rather than victims by having complacently occupied a *petit bourgeois* position at the expense of the people. This recognition marked a great turning point in our movement . . . We finally arrived at self-criticism and self-denial, through which we clearly foresaw the possibility of alliance with the working poeple.[37]

This shift of attitude from a sense of victimization to a sense of victimizing came to characterize that generation of medical students who in 1967 launched another protest movement against the Doctors' Registration Law, and soon the new attitude spread to the students of other faculties, who thus came to support the strike of the medical students. The attitude permeated the privileged students of the University of Tokyo with soul-searching effect and soon spread also to less privileged students on other, less prestigious campuses. At last it came to embrace the full 19.4 percent of the Japanese population who as university students were all victimizers by very force of the fact that their positions were more privileged than those of the majority of the population to whom university doors were closed. Meanwhile, internationally, the attitude came to be extended as follows:

> We on mainland Japan could not evade our responsibility for having left the Okinawans for more than twenty years since the end of the war without the benefits of our new constitution, Labor Standards Act, and even Prostitution Prevention Law. We have passed two periods of decision concerning the status of Okinawa, viz., in 1951 and in 1960. But on both occasions, we permitted the conservative administration to stay in power half permanently, for we were unable to abolish the Japanese-American security system. Thus we ourselves became inflictors of injustices upon the Okinawans in double and even triple meanings.
>
> *   *   *   *   *
>
> What does the security treaty mean to us? Viewed from the point of view of Asians, above all it places us Japanese in the position of "victimizers." All the existing parties, from the Liberal Democratic Party to the Communist party, overlook this point of view. However, this is the only point of view through which we can organize an antisecurity treaty campaign on an international basis.[38]

As already shown, existential rather than directly political goals predominantly motivated the supporters of Zenkyōtō; in other words, internal change was more important to them than external change. In the final analysis, however, their existential orientation has illuminated both national and international problems for them in a basically humanistic way, enabling them to identify in both sympathy and solidarity with those who have suffered on account of a former failure of understanding. Viewed in this humanistic light, the problem of Okinawa is a thorn in the heart of the Japanese.

Toward Independent Collectivism: Standing on One's Own Feet

Another shibboleth in wide circulation among the students of Zenkyōtō and anti-Communist party factions is the expression *jiritsu*, which in Chinese characters, as first used by Ryūmei Yoshimoto in the title of a book he published in 1966,[39] means "standing on one's own feet," although students sometimes use its vernacular form *jibun de*, which means "of one's own accord." Whereas members of the Democratic Youth League had long used a different shibboleth, *dokuritsu*, which means "independence" primarily in a political sense, members of Zenkyōtō distinguish themselves by employing the new terminology of *jiritsu* instead of the old one of *dokuritsu*. In the same way they distinguished themselves from conventional student self-governments, membership in which is automatic and compulsory with registration in all Japanese universities. Membership in Zenkyōtō, however, was to be entirely voluntary, rather like membership in a faction, except that it includes nonsect leaders who, unlike the leaders of sects, did not embrace any specific theory of revolution. A leading member of Zenkyōtō at the University of Tokyo draws this picture of his group:

> The Struggle Congress is just a group, somewhat lesss than an organization. It exists only for the individuals who formed it. Whenever we talk about it everyone of us qualifies his view of it by saying, "according to *my* opinion," and refers to the group as "*my* Struggle Congress."
>
> *   *   *   *   *
>
> I never try to confirm whether another's view is the same as mine in order to

establish solidarity between him and me. I feel solidarity with anyone who actually struggles hard to do something. But I cannot feel solidarity with those who talk big but do nothing but sit, looking down upon "the ignorant masses."

* * * * *

All the hitherto existing student organizations have been more or less formed after the image of the Japanese *ie* [the family]. I refuse to cooperate with those who are unaware of this fact. For instance, some self-styled leftists often conform to the traditional wedding ceremony, justifying themselves by acknowledging "a more compromise." I cannot stand that sort of sticky behavior. I feel it necessary for each one of us to establish separate identities as individuals, distinct from one another's, before we can enter into a relationship of solidarity. But even then we should constantly be aware of the fact that "I am I" and "You are you" and that you and I should not be put together to form any stereotyped category. This is why I am repelled by the Democratic Youth League and the Communist party. The cause for my repulsion lies not so much in their revolutionary tactics as in their habit of disregarding separate and individual identities.[40]

This statement reveals the essential attitude of Zenkyōtō students, for they have addressed themselves to the difficult task of overcoming the shortcomings endemic to the course of modernization in Japan. The traditional pattern of behavior related to the family system and emperor system based on it is what I call "dependent-collectivism," in which individuals are submerged in the group, say, of the family, the party, or the state and depend upon the group-mind for their decision-making at the same time that their goal-orientation is collectivist.[41] Paradoxically, the Communist party, which was the staunchest opponent of the emperor system in the 1930s, could not overcome its own inherent dependent-collectivist mentality. And although the Bund tried to do so from its inception in 1958, it failed even to survive the 1960 campaign. Consequently, it seems to have become a compelling objective of the Zenkyōtō of the University of Tokyo to succeed where the Bund failed.[42] The oft-quoted handwriting discovered on the wall of the University of Tokyo's Yasuda Hall after its fall on January 19, 1969, expresses the basic attitude:

We who are in quest of solidarity shall not be afraid of temporary isolation. We who are willing to fall in pursuit of our struggle refuse to give up before having exhausted all of our energies and resources of battle.[43]

The statement elicits reconsideration of the differences between *jiritsu* and *dokuritsu*.

According to Zenkyōtō logic, to be fighting on one's own to the best of one's ability is the only necessary prerequisite to political cooperation at any level, whether among individuals or groups, whether national or international, and whether for or against capitalism, socialism, or communism. With this logic the leaders of anti-Communist radical factions agree, except for certain political reservations. For example, in order to bring about revolutionary change throughout the world, the anti-Communist factions proposed to form united fronts on a wide scale among those national groups fighting against the imperialism of their own countries.[44]

The two words *dokuritsu* and *jiritsu* should not be translated indiscriminately as "independence," although there is no exact English equivalent for *jiritsu*. As mentioned earlier, for the Democratic Youth League and the Communist party *dokuritsu* is a political concept, meaning "independence" and implying specifically the independence of the Japanese proletariat from American imperialism. For those who use the expression, *jiritsu* has, by contrast, at least three levels of meaning. First, when Yoshimoto made its application in his 1964 essay, he called it *jiritsu shugi* ("standing on one's own feet-ism") and defined it as the nationalism of the common man, claiming that common indigenous ways of thinking as distinguished from those of the elite had never been given due consideration in Japanese intellectual history and asserting that he would himself therefore be responsible for interpreting the ideas and feelings of the masses. Accordingly, in his context, *jiritsu* meant a quest for an indigenous pattern of thinking that could be universalized not only as an instrument of interpretation but also as an instrument of change. He called his application the nationalism of the common man, because it repudiated all exogenous means that would analyze and change Japanese society. Although similar to the concept of *dokuritsu* in that its reference is national rather than international, its emphasis upon common men differs considerably from the emphasis of the Communist party upon a class-conscious proletariat. By "common men" Yoshimoto meant "those who would not and could not leave the sphere of their daily lives that lies between their homes and work places, and those who live and die indifferent to whatever political rule they are placed under."[45] Second, as derived from Yoshimoto's view and its circulation among Zenkyō-tō members, *jiritsu* has taken on an existential orientation, whose individual reference is selfhood and whose group reference is humanity as a whole. Third, among the leaders of anti-Communist party factions, *jiritsu* has taken on political implication through which those national groups fighting native imperialism may eventually achieve the solidarity of an international revolutionary cause.

Public Assessment of Student Movements in 1969

In a nationwide *Asahi* newspaper public-opinion poll conducted among 3,000 respondents at the end of May, 1969, Japanese attitudes toward radical student movements showed the following distribution:

Acceptance of violent actions as inevitable in present circumstances	6%
Sympathy with student point of view but opposition to their methods	71%
Disapproval of both student point of view and their methods, to the extent of advocating repression	17%
Others	1%
No answer	5%[46]

A similar *Yomiuri* newspaper poll also conducted among 3,000 respondents at the end of June in the same year showed the following distribution:

Sympathy with student point of view	2.3%
Understanding of student point of view but opposition to their methods to the extent of advocating repression	58.6%
Condemnation of student movements as deplorable	9.3%
Advocacy of repression	16.3%
Disinterest in the issue	4.2%
Ignorance of the issue	1.3%

Others   0.8%

Don't know   7.2%[47]

In both surveys, despite their disapproval of the violence of student methods, a majority of the respondents sympathized with the point of view and the goals of the students. As for the causes of campus unrest, in a range of multiple choice possibilities, 63 percent of the *Asahi* respondents blamed the government; 52 percent the student themselves; and 48 percent, the universities, while 43.9 percent of the *Yomiuri* respondents, the largest percentage, blamed dissatisfaction with the existing Japanese social and political system. As for the opinions of the students themselves with respect to the causes of campus unrest, in a poll conducted by the *Yomiuri* in February, 1969, among 1,425 respondents in twenty-one universities all over the country, although the majority of the students expressed disapproval of violence, 43.9 percent of them blamed dissatisfaction with the existing Japanese social and political system and 35.1 percent the poverty of the government's educational policy. Compared with a similar survey the *Yomiuri* had conducted in August, 1968, the 1969 poll showed a considerable increase in student dissatisfaction with their education as well as in criticism of Japanese economic, social, and political conditions.[48]

The two obvious facts indicated by these polls is: (1) that despite widespread sympathy with the point of view and goals of the student movement, both the Japanese public and students themselves opposed student use of violence, and (2) that despite their opposition to violence, both the Japanese public and students themselves were aware of the defects in existing Japanese social and political conditions as well as in the Japanese university system. In the *Asahi* poll, 38 percent of the respondents supported the Sato government and 35.4 percent opposed it. In both cases, the percentage of those who felt dissatisfaction with social and political conditions to be the cause of campus unrest was higher than the percentage of those who opposed the Sato government. It would seem, then, that even among those respondents who expressed support for the government a considerable number sympathized with the point of view embodied in the student movement and considered the government responsible for it. Inherent in this view may be an indication that the radical students' movement at least shocked both the general Japanese public and the nonradical student masses into some awareness of the causes of campus troubles.

According to the *Yomiuri* poll taken in June, 1969, 20.5 percent of metropolitan inhabitants responding and 16.3 percent of total respondents, including rural inhabitants, expressed their willingness to join a nonviolent demonstration such as the one staged on June 15, 1969. Interpreting these results as a sign of wider dissemination of a critical spirit among the people, Suzuki Hiroo, a lecturer at Tokyo University of Education, has pointed out that 16 percent of the total number of Japanese voters amounts to about ten million men and women. Granted that not all of those who said they were willing to do so would actually join a demonstration, he nevertheless maintains that this imaginary number is overwhelmingly and ominously larger than the actual number of demonstrators in 1960.[49]

4. Implications of 1969 for the 1970s: Conjectures

The Zenkyōtō movements of 1969 have led up to the second postwar peak of the student movement since the first peak was reached during the antisecurity treaty campaign of 1960. Suppression of the movements, however, by the introduction of mechanized police forces on almost all the campuses where disturbances occurred seems to have led to their definite decline by the end of 1969. The death of a cycle of student movements tends to germinate a new cycle, which bears the mark of its predecessor. This was true with the 1960 antisecurity treaty movements, and this would also apply to the Zenkyōtō movements of 1969. What, then, are the legacies of the Zenkyōtō movements that might affect the student movements in the 1970s?

First, we can point out the fact that the anti-Communist-radical students' mobilization potential went up during June, 1970, in comparison to that of June, 1960, as well as to that of June, 1969. During the month of June, 1970, antisecurity treaty demonstrations were staged by various organizations and opposition parties. The New Left organizations, including Zenkyōtō, Hansen Seinen Iinkai and Beheiren, planned to stage the largest demonstration on June 14 to commemorate the tenth anniversary of the death of Miss Kanba, while the Socialist and Communist parties gathered their forces to accentuate their demonstartion against the security treaty on June 23, when the original ten-year term of the treaty was up, and the treaty was to be extended automatically. On June 14, Zenkyōtō, Hansen Seinen Iinkai and Beheiren, having reached an agreement not to use *Gewalt* staves while demonstrating, 72,000 persons turned out to join the demonstrations sponsored by those organizations in the city of Tokyo alone.[50] This meant an even larger turnout than their demonstration on June 15, 1969, when their movements were on the upswing. On June 23, the total of demonstrators, including those mobilized by the Socialist and Communist parties, amounted to 774,000 all over the country, and 157,000 in Tokyo alone. These numbers surpass by far the number of demonstrators during the antisecurity campaign in 1960, which totaled 505,000 for the country as a whole and 130,000 for Tokyo alone. Out of the total participants on June 23, 1970, the New Left organizations had expected some 8,000 to attend the meeting sponsored by them. Actually, however, 57,000 demonstrators, according to their own estimate, joined their meeting. Even the estimate made by the police, which amounted to 20,000 persons attending the meeting, surpassed the number originally expected by the sponsors.[51] The increase of the mere number of participants in those demonstrations confirms the previously quoted prediction in 1969 of the commentator to the effect that the joiners of the demonstrations against the security treaty in 1970 would be larger than those in 1960, if the demonstrations were conducted without the use of violence on the part of the demonstrators. It should also be noted that the New Left organizations are now more capable of mobilizing students and nonstudent citizens than they were ten years ago, if their demonstrations are conducted on the nonviolent basis.

The partial success of the June demonstrations points to a possibility that ordinary Japanese citizens and students together may form a united front to stage movements of protest on a nationwide basis without recourse to violence, on the model of the demonstration of June 14, 1970. If this is continually the case, then public protest against the security treaty, the Vietnam War, the continued militarization of Okinawa, discrimination against alien residents in Japan, especially the Koreans and Chinese, possible enforcement of a conscription system may be effectively organized in the foreseeable future.

There are some counter-developments, however, among student movements that make the prediction of the formation of such a united front too optimistic. Just as in the period that immediately followed the antisecurity treaty campaign in 1960, now is the time for severe schisms between the pro-Communist-party sect and anti-Communist-party sects, and among the anti-Communist-party sects themselves. Violence is now used not against the police forces, but free-handedly in intersect struggles, causing injury and death among sect leaders, and involving suicide among nonsect students. If the intersect violence persists, the student movement groups may be either isolated from other citizens' protest organizations, making the former ineffective, or the citizens' organizations might be contaminated with the schisms among the student groups and as a result also become incapacitated. Whether or not the New Left student movements become effective as an agent of political protest in the 1970s seems to hinge upon their capacity to get themselves successfully allied with a wide range of independent citizens' protest movements.

Second, whatever the political fate of the Zenkyōtō movements might be, the basic propositions they raised will remain a legacy in the ways of thinking among the participators in the movements and upon succeeding generations of students. These propositions are, as we have discussed, the recognition of oneself as the victimizer rather than the victim of the present system; the determination that what one says and what one does should coincide; and the idea that one should become the locus of one's own judgement and at the same time should work toward a collectivistic goal. With these ethical propositions, the students try to point out the basic shortcomings of the present-day university system in Japan, and of the way in which science and technology are organized and pursued. They also attempt to apply those propositions in their approach to national issues, such as environmental disruption, and to international issues, such as discrimination against the Korean and Chinese residents in Japan, as revealed currently in the proposed legislation to strengthen government control over aliens entering or residing in Japan.

Political activism is a vital but not the only vital aspect of student movements. The effects of the ways of thinking that emerge out of the movements are just as significant as the indicators of their influence. Political activism of the student movements might temporarily take the extreme form of violence, which might annihilate their purposes. Nevertheless, the new ways of thinking that they have evolved may have more lasting effects on the students themselves and perhaps on adults also.[52]

1. The number and the percentages of the university and college students were checked with the Ministry of Education on May 28, 1969.
2. *Yomiuri Shimbun*, August 2, 1969.
3. Tsurumi, Kazuko, *Social Change and the Individual: Japan before and after Defeat in World War II*, (Princeton, N.J.: Princeton University Press, 1970), p. 335.
4. *Ibid.*, pp. 324–325.
5. Nagai, Michio, "University Problems in Japan," *Bulletin*, The International House of Japan, No. 23, April, 1969, p. 10.
6. *Yomiuri Shimbun*, February 24, July 30, 1969.
7. The Student Autonomy of the Medical School of the University of Tokyo went on strike in January, 1968, for an indefinite period, protesting against the revised Medical Doctors' Law and demanding collective bargaining to conclude an agreement on the conditions of internship with the Medical School. Later the strike spread to the rest of the faculties of the university. The University of Tokyo struggle was directed primarily against the outmoded structure of the relationship between professors and their disciples and among professors themselves. For a historical account of the University of Tokyo struggle, see *Tokyo Daigaku Shimbun Kenkyūjo* (The Institute of Research on Journalism, University of Tokyo), (ed.), *Tōdai Funsō no Kiroku* (Record of Struggle at the University of Tokyo), Nihon Hyoronsha, Tokyo, 1969.

In May, 1968, about ten thousand students of Nihon University demonstrated in front of the university administration building to protest against shady dealings in university money, amounting to 3.4 billion yen, for whose expenditure the board of directors, headed by Jujiro Furuta could not publicly account. Nihon University is a mammoth private university of one hundred thousand students. It was considered to be an extra conservative university with generally apathetic and submissive students. So it came as a shock when student protest started on that campus and was primarily directed against corruption and the shady handling of university money on the part of the university authorities. For an account of the history of the struggle at Nihon University, see *Nihon Daigaku Bunrigakubu Tōsōiinkai Shokikyoku* (The Secretariat of the Struggle Committee, Literature and Science Faculty of Nihon University), (ed.), *Hangyaku no Barikeido* (The Barricade of Revolt), Tokyo Sanichi Shobo, 1969.
8. For the history of the Bund, see Tsurumi, *op. cit.*, pp. 329, 342.
9. Kitakōji Satoshi, *et al.*, "Gakusei Undō no Genjō to Tenbō" (The Present Situation

and the Future Prospect of Student Movements) (A Symposium), *Shisō no Kagaku* (The Science of Thought), No. 62, May, 1967, p. 22.

10. Lifton, Robert Jay, "Youth and History: Individual Change in Postwar Japan," Erikson, Erik H., (ed.), *The Challenge of Youth* (Garden City, New York: Doubleday & Co., 1963), p. 274.

11. Takeuchi's essay, "Minshu ka Dokusai ka" (Either Democracy or Despotism) was published in *Tosho Shimbun* on May 31, 1960. He also delivered a speech to similar effect on June 2, 1960, at a public rally held at Bunkyō Town Hall in Tokyo. Subsequently he resigned from Tokyo Metropolitan University as a protest against the Kishi government.

12. Hidaka, Rokurō (ed.), *Issen Kyūhyaku Rokujūnen Gogatsu Jūkunichi* (May 19, 1960), (Tokyo: Iwanami Shoten), pp. 93–94.

13. The author's interview with Shima on July 29, 1962.

14. For the distinction between hedonistic versus ascetic revolutionaries, see Feuer, Lewis S., *The Scientific Intellectual* (New York: Basic Books, 1963), p. 8.

15. For further explanation of eclectic Marxism, see Tsurumi, *op. cit.*, pp. 346–350.

16. This four-page leaflet was signed by Hiroshi Tonami of the Jimukyoku Faction of the Socialist Student League.

17. Tsurumi, *op. cit.*, pp. 37–40.

18. For a detailed account of what actually happened on that day, see the Section, "Rokugatsu Jūgonichi kara Jūkunichi Gozen Reiji made" (From June 15 to 12:00 A.M. of June 19), *Anpo: 1960*, Usui, Yoshimi (ed.) (Tokyo: Chikuma Shobo, 1969), pp. 183–231.

19. Yoshimoto, Ryūmei, *Jiritsu no Shisōteki Kyoten* (Intellectual Basis for Standing on One's Own Feet), (Tokyo: Tokuma Shoten, 1966), p. 195.

20. We shall later discuss what is meant by "standing on one's own feet."

21. For a detailed account of the different factions that existed in July, 1969, see *Shakai Mondai Kenkyūkai* (The Social Problems Study Group), (ed.), *Zengakuren Kakuha —Gakusei Undō Jiten* (The Factions of Zengakuren—Dictionary of the Student Movement), (Tokyo: Futabasha, 1969).

22. The following list shows the relative strength of the factions in September, 1962. The numbers stand for seats occupied by the representatives of each faction at Zengakuren Plenary Meetings in 1961 and in 1962.

		1961	1962
	Marxist Students League	145	183
Anti-Communist-	Socialist Students League	90	98
Party Sects:	Social Youth League	19	40
	Revolutionary Communist League-Kansai Faction	13	26
Pro-Communist-Party Sect:	Democratic Youth League	110	113

Junpō Gakusei Seinen Undō (Tri-Monthly Review of Student and Youth Movements), Tokyo: Nihon Kyōiku Kyōkai, No. 107, September 1, 1962, p. 19.

23. The Editorial Board, "Tōdai Tōsō to Gakusei no Ishiki" (The University of Tokyo Struggle and the Consciousness of the Students), *Sekai* (the *World*), Vol. 286, September, 1969, pp. 63–71.

24. "Zenkoku Kageki Daigaku Shin Chizu" (The New Map of Japan's Radical Universities), *Shūkan Gendai* (Weekly Contemporary), August 21, 1969, pp. 122–127.

25. Tsurumi, Kazuko, "Kyōiku niokeru Sanka Minshushugi" (Participatory Democracy in Education) *Tenbō*. No. 117, September, 1968, pp. 14–15.

26. The range and the extent of student participation in university affairs at present differs according to universities. But students of many universities sometimes organize their own lecture series and seminars called "autonomous lectures" and "autonomous seminars," selecting and hiring instructors *on their own*.

Often assistants and graduate students are asked to be instructors, as in the case at the University of Tokyo. These autonomous seminars and lectures were initiated by the Zenkyōtō students of various campuses while they confined themselves within barricaded university buildings. This new style of group studies has now spread even to those campuses where no barricades exist or strikes are going on. The situation is comparable to what American students call "parallel development."

27. A medical report of the casualties caused and a chemical analysis of the gas used by the police during those days, together with parliamentary proceedings concerning the kinds of the gas used, were published in *Kokuhatsu* (Indictment) No. 1, edited and published by a group called Eye Stare, Tokyo, June, 1969.
28. Weber, Max, *The Theory of Social and Economic Organization*, translated by Henderson, A. H. and Parsons, Talcott, (Glencoe, Ill.: the Free Press of Glencoe, p. 156).
29. Iida, Momo, *et al.*, *Tōron: Shichijūnen o Dōsuru* (A Symposium: How Do We Fight in 1970), (Tokyo: Denen Shobo, 1969), p. 167.
30. *Ibid.*, p. 169; p. 173.
31. *Ibid.*, pp. 284–8.
32. Ōno, Akio, *Shiichjūnen wa Dōnaru* (What Will Become of 1970), (Tokyo: Kodansha, 1969), pp. 207–09.
33. The *Sekai, ibid.*, p. 64.
34. *Ibid.*, p. 68; p. 71.
35. Levy, Marion J., Jr., *Modernization and the Structure of Societies* (Princeton: Princeton University Press, 1966), p. 27.
36. *Toride no Ueni Warera no Sekai o, ibid.*, p. 214.
37. For the history of the Bunds, see Tsurumi, *op. cit.*, pp. 329–42.
38. Ōno, *Shichijūnen wa Dōnaru, op. cit.*, pp. 162–163.
39. Yoshimoto, *op. cit.*
40. *Tōdai Zengaku Joshu Kyōtō Kaigi* (The All Campus Struggle Congress of the Assistants of the University of Tokyo) (ed.), *Todai Zenkyōtō* (The All Campus Struggle Congress of the University of Tokyo), (Tokyo: Sanichi Shobo), pp. 215–223.
41. Collectivistic goal orientation is synonymous with Levy's pattern variable "responsible," by which he means that "the emphasis is placed on one (or more) of the members of the relationship safeguarding the relevant goals of the others if he is (or they are) to achieve his (or their) own goals at all." "Responsible" goal orientation is contrasted, by Levy, to "individualistic" goal orientation. Levy, *op. cit.*, pp. 147–9. In Levy's scheme, the locus of decision-making is also included in these paired pattern variables. However, in my scheme I separate two aspects: first, the locus of decision-making, which can be classified by the variables, dependent-independent, and second, the goal orientation, which can be analyzed in terms of individualistic-collectivistic. For further discussions see, Tsurumi, *op. cit.*, pp. 18–19.
42. *Tōdai Zenkyōtō, op. cit.*, p. 221.
43. *Toride no Ueni Warera no Sekai o, op. cit.*, p. 7.
44. *Tōron: Shichijūnen o Dōsuru, op. cit.*, pp. 134–5.
45. *Yoshimoto, op. cit.*, p. 198.
46. *Asahi Shimbun*, June 15, 1969.
47. *Ibid.*, August 7, 1969.
48. *Ibid.*, February 24, 1969.
49. *Ibid.*, August 7, 1969.
50. *Asahi Shimbun*, June 15, 1970.
51. *Ibid.*, June 24, 1970.
52. This paper, written in June, 1970, is a comparison of the student movements at their two postwar peaks, the *Zengakuren* of 1960 and the *Zenkyōtō* of 1969. Although the direction and styles of the movements have changed since then, most of the basic problems they addressed themselves to in those periods still persist.
For a more recent publication in English on the Japanese student movements, I recommend *Japanese Radicals Revisited* by Ellis S. Krauss (University of California

Press, 1974). This is the only empirical and analytical work, as far as I know of, that deals with the change and continuity of political attitudes of the student activists at least for the first ten years after they have left universities. This book throws light on the significance of the student movements of the 1960's, which I have discussed in my paper, in the wider perspectives of the changing Japanese society.

Kimitada Miwa

In the Shadow of Leaves and Mishima's Death[1]

1. Mishima's Suicide and Its Repercussions

A few minutes after noon on November 25, 1970, Yukio Mishima committed harakiri in the office of the commander in chief of the Ground Self-Defense Force Eastern Corps at Ichigaya, Tokyo.[2] Judging from the appeal he prepared in advance as commander of his private army, called the Shield Society,[3] and the speech he made from the balcony in front of Self-Defense Force personnel, the purpose of Mishima and the four comrades who accompanied him was to arouse the Self-Defense Force men into action so that a revision might be effected in the provisions of the Constitution, which had been "degrading them," and also so that they might be restored to the position of glorious duty to defend the fatherland as the army of the emperor.[4] Mishima planned this action as a samurai and put it into practice with the determination to administer justice to himself as a samurai when his mission failed. Mishima's death was understood to have observed the ancient formalities of Bushido prescribed for harakiri, but actually it was made complete when Masakatsu Morita, 25, a member of the Shield Society, assisted him by ritualistically beheading him.[5] Morita himself then performed harakiri and died when another member upon his request beheaded him. Mishima was forty-five years old. His literature had just reached a peak of maturity, as evidenced in the last portion of the manuscript for *The Sea of Fertility,* which had been handed to a man from his

229

publisher that very morning.[6] His physique as a result of constant vigorous exercises, did not show any sign of decay but in fact still preserved the form of an ideal youth, into which he had once wanted to remould himself.[7]

As a consequence the public was puzzled as to the true meaning of his death, so much so that they were liable to make a mistake by taking the political objective as his true motivation. Only those who had perchance observed Mishima's creative motivation while reading his literary works could realize that the significance of his death was a more private one. If a man is an activist, rightist or leftist, he can hardly reach the depths of literature by emotionally involving himself in it. It was only natural, therefore, that people should have been profoundly moved or shocked by looking only at the political implication of Mishima's death.

Equally it was not surprising to find misunderstanding as to the implications of Mishima's death as discussed in foreign journalism. In fact, as we look in foreign newspapers, we discover that those that are better acquainted with conditions in contemporary Japan, including Mishima's literature, seemed to give less political significance to this event, and in contrast, those who knew practically nothing about Mishima seemed to draw a hasty, pseudo-historiographical conclusion that "militarism" was to be now reborn in Japan.[8]

Nevertheless, there is no denying that Mishima performed the task of popularizing Bushido when it was regarded by journalists not only in Japan but also abroad as something dreadful and despicable. He popularized it to the same extent that Akira Kurosawa and Toshiro Mifune have popularized the samurai as an admirable type of man. For some time to come, people in foreign lands may not be able to think of the meaning of Bushido without relating it to Mishima's death. Thus it seems that the Bushido which used to be considered the basic moral precepts of ancient Japan has now amplified its attributes by incorporating the life and death of Mishima, and that the name of Mishima may be remembered always as the restorer of Bushido to its old significance.

2. Inazo Nitobe, *Bushido,* and *In the Shadow of Leaves:* Background Materials for an Understanding of Mishima

When we discuss Bushido in this manner, we naturally think of Dr. Inazo Nitobe. It is not simply because Nitobe was the first man to introduce Bushido to the Western world by writing a book in English. His book was simultaneously translated into Japanese and published in Japan. It found a broad reading public. During the Pacific War, it was read along with Tsunetomo Yamamoto's book on Bushido, *In the Shadow of Leaves,* which had been in existence since 1716, by university students who were bound for the front, obviously not without considerable influence.[9]

Nitobe's English original of *Bushido: The Soul of Japan* was published in 1899, but for it to find a wide reading public it had to wait till after the Russo-Japanese War (1904—1905). This book was to help solve the riddle of how a small insular nation of the Orient could defeat the great continental empire of the Occident. It is an interesting historical fact that chauvinistically inclined Theodore Roosevelt as President of the United States was greatly impressed by this book. It was also noteworthy that a cultural anthropological study of the Japanese prepared during the war by Ruth Benedict, *The Chrysanthemum and the Sword,* drew heavily upon Nitobe's *Bushido* for its theme. It is even argued that, had Nitobe's book not been read by President Harry S. Truman, the United States would have chosen to conclude the war by merely using conventional weapons. It is pointed out that a passage in *Memoirs* by Harry S. Truman can be construed to mean that the decision to use the atomic bomb against Japan was taken as the only effective way to fight Japanese soldiers who take death so easily, as manifested in harakiri.[10]

Upon hearing the news that Mishima's death had taken place in the form of harakiri, which met all the ancient prescriptions of Bushido, foreign journalists promptly concluded there was a revival of militarism in Japan. We might well ask them what they would propose as a measure against this so-called militarism. Would they come up with as rash a proposal as Truman's atom bombs?

I take the stand that Yukio Mishima's death was first and fore-most of very private significance. That is so, no matter how politi-cal his death may be made to appear by the appeal he did indeed present to the personnel in the Self-Defense Force and the cir-cumstances of his death. I believe that it was more deeply related to his eroticism.[11]

Mishima's life as a man may be divided broadly into two parts. It is divided by the decision Mishima made about life when he published his first successful novel, *Confessions of a Mask* (1949), which skyrocketed him to fame. Up to this point, the overly self-conscious little boy who was Mishima was trying to overcome various things that frightened him by moulding his physical de-licacy into a prematurely poetic spirit. On account of his delicate constitution he felt a strong longing for a nearly barbaric mascu-line presence, which seemed to have been conquered by the train-ing of his spirit. Yet when he had to recognize that it was related to his powerful carnal desire, Mishima was made to realize that physical defect could not be overcome merely by the spirit. From this sense of defeat that Mishima felt about his literary stoicism, he anticipated that the logic of physique, not the abstract logic of poetry, would turn him into a complete man. It materialized into the work entitled *Confessions of a Mask*.[12]

Mishima, who had already spoken through a mask, must have been surprised at what a world of freedom opened itself up before him. He commenced to extend his life into those corners that had been closed against him until only yesterday. He cultivated parts of the wilderness of his life that before he had consciously avoided clearing in order not to disturb his endeavor to make his poetic spirit more delicate and refined. He began to take up those attributes of masculinity that had frightened him as a physical weakling, with the ferocious determination of a stoic. And because it was muscles that enamored him above all, it was only natural that his first efforts should be directed toward the acquisition of a masculine appearance. The will power that had once sharpened his literary skill soon began to produce effects when it was directed toward cultivating his physique. It is not unlikely that the achievement of his stoicism, which was visual and could be touched with hands, appealed to Mishima as something more certain than his literary success and prompted him to higher levels of stoicism. Any professional physical culturist would have admired Mishima's stoic determination, and with it Mishima succeeded in a short period of time in acquiring a physique that he could proudly present to the public.

The moment Mishima believed he had conquered all that had frightened him as a child, the masculine appearance he had acquired for himself through his stoicism now began not only to control his muscles but even to demand a certain manliness in his behavior. This moment must have coincided with the time when he himself began to have some doubts about the mode of life that he had believed would be justified by the Hellenistic ideal body he had come to possess. Mishima apparently had failed to construct a system of morality that the Hellenistic physique would admit, a system that would accept and support his life in totality. Inasmuch as it was to support his particular life in totality, it was required that this system of morality have universal applicability. Although Hellenism might have meant something in literature, it could not go very far in justifying real life. It was at this juncture that Mishima picked up the Bushido of *In the Shadow of Leaves* out of the indigenous cultural heritage of Japan in order to relate his particular life to the reality of Japan.

Mishima's first encounter with the book was toward the end of the war when nobody knew for sure if he would be alive the next day. Nocturnal air raids over Tokyo had become nearly incessant, and Mishima, standing at the entry to the underground shelter, would glimpse remote parts of the metropolis aflame from incendiary bombs. He would think of the glory of dying for his country and for his emperor. When at last a red postcard to call him into service was delivered to him, he composed his will. In it he thanked his parents for their loving care and regretted that he had not yet reciprocated with his filial piety. He, who was about to go off to the front to die a brave death as a solider of the emperor, encouraged his younger brother to emulate him. In all it was a model will. It was a vivid expression of the ethic that a samurai should handle his life as lightly as a feather. Is this the evidence of how Mishima read *In the Shadow of Leaves*?

Indeed *In the Shadow of Leaves* gives its theme in a single forceful sentence: "Bushido is a way of dying." And then it goes on to explain:

> It is to choose death, when one is to choose between life and death. There is no more meaning to it than that. Go ahead with determination. That is all.

It also states in no ambiguous terms:

> A man of true valour is the one who leaves his place without a word to meet his death. It is not necessary to kill the opponent. The truly valiant is the one who is slain to death without uttering a word.

If this was all that was required to prove that he was a man, Mishima could do it in his total self-denial for the sake of the emperor. But Mishima's body then was such a far cry from the conceptual incarnation of heroic prowess that, when he reported to serve in the Imperial Army, he was mistakenly diagnosed as suffering from pleurisy and was ordered to return home immediately.

The war came to an end, without a battle being fought on any of Japan's main islands. The time had passed forever for him to become a true man by merely getting killed in total self-denial. In addition, the emperor, who had been believed to make such a death a death of valour, now declared that he was not a god, and that the people instead of dying in glory were now to live for the cause of peace. Deprived for the moment of the meaning of dying for the emperor, Mishima became something similar to the mediaeval boy Henry in his short story *The Seas in the Evening Glow* (1955), who in response to the command given by a visionary Christ organized a regiment of crusaders and believed that the seas would part before his own eyes and allow him to pass into the Holy Land. Was it not that Mishima wanted to reflect in Henry's recollections his own belief that his self-denying devotion to the emperor toward the end of the war would save the fatherland?

He looked at the sunset, and its reflection on the seas. He could not help recollecting that mysterious experience he had in the early part of his life. That strong craving for something miraculous, something unknown. . . . And the thing that comes back to his mind last is the memory of the seas, of quiet waves coming to the shore glittering in the settling sun, when he prayed at the pier of Marseilles surrounded by many children.

Perhaps, if the seas were to part, it could have happened only at that moment. And yet even at that very moment, the seas were mysteriously quiet and wide before his eyes, shining like a fire in the evening glow. . .

Mishima, who recollected his wartime determination to die and the miracle that was to accompany it in this manner, for the first time since the end of the war made public his own understanding of *In the Shadow of Leaves* in his essay "The Vacation of a Novelist" in the same year (1955) as *The Seas in the Evening Glow*.

This is not a book of cynical paradoxes, but an incomparably mysterious book of morals, which beget paradoxes of themselves from wisdom and determination or action. It is a humanistic book full of spirit and full of cheerfulness.

It was in this year, 1955, that Mishima started taking lessons in body building. It could not have been a mere coincidence that *The Seas in the Evening Glow*, his rediscovery of *In the Shadow of Leaves*, and esthetical excercises for masculinity all took place in the same year. It must have been a consequence of his cheerful return to the country, having cured his self-hatred through his trip to Greece. A need for reading fresh interpretations into *In the Shadow of Leaves* had arisen.

Seven years later in 1967, Mishima further clarified his interpretation of the book in his short commentary, "In the Shadow of Leaves and I":

The sentence "Bushido is a way of dying" is in itself a paradox that symbolizes this book in totality. This is where I found the greatest reason for drawing power for living from this book.

and also that:

. . . [the book I was looking for] was something that would become the core of my morality, and at the same time would accept my particular youth as it was acknowledging it. It was to be something that would hold with both hands my loneliness and my anticontemporary stand. Furthermore, it had to be a forbidden book of the age. "In the Shadow of Leaves" met all these requirements.

The book, which Mishima called a book of paradoxes and found meeting all of his personal requirements, was about to be read as a book of thought held by people living a leisurely life in time of great peace. This book, which recommends camaraderie between men by saying that "the supreme love is a hidden love, an emotion kept secret from its object," was indeed to support Mishima's particular life in its entirety.

In addition, it contains a passage that comes very close to Mishima's existentialist nihilism:

> A man's life is very short. He should live as he pleases. It is a folly to live a life of suffering by doing nothing but what he does not like. But this fact becomes harmful, if misconstrued. So this should be handled as a secret which should never be let known to young men.[13]

Thus the book adopted by Mishima as the core of his morality, coupled with his adoption of the Wang Yang-ming philosophy of activism that commands that action correspond to speech, began to remodel Mishima into a hedonistic man of self-denial and nihilistic utopianism.[14]

Upon consideration, was it possible that his "toy" soliders were only taught to serve their nation through their self-denial and comradeship but were never allowed to know the secret that would lead them to hedonistic impulsiveness?

Now what was to happen to Mishima, who had turned the book's major theme, "Bushido is a way of dying," into the source from which he was to draw a reason for living? Earlier in his literary career (1950), Mishima had written an interesting passage in his essay on Oscar Wilde:

> A paradox may serve as a momentary excuse, but it can never become a true one. By chasing himself into a corner, a man in the end deprives himself of all of his rights to excuses. It is for this reason that a man of paradoxes comes closest to God, nearly touching Him. God is the last excuse of a man, and possibly, paradoxes are a short cut to God.

We are surprised to realize how realistically these words corresponded to the last moment of Mishima's life. Mishima, who believed that he had been living a life of paradoxes, as interpreted from the Bushido of *In the Shadow of Leaves*, had actually chased himself into a position the only way out of which was for him to die a warrior's death, this through his depriving himself of all excuses for his hedonistic life.

And the last excuse he chose was a god whom he called the emperor. The greatest paradox of all is the fact that the moment he committed harakiri after exclaiming three *banzai* for the emperor, he returned to the starting point of *In the Shadow of Leaves*: "Bushido is a way of dying." It somehow reminds us of the dazzling sight of the picture of Dorian Gray when it snapped back to its original splendor of youthful manhood the moment it was stabbed with a knife by Gray himself.[15]

3. The Spirit of Perfect Death

In 1899 when Nitobe wrote *Bushido,* he bade a determined farewell to those elements in Bushido that were found antimodern and anti-Christian while Japan had to modernize itself to get along with Western powers as their partner. He controlled his nostalgia, expressing it only in subdued lyricism. He concluded his book as follows:

> Bushido as an independent code of ethics may vanish, but its power will not perish from the earth; its schools of martial prowess or civic honour may be demolished, but its light and its glory will long survive their ruins. Like its symbolic flower, after it is blown to the four winds, it will still bless mankind with the perfume with which it will enrich life. Ages after, when its custom will have been buried and its very name forgotten, its fragrance will come floating in the air as from a far-off, unseen hill, "wayside gaze beyond"; —then in the beautiful language of the Quaker poet, "The traveller owns the grateful sense of sweetness near, he knows not whence, and, pausing, takes with forehead bare the benediction of the air."[16]

We wish we were in the position to conclude this short study in the same manner as Nitobe did. But it seems that Mishima's death has awakened from its slumber the system of ethics that once belonged to an age considered long past. Not its fragrance but its bloody sight has shaken people. In this conjunction, however, we do not intend to discuss whether Nitobe's views of Bushido were a beautified illusion or not. All that we want to do is to conclude this study by referring to the response of a younger generation of this country.

The young man K had once been a radical student activist. He had perhaps been at the auditorium of the University of Tokyo in January, 1969, when he and his comrades fought a losing battle with riot police. In the end they surrendered, beaten by water and tear gas. Nobody had jumped off the tower to die a heroic death of protest. Mishima for one had been disillusioned about the lack of heroism in the samurai tradition. The young man K must have been present at the public debate between the University of Tokyo student activists and Yukio Mishima, which was held shortly after the fall of their revolutionary bastion, where, it was known later, Mishima presented himself with the determination of killing himself as a samurai with a sword should he have been humiliated.[17]

Upon hearing the first newscast that Mishima had committed harakiri, the young man K wished that "Mishima's life should be saved. . . . . It is unfortunate if he dies splendidly. Instead, he should fail miserably in his attempt at suicide just as General Hideki Tojo did."[18]

The Mishima who in fact succeeded in dying a perfect death seemed to him to have dealt a moral blow to him as a revolutionary activist with a message: "Hey, you, you can't die like me?" Mishima's death, which was in fact the ultimate expression of the Wang Yang-ming philosophy that action should follow speech, produced such a response in the young man K, who, as a revolutionary activist himself, had been feeling the need of reactivating the philosophy. On top of that, the death performed in the ritualistic form of harakiri, which has long been considered as the most manly form of action in the indigenous culture of Japan, seems to pose a question: "How manly are you?" It is true that Mishima and radical student activists were not the same but were divided into two opposing groups, Emperorist Rightists ("emperorism is my own coinage for *sonso*, literally "respect the emperor," since "imperialism" has a different connotation) and Anti-Establishment Leftists, but when he questioned their manliness in activism in this manner, the self-identify of the latter group as revolutionaries was bitterly shaken.

The spirit of Mishima looms over all the people, rightist and leftist alike: he will remain a hero of activism even with his enormously oppressive demoniac majesty.

1. This paper was read at the International House of Japan on February 18, 1971, for the monthly Diplomats Luncheon presented by the American Friends Service Committee.

2. The building, with its modified Gothic clock tower, stands in a spacious compound and once housed young cadets of the Imperial Military Academy. Such notable— or notorious—military leaders as General Tomoyuki Yamashita, the conqueror of Singapore, Colonel Kanji Ishihara, the mastermind of the Manchurian Incident, and General Hideki Tojo, premier of Japan's war cabinet of 1941–44, were all graduates. After Japan's defeat, this same building was turned into the site of the International Military Tribunal Far East. Many army leaders, along with others, were tried here and sentenced to death by hanging. Another graduate of the Military Academy, General Korechika Anami, then war minister, committed harakiri as a token of his apology to the emperor when the decision was taken on August 14, 1945, to accept the Allied surrender terms.

3. The Shield Society (*tate no kai*), which took its name from the proverbial ancient phrase *shiko no mitate,* meaning literally "an ugly and unworthy but strong shield for the emperor," was organized by Mishima in March, 1968, with some twenty student volunteers, and the ultimate number was to reach one hundred very rapidly. Previously, Mishima had plans of organizing militia corps for the defense of his country, in the belief that the last resistance against invading forces (or insurrections) would be successfully carried out by local people armed with conventional weapons. He had based these plans upon an extended study of conditions of militia in various foreign lands, from Britain to China. After his death, the monthly journal *Gendai* (Contemporary Age) published in its February, 1971, issue a mimeographed circular prepared by Mishima and entitled "Why Do We Need a Fatherland Defense Corps?" This document was dated January 1, 1968. The circular was apparently distributed among top leaders in Japanese politics, business and journalism but did not produce any of the desired results. Thereupon, so it seems now, Mishima gave up the plans, at least for the moment, and established a more playlike soldiery with student volunteers who were selected by Mishima himself in the beginning and later by his lieutenant, Masakatsu Morita, and clothed in a toy soldierlike uniform designed by the designer of General de Gaulle's uniforms, according to Mishima's specifications, with long side vents with red piping for a martial effect.

4. The written appeal, which had been prepared beforehand, read in part as follows: Four years ago I entered the Self-Defense Force with a determination of my own, and in the following year, I organized the Shield Society. The basic idea of the society lay nowhere but in the determination to sacrifice one's own life for the sake of re-making the Self-Defense Force into a national army, an honorable national army when it should awake at last. If it is true that a constitutional revision is difficult under the parliamentarian system as it exists today, the best chance was to arrive when it was to be called in for the preservation of peace and order. Then we were to contribute our lives, acting as the vanguard of the Self-Defense Force mobilized for the purpose of preservation of peace and order, and were to become the cornerstone for the rebuilding of a national army. It is the army that is to defend the national

polity, while it is the police that defends the political regime. The first time the police reach the stage where they can no longer defend the political regime all by themselves, the army will be mobilized, thereby clarifying what the national polity is, and the army will regain the true significance of its having been brought into existence at all. The true significance of the very creation of the Japanese army lies nowhere but in the idea of "defending Japanese history, culture, and traditions with the emperor at the center" of them all. For the mission of correcting the twisted principle of the nation, we, few as we were, had been receiving training and were ready to undertake the difficult task.

5. The autopsy showed that Mishima's harakiri performed with a short sword consisted of a cut two inches deep and over six inches long, some two inches below the naval. Intestines were protruding from the gash. As a result of the beheading, there were three cuts around the neck and another on the right shoulder. Morita's harakiri was a cut five inches across the belly but so shallow that it scarcely bled. At the time of harakiri, Mishima had taken off his uniform jacket. Underneath, he wore nothing. He and Morita each wore a loincloth of fresh white cotton (*Asahi Shimbun*, November 26, 1970).

Mishima's death, as a public affair, is understood to have taken place in the form of *kanshi* (death of admonition) for the purpose of arousing the Japanese conscience from its beguiling slumber in economic prosperity and its accompanying moral degradation. It is said that in Japanese history this type of death had rarely taken place. One source cites a few examples. Among them are Masashige Kusunoki (ca. 1294–1336), a royalist hero of Japan's warring period; Shōin Yoshida (1830–59), an anti-Bakufu ideologue in the dawning years of modern Japan, whom Mishima admired so much as to identify himself with him; and Takamori Saigō (1827–77), a major politico-military leader of the Meiji Restoration and exponent of the "Conquer Korea" argument, who later led the Satsuma Rebellion against the Meiji government. (Chōgorō Kaionji, "Shisō de sekai wa ugokanai" (The World Does Not Move with Ideology), *Shokun* (Tokyo: Bungei Shunjū Sha, February, 1971, pp. 18–20.)

For Yoshida, the ideologue of anti-Bakufu emperorism, Mishima had a special place in his heart. Publicly he admired him, referring to him always eulogistically. His apparent insistence upon the date of November 25 for action seems to be another proof of his devotion to Yoshida, for this was the day (converted from the lunar calendar) one hundred and eleven years before when he died by harakiri. This insistence, by the way, was the single most convincing evidence that Mishima did not actually mean to lead a coup d'état, or it was at least secondary to his purpose, for even though he had come to know that the regimental commander who might have acted in accordance with Mishima's appeal would be away, Mishima carried out the plan on the date decided.

Whether this day was of special significance to Mishima because of Shōin Yoshida has not been verified as yet by Mishima's own words or anything of similar authority. But the fact remains that this was the day in 1948 he set for starting to write *Confessions of a Mask*, his first full-length novel, which established his name in the Japanese literary world. It was also on that date in 1970 that he wrote the last line in his manuscript of the last volume of *The Sea of Fertility*, which had, more or less in final form, actually been completed during the summer of that year.

I do not believe that Yoshida's life had become so important a concern of Mishima's as early as 1948. I would rather think that it was related to something more personal in his life or memory, like his love for the model in the story *Confessions of a Mask*, or more specifically someone like Zemmei Hasuda, who lavished complimentary remarks upon Mishima's prodigious talent when one of his earlier short stories (*Hanazakari no mori*) was printed in Hasuda's literary journal. Mishima then was only sixteen. And four years later, Hasuda as an army officer shot his regimental commander to death with his revolver and then shot and killed himself. His patriotic sense could not stand the "disloyal" remarks his superior had made about the emperor immediately after the radio broadcast of His Majesty's surrender rescript of August 15, 1945. In November (exact date not given) of the next year, Hasuda's literary friends got together to hold a memorial service for the repose of his soul. Mishima expressed his sorrow and regrets over Hasuda's death in verse:

You, who loved the cloud of ancient times,
disappeared into it, while incarnating them.
But I am left behind in this modern age,
vainly longing for clouds vigorous and growing.
Yet my body looks like being about to be buried
under the vast expanse of dusty soil.

(For this verse and other information referred to above, see Nejiro Odaka, "Hasuda Zemmei to sono shi (Hasuda and His Death)," *Shokun*, March, 1971, pp. 61–64.)

Visually, Saigō's death comes closest to Mishima's. At the time of his death, Saigō was fifty years old and Beppu Shinsuke, who beheaded him upon request, was twenty years his junior. Another parallel of historical significance may be drawn in terms of foreign impact and nationalist reactions. Saigō's rebellion against a modern stand took place in 1877, some twenty-five years after the arrival of Commodore Perry's squadron, which resulted in the opening of Japan. Mishima's death for a nationalistic cause occurred exactly twenty-five years after Japan's defeat and "second opening to the world." But metaphysically, they seem to be far apart. While Saigō was a deist, or even a theist perhaps, and a humanitarian, as his pet phrase "Respect Heaven and Love People" indicates and his life testifies, Mishima's life was clearly humanistic, if anything at all, but not humanitarian; and he apparently wanted to deify himself by his death. This point is made in a dialogue between Jun Etō and Mitsuo Nakamura, "Mishima Yukio no bungaku" (Mishima's Literature), *Shinchō* (special issue, January, 1971, pp. 252–3).

This apparent difference must have been a major reason why Mishima did not make a reference to Saigō at all in speaking of Wang Yang-ming and his teachings of activism. Another reason could have been the similarity in their sexual proclivity, which Mishima found embarrassing to call public attention to. In this manner, Saigō, a most overwhelming hero of all ages in Japanese history for his selfless manly virtues, remained a fearful image for his boyhood and young manhood. In a way, it seems to me, his whole life was one continuous battle to overcome this image and to come out triumphant over the hero legend of Saigō. That seems to have been exactly what he meant to achieve at the Ground Self-Defense Force Eastern Corps Headquarters on November 25, 1970.

During feudal times, ritualistic beheading was customary when a samurai criminal was sentenced to death by harakiri as an "honored privilege" of his class. It was both to facilitate the process of death and the procurement of the head as evidence of sentence having been successfully executed. But when a man chose harakiri of his own accord as a form of death, he did not ordinarily use an assistant to behead him. So General Maresuke Nogi died only after long agonizing hours from the cut in the belly that did not bleed fast enough, when he close this form of death in 1912 to follow the late Emperor Meiji to the grave. In 1944, Seigō Nakano, emperorist nationalist, died in a similar manner when he preferred harakiri to arrest by the military police as a heartily hated opponent of General Tōjō, the prime minister.

We have already drawn parallels between Mishima and Saigō. Why did Mishima use an assistant to behead him? There may be a number of answers. But could it be possible that like Saigō, who had clearly committed an offense against the state, Mishima wanted to administer a "criminal" punishment upon himself?

6. *The Sea of Fertility* consists of four volumes, each of which may be read as a separate story, but they are all woven together with a thread of transmigration and reincarnation. The first installment of the first volume was first printed in the September issue of the literary monthly *Shinchō* in 1965. Thus it took over five years for the work to be completed. Mishima kept saying that he had been pouring everything he had

learned from life into this work, so he did not know what to do after its completion. It was a taboo within his household to discuss his plans after the completion of a this work.

According to Professor Donald Keene the title suggested to him that "it was [Mishima's] metaphor for life constantly renewing itself, meaningless perhaps but indestructibly fertile." But Mishima's answer to his inquiry "sent a chill" through him:

> The title "The Sea of Fertility" is intended to suggest the arid sea of the moon that belies its name. Or, I might go so far as to say that it superimposes the image of cosmic nihilism with that of the fertile sea. (Donald Keene, "Mishima," *The New York Times Book Review*, January 3, 1971, p. 5.)

After having read the first two volumes, Japan's Nobel Prize winning novelist Yasunari Kawabata commented:

> . . . as if I had been struck by a miracle, I was moved and overjoyed. On the happiness that I am also a contemporary of Mishima, who has produced a master-piece of all ages comparable to none, I would honestly like to congratulate my-self . . . In this work Mishima's dazzling talent has been purified and sublimated to reach dangerous proportions of violent emotion. Probably this new, fatal classic will survive the difference of countries, the age and critiques. (Quoted from the jacket of the twenty-first printing, 1970, of the first volume originally published in 1969 by Shincho sha, Tokyo.)

In the second volume the hero, a young nationalist (twenty) characteristically ends his life by harakiri after having assassinated a financial tycoon all by himself. It so happened that on the very morning of November 25, 1970, I picked up the volume, which I had taken to bed the night before but had been unable to read very far. I wanted at least to know how the story ended. Thumbing through the book, when I came to the last scene and read it, I sighed, "Oh, again!" I felt that Mishima had repeated the heroic but gruesome scene too often. (He had not only written a short story entitled *Yūkoku* [Patriotism] in 1960, in which a young officer, an accomplice in the planning but not in the actual uprising of the February 26, 1936 coup d'état, takes his own life by harakiri before the eyes of his wife, who was also to kill herself to follow him to death, but even made it into a self-directed, self-acted motion picture in 1965.) Then I went to my office at Sophia University, and shortly before noon I asked a research assistant of mine to take a book, which was long overdue, back to a library in the same building where the last minutes of Mishima's life drama were taking place. From the university, the Self-Defense Force corps headquarters is only a long city block away. The assistant came running back in a few minutes, saying, "A coup d'état must have taken place, since the gate is blocked by riot police trucks, etc." I immediately responded, saying, "Don't be silly. Nothing like that could ever happen. Those men up there whom I had chances of observing while going to the library did not look a bit brave and strong!" But, as it turned out, that was exactly what Mishima was trying to lead them into becoming—at least as implied in his written appeal and his speech—at that very moment!

7. Some of his close friends and associates revealed after his death that Mishima had in fact been concerned with the apparent beginning of his physical decay. But to the general public, he was physically as perfect as before.

8. For example, as reported in the *Asahi Shimbun* (November 26, 1970), *The New York Times* (November 25) was the only exception. It came out with a eulogistic treat-ment of Mishima as a writer, calling him Japan's Hemingway, Japan's Renaissance man, and compared him to such literary giants as Balzac and Flaubert.

9. "In the Shadow of Leaves" is my translation of the title of the book *Hagakure*.

Yamamoto was a samurai of Saga *han*. At the age of nine, he began serving his lord, Nabeshima Mitsushige, as a page. His life was one of total devotion to his lord, an exemplar for others. In 1700, when he was forty-one years old, his lord died. He wanted to follow him to the grave by harakiri. But the *han* statute proscribed such an act. In the following year, he had his hair shaved off to become a monk. His wife followed suit. They retired into a woodland away from the castle town. Here the book began to take shape from a dialogue he carried on with his friend Tsuramoto Tashiro, a samurai of Saga *han* whose career had been very similar to his own. (See the introductory essay in Naramoto, Tatsuya [ed.], *Hagakure*, vol. 17 of *Nihon no meicho* [Tokyo; Chūō Kōron Sha, 1969], pp. 16–23.)

10. Yagiri, Tomeo, "Seppuku no bigaku" (Esthetics of Harakiri), in *Shimpyō*, special edition, January, 1971, p. 196. At the time of preparation of this article, I was unable to establish the authenticity of Yagiri's reference to the Truman *Memoirs*. He has been writing for such a reputable publisher as Chūō Kōron Sha, and I hopefully depended for his reliability upon this social mark of distinction.

11. Commenting upon "Patriotism' Mishima himself wrote :

> The story that makes up "Patriotism" is nothing more than an unorthodox version of the February twenty-sixth Incident. But what I described in here—the scenes of love and death, and the perfect unification and multiplication of eros and patriotic loyalty—are the one and only supreme bliss I expect of this life. (From the commentary added to a popular paperback edition of Mishima's selection of his short stories, *Hanazakari no mori, Yūkoku* [Tokyo: Shincho Sha, 1968, p. 261].)

After Mishima's death, there were many who saw significance in this connection of his eros and desire for death by harakiri. Tadasu Iizawa, a novelist, was one of the first to make a comment to this effect. He said:

> [Mishima's] sense of beauty was always connected with his sexuality. He always handled sexuality as something pathetic. And as such he seems to have been drawn towards harakiri . . . Mishima who had long despaired of things political could never have thought of staging a coup d'état. (*Asahi Shimbun*, November 25, 1970)

But most revealing of all was popular novelist Kōichiro Unō's "Kanno bi no shori" (The Triumph of Sensual Beauty), *Shincho* (special edition, January, 1971, pp. 181–9). Unō speaks of the eroticism of harakiri by recalling his own boyhood experience. His mother was a descendant of a samurai of Yamamoto Tsunetomo's Bushido tradition. She was wont to say to him, "As a child of a samurai, you are expected to be capable of performing harakiri." Whenever this was told him, he can distinctly remember, he was immediately sexually aroused and was embarrassed. "I could not understand why Mother could tell me such an embarrassingly sexual thing shamelessly." (*Ibid.*, p. 184)

Unō's associations of *hachimaki* (headband) and loincloth were just as embarrassingly erotic to him. Pointing to the fact that these are very particularly Japanese, and also to the fact that both Mishima and Morita on that fateful day not only wore *hachimaki* but also wore nothing underneath their uniform except a loincloth, Unō surmises that death developed very naturally out of this type of sensuality, and these three components of Mishima's death may very well hold a secret key to the Japanese philosophy of life and death. (*Ibid.*, p. 185).

Further, Unō makes an extremely interesting observation when he calls a defeated samurai's harakiri before the eyes of the victor the last attempt at winning the match:

> The defeated, who in front of the victorious, bares the abdomen, which is least protected and most sexual, seems after all . . . to be attempting for the last time to conquer his adversary by the sensual beauty [of harakiri] that will lead to death. Is it not the efforts by the man, who had been physically beaten in this world, to overwhelm his opponent spiritually, even though what can be won may not exceed

the admiration of the enemy marshal and the general public, at least on the surface
. . . (*ibid.,* pp. 186–187).

It is indeed quite possible that Mishima's choice of harakiri as his form of death
was a consequence of his efforts to conquer all the things that had frightened him as a
child, among which were the physical prowess of imperial soldiers and Saigo's activism
and death. When Mishima harangued Self-Defense Force men to rise with him, which
they did not do (this was a sign of their weakness), and when he performed harakiri
more masterfully than many brave men, he conquered them all, even those who had
despised him for his narcissistic and chaotic activities, which included acting and
singing on stage and screen, boxing and karate, posing for nude photographs, as well
as gruelling field exercises with Self-Defense Force men in the biting cold of winter at
the foot of Mount Fuji, which led to his organization and command of the Shield
Society "toy" soldiers.

12. The book was prefaced, so to speak, with a lengthy quotation from Dostoyevsky's
The Brothers Karamazov that read as follows:

> Beauty! I can't endure the thought that a man of lofty mind and heart begins
> with the ideal of the Madonna and ends with the ideal of Sodom. What's still more
> awful is that a man with the ideal of Sodom in his soul does not renounce the ideal
> of the Madonna, and his heart may be on fire with that ideal, genuinely on fire,
> just as in his days of youth and innocence. Yes, man is broad, too broad, indeed.
> I'd have him narrower. The devil only knows what to make of it! What to the mind
> is shameful is beauty and nothing else to the heart. Is there beauty in Sodom? . . .
> But a man always talks of his own ache. (From the Modern Library edition, trans-
> lated by Constance Garnett, 1950, p. 127.)

13. "Existentialist nihilism" is one of the terms with which Momo Iida characterized
In the Shadow of Leaves in his collection of essays, *Mishima Yukio* (Tokyo: Toshi
Shuppan Sha, 1970). Iida was one of Mishima's classmates from Tokyo Imperial
University Law Department. He considered himself ideologically diametrically op-
posed to Mishima. I owe it to Iida to have found the significance of the passage from
the Bushido book that follows in the text. (*Ibid.,* p. 131.)

This particular passage is usually played down in its significance, for it seems rather
out of place in the generally serious context of this Bushido book. It is the case with
the aforementioned Naramoto edition. Interestingly enough, it is also the case with
Hagakure Nyumon (An Introduction to *In the Shadow of Leaves* which Mishima
himself prepared and which was published by Kobun Sha in 1967. Mishima gives a
contemporary Japanese translation (p. 257) along with other passages but does not
bother to elaborate on it as others do.

14. Mishima himself wrote a book, *Kodo gaku nyumon* (An Introduction into the Learning of Activism), Tokyo: Bungei Shunju Sha, 1970. It was published early in November, only a few weeks before his death. A part of it had been printed in the September
issue of a journal. Commenting upon this portion, Professor Yoshiaki Iisaka of
Gakushuin University wrote a newspaper column saying that Mishima was making a
big thing out of the Wang Yang-ming philosophy by "projecting his own violent emotions," and also that these violent emotions were "a type of activist nihilism, and this
nihilism, as it is wont with him, will manifest itself in an abrupt and resolute action
on the one hand, and on the other in the form of demoniac estheticism." (See the commentary by Professor Iisaka in *Shokun,* February, 1971, p. 233.)

15. *The Portrait of Dorian Gray* is the only novel of Oscar Wilde, a prolific, Irish-born,
Oxford-educated playwright. It was first published in 1890. In the following year,
he wrote *Salome* in French. This latter is the book that Mishima called "the book that
I chose with my own eyes and made my own property," in the same essay on Wilde
referred to above. (This and other essays are collected in a variety of volumes, but I

used *Mishima Yukio bungaku ron shu* [Mishima's Literary Essays], Tokyo; Kodansha, 1970.) See p. 464.

Raymond Radiguet, who had made a name for himself in the honored history of French literature before his premature death in 1923 at the age of twenty, became the idol of Mishima before the end of the war, for he surely thought he would be killed soon. He was then just about twenty. Mishima consciously imitated the fiction writing style and technique of this boy-prodigy of France, especially his *Le Bal du Comte d'Orgel*, which was completed just before his death. But as he began to live longer than the French novelist, this novelist ceased to be his idol. Obviously, Mishima was to learn more about life from the older Irishman. It may not have been a mere accident that he chose *Salome* to be presented after his death by the Roman Theater, the troup he had brought into existence primarily to present his plays, including a successful three-act play, *My Buddy, Hitler* (1968). *Salome* in Konosuke Hinatsu's translation, which had been presented as produced by Mishima first in 1960, at the very moment when all of Japan was engulfed in the resounding calls of opposition to the Japan-U.S. Security Pact, was again to be presented in 1970, the year of the automatic extension of the pact. Mishima auditioned actors and actresses. He designed the stage effects and costumes. He attended to other details as well. He said that there should be plenty of incense smoke. He even suggested that he might play the role of John the Baptist. He said that there should be plenty of blood spilling off the silver tray. (See *Roman gekijo* No. 7, February 15, 1971, 56 pages.) To me, as a spectator among the capacity crowd of the second night, it appeared in rather bad taste. It could have been Mishima's head itself on the tray, should he have chosen to live long enough to act out the play!

16. *Bushido: The Soul of Japan* (New York, 1905), pp. 192–193.

17. As reported in *Sandei (Sunday) Mainichi*, June 1, 1969, Mishima told the activist students of the University of Tokyo:

> To you my activities may appear unsightly, entering the Self-Defense Force, and wearing a military uniform. But if you allow me, I will say that those towel masks you used to wear were just as unsightly as the look of chimney sweepers. As for the ineffectiveness of actions, we are mutually not much different, I believe. To lead them to effectiveness the moment is when we attempt killing each other. If this is the moment, then we will kill each other. Until we get to that point, we shall be unable to arrive at an agreement. This is what I want to tell you. (This passage is reproduced in *Sandei Mainichi*, special issue, December 23, 1970, p. 29.)

A full record of the debate, with some supplementary remarks, is available as a book, *Toron Mishima Yukio vs. Todai zenkyoto* (Tokyo: Shincho Sha, 1969).

18. *Shūkan Bunshun*, December 28, 1970, p. 146.

On September 11, 1945, when General Tojo was about to be arrested at his home as a war criminal, he tried to kill himself with a revolver. But his shots were not fatal. He faced trial before the International Military Tribunal Far East and was sentenced to death by hanging.

Bibliographic Note

In the course of putting notes to the text, I have already made comments upon some of the sources I referred to, but it seems in order to give a bibliographical commentary no matter how brief it may be.

The news of Mishima's dramatic and violent death caused nationwide consternation. Nearly everybody in Japan became a commentator. Weekly maga-

zines covered opinions of people in the street, as well as more professional commentaries and criticisms by men in high government positions. Yet some professional commentators kept silence for the moment, or eventually for good,
for various reasons. Mishima's death indeed produced a situation where to
be asked what opinion one held about Mishima's death was almost like being
tested on one's fundamental beliefs as to life, death, national defense, the constitution, or sexuality. That is to say, it acted in a way as a catalyst to draw
out from the unconscious or the historical memory of the recent past of every
Japanese his concern about the present and immediate future of Japan.
Thus, if interested, one could make an extremely interesting study of Japanese
reactions to Mishima's death that would involve self-image, nationalism, and
so on. But my immediate interest was the meaning of Mishma's personal death.

To get a quick pictorial appreciation of what format weekly journals used
to report Mishima's death and to comment upon its meanings, the most con-
venient manual is *Zenkan Mishima Yukio taikan*, a special issue of *Shimpyō* (Tokyo:
Hyōron Shin Sha, January, 1972). It is also good for a complete listing of reports
and articles concerning the event that appeared in both weekly and monthly
magazines within the first month after his death. Its chronology about
Mishima's life and works is also useful.

But if one is to choose one, most dependable collection of commentaries
upon Mishima's death, it will be the January, 1971, special issue of *Shinchō*,
subtitled "Mishima Yukio tokuhon" (Tokyo: Shinchō Sha). One important
document, Mishima's plans for introducing a militia as part of Japan's defense
system, was printed in *Gendai* (Tokyo: Kodansha, February, 1971). Incidentally, Mishima's serious literary works had been published almost exclusively
by those two publishers.

It is surprising to note, however, that the May, 1970, special issue of *Kokubun-
gaku* (Tokyo: Gakutō Sha), which was published half a year before Mishima's
death with the subtitle "Mishima Yukio no subete," includes literary criticism
on Mishima's major works that easily supercedes many commentaries after his
death in shedding light upon the meaning of his then-not-yet-enacted death.
The dialogue between Mishima and Yukio Miyoshi, which is also included in
this issue, is very revealing of Mishima's thought about his own literature and
his already planned death.

Of the public statements Mishima made before his death, the most revealing
of his impending death is found in a dialogue he had with Sho Furubayashi,
which is printed in *Tosho shimbun* (Tokyo: Tosho Shimbun Sha, January 1,
1971). Also, one week before his death, Mishima handed a manuscript to a
publisher. This is printed in *Ushio* (Tokyo: Ushio Shuppan Sha, February
1971), as "Waga dōshi kan" (My View of Comradeship).

To fully appreciate the situation in which he made the final move toward
his death, it is enormously helpful to listen to the phonographic record of Mishima's efforts to speak to the Self-Defense Force men and their booing of him,
for it becomes further apparent that his primary objective of the day was to
kill himself rather than arouse them into action with him. Should he have really

wanted to lead them by his appeal, he should have spoken into a microphone connected with an amplifier. His voice was almost inaudible. A sonosheet, entitled "Mishima Yukio saigo no zekkyō" (The last cry-outs of Mishima), is included in a special issue of *Shūkan Sankei* (Tokyo: Sangyō Keizai Shimbun Sha, December 31, 1970).

Very little has been said about Masakatsu Morita, who beheaded Mishima and then killed himself. An article about Morita by a friend of his is included in the special edition about Mishima and the Shield Society of *Nijusseiki* (Tokyo: Nijusseiki Sha, January, 1971). Morita's diaries as a student at a Catholic missionary school for boys in Yokkaichi City, Mie Prefecture, and as a rightist student activist at Waseda University, Tokyo, during the years of campus disturbances appear in book form: Masakatsu Morita, *Waga shisō to kōdō* (My Thought and Actions) (Tokyo: Nisshin Hōdō Shuppan Bu, 1971).

No matter how selective and brief I might want to make it, this bibliographical note would not be complete if no word is said about Donald Keene's contribution to commentaries, after Mishima's death, which appeared in *The New York Times Book Review* (January 3, 1971). This is the best of all commentaries both in Japanese and English I have come to read. The author, well-known professor of Japanese literature at Columbia University, had been a close friend of Mishima's for over sixteen long years. His representation of Mishima as a writer seems admirably balanced, and his insight into the depth of Mishima's hollow mind about life and the world is chillingly convincing. Yet one can see between the lines Professor Keene's highly controlled love and sorrow for Mishima. A Japanese translation of the Keene article was printed in the March, 1971, issue of *Chūō kōron* (Tokyo: Chūō Kōron Sha). But what a surprise it was to read it in Japanese: nothing of the noble sentiment of the original was transmitted. Something was lost in the process. It sounded as if it had been written by some clever news reporter who had come to know Mishima only from his quick interview between curtain calls.

The following is a partial list of Mishima's literary works that have been translated into Western languages. This is adopted essentially from a list prepared by Katsuhiko Takeda and Ryoko Aburano for *Gendai no esupuri* (L'Esprit d'Aujourd'hui), No. 48 (Mishima Yukio), edited by Izumi Hasegawa (Tokyo: Shibundō, 1971):

Kamen no kokuhaku (1949)
    Confessions of Mask. Translated by Meredith Weatherby. New Directions, 1958.
    Confessiones de una Mascara. Published by Seix y Barrel, 1962.
    Geständnis einer Maske. Translated by Helmut Hilzheimer. Rowohlt, 1964.
    Confessioni d'una Maschera. n.d.
"Kaibutsu" (1949)
    "The Monster". Translated by David O. Mills, Occasional Papers, No. II.
Japanese Culture II. University of Michigan Press, 1969, pp. 159–211.
Ai no kawaki (1950)
    Thirst for Love. Translated by Alfred H. Marks. Knopf, 1969.

Kinjiki (1951–53)

Forbidden Colors. Translated by Alfred H. Marks. Knopf, 1968.

Yoru no himawari (1952)

Twilight Sunflower. Translated by Sigeho Sinozaki and Virgil A. Warren. Hokuseidō, 1958.

Manatsu no shi (and other stories) (1952–1963)

Death in Midsummer and Other Stories. Translated by Edward G. Seidensticker, Donald Keene, Ivan Morris and Geoffrey Sargent. New Directions, 1966.

Shiozai (1954)

The Sound of Waves. Translated by Meredith Weatherby. Knopf, 1956.

Sumor Balovo. Translated by Ivan Slanig. Zora, 1958.

Die Brandung. Translated by Oscar Benl. Rowohlt. 1959.

La Voce Delle Onde. Translated by Liliana F. Somimavlla. Feltrinelli, 1961

Bruset av Vagov. Translated by Sonja Bergvall. Albert Bonniers, 1956.

A Norwegian translation, published by Gyldendal, 1967.

Le Tumulte des Flots. Translated by G. Renondeau. Gallimard, 1969.

"San genshoku" (1955)

"Three Primary Colors". Translated by Miles K. McElrath. Occasional Papers, No.II. Japanese Culture 11. Michigan University Press, 1969, pp. 177–194.

"Kujaku"

"The Peacock". Translated by David O. Mills. Also included in the same volume as above, pp. 213–225.

Kinkakuji (1956)

The Temple of the Golden Pavilion. Translated by Ivan Morris. Knopf, 1959.

Le Pavillon d'Or. Translated by Marc Mecreant. Gallimard, 1961.

Il Padiglione d'Oro. Translated by Mario Teti. Feltrinelli, 1962.

El Pabéllon de Oro. Translated by Juan Marsé. Seix y Barrel, 1962.

Den Gyllene Paviljongens Temel. Translated by Torsten Bromkvist. Albert Bonnier, 1962.

Det Gyldne Tempel. Translated by Ida Hammerich. Gyldendal, 1965.

Kindai nōgaku shū (1956)

Five Modern Nō Plays. Translated by Donald Keene. Knopf, 1957.

La Mujer del Abanico : Seis Piezas de Teatro Noh Moderno. Translated by Kazuya Sakai. Mandragora, 1959.

Sechs Moderne Nô-Spiele. Translated by Gerdav Uslar. Rowohlt, 1962.

Per erik Walund. Published by Albert Bonniers, 1963.

Fem Modern Nō-Spil. Published by Gyldendal, 1964.

Cing Nos Modernes. Translated by Georges Bonmarchand. Gallimard, 1970.

Utage no ato (1960)

After the Banquet. Translated by Donald Keene. Knopf, 1963.

Efter Festen. Translated by Ida E. Hammerich. Gyldendal, 1964.

Dopo il Banchetto. Translated by Livia Livi. Feltrinelli, 1964.

Après le Banquet. Translated by G. Renondeau. Gallimard, 1965.
Nach dem Bankett. Translated by Sachiko Yatsushiro. Rowohlt, 1967.
Posle Banketa. Translated by Ivan Slanig. Zora, 1967.
Efter Benketten. Published in 1969.
"Nettai ju" (1960)
Japan Quarterly, 11 (1960), no. 2: 174–208.
"Tropical Tree." Translated by Kenneth Strong. *Japan Quarterly,* 11 (1960), no. 2: 174–208.
Utsukushii hoshi (1962)
Den Vackra Stjärnam. Translated by Erik Sundström. Albert Bonniers, 1970.
Gogo no eikō (1963)
The Sailor Who Fell from Grace with the Sea. Translated by John Nathan. Knopf, 1966.
Sjömannen som föll i onad hos havet. Translated by Birgit and Morten Edlund. Albert Bonnier, 1967.
Il Sapore pella Gloria. Translated by Mario Teti. Arnoldo Mondadori Editore, 1967.
Le Marin Rejeté par la Mer. Translated by G. Renondeau. Gallimard, 1968.
Een Zeeman Door de Zee Verstoten. Published in 1970.
Sado kōshaku (1965)
Madame de Sade. Translated by Donald Keene. Grove Press, 1967.
Taiyō to tetsu (1968)
Sun and Steel. Translated by John Bester. Tokyo: Kodansha International, Ltd., 1970.
Haru no yuki (1965–1967)
Spring Snow. Translated by Michael Gallagher. Knopf, 1971.

Yasuhiro Kawanaka

The Canons of Journalism
and Trends in Japanese Dailies

During the past years, a new sense of the social responsibility for the press has been growing among citizens as well as practioners in democratic countries.

The Canons of Journalism adopted by the Japanese Newspaper Association states:

> The principal difference between newspapers and other commercial enter-
> prises is that newspapers in their reporting and editorial activities exercise
> great influence over the public. The public depends chiefly on newspapers as
> its source of information and the basis of its judgment of public events and
> problems. From this distinction arises the public character of journalistic
> enterprises and the special social status of journalists. The realization of their
> responsibility and pride by journalists is fundamental in ensuring their
> special status. Those two points must be observed by each individual jour-
> nalist.[1]

A similar concept of the social responsibility of the press has been expressed by the Royal Commission on the Press at the instigation of the National Union of Journalists in the United Kingdom. The commission suggests in its report three hypothetical standards for judging the performance of the press.

First, the press may be judged as the chief agency for instructing the public on the main issues of the day.

Second, it may be judged by the standard enunciated by its own spokesmen (which does not differ very much from the first but is somewhat lower).

Third, it may be judged as a great industry, rather than a public service, concerned with the collection and diffusion of news.

Discussing these hypothetical standards, the commission arrived at two essential requirements that are more modest and realistic than the first and second standards and more in accordance with the aspirations of the press than the third:

1. If a newspaper purports to record and discuss public affairs, it should at least record them truthfully.

2. The number and variety of newspapers should be such that the press as a whole gives an opportunity for important points of view to be effectively presented in terms of the varying standards of taste, political opinion, and education among the principal groups of the population.[2]

The commission concluded that if the press is giving its readers the material for forming judgments on the problems of most immediate interest to them, it is perhaps serving their needs at present.

The concept of the social responsibility of the press is explicitly formulated in five requirements by the Commission on Freedom of the Press in the United States in its report entitled *A Free and Responsible Press*. The commission states:

1. The press in contemporary society should give "a truthful, comprehensive, and intelligent account of the day's events in a context which gives them meaning."

2. It should serve as "a forum for the exchange of comment and criticism," though it should not be subject to legal obligations.

3. It should project "a representative picture of the constituent groups in society," because it can provide people with the images with which they make decisions, either favorable or unfavorable.

4. It should assume a responsibility like that of educators in stating and clarifying "the values and goals of our society as a whole."

5. It should provide "full access to the day's intelligence," because the citizens in a modern industrial society need to know more than in earlier days.[3]

The significance of the social responsibility theory has been discussed by American scholars. Professor Theodore Peterson, dean of the College of Journalism, University of Illinois, discusses the significance of this theory against the intellectual background of authoritarian, libertarian and Soviet Communist theories in *Four Theories of the Press*.[4] Professor Wilbur Schramm, director of the

Institute of Communications, the East-West Center, further elaborates the concept of social responsibility of the press in his *Responsibility in Mass Communication*.[5] My recent book *Freedom and Responsibility of the Press* was another attempt to elaborate the same concept for Japanese readers.[6]

Underlying all these statements is the acknowledgment that the press has a social responsibility to provide readers with knowledge of events of the day that are likely to affect their lives. The present inquiry is: to what extent has the Japanese press assumed the responsibility for providing information on the events of the day? First, I trace briefly the growth of the Japanese press since the Meiji period, when the Japanese press we know today came into existence. Second, I shall trace the origin of social resposibility in the postwar period, when Japanese newspapermen came to formulate their own codes of professional ethics. Finally, I review the trends in the contents of the Japanese press by content analysis of the leading Japanese dailies.

1. Growth of the Japanese Press

The first Japanese newspapers were the *kawaraban*, or tile block prints, published during the Tokugawa period.[7] They featured such news as fires, earthquakes, and floods. They carried a lot of illustrations of the Westerners at the coming of the Black Ships, or steamships, toward the end of the Tokugawa period. Vendors sold the *kawaraban*, reading them aloud in the streets. Though legally forbidden by the shogunate, the *kawaraban* was an important source of information for the common people.

The Tokugawa Shogunate, which had decided to shut Japan's door against the rest of the world, obtained overseas information from the Dutch Reports prepared by the Dutchmen who had been permitted to engage in trade at Dejima, Nagasaki. These reports were the exclusive source of information, which was accessible to the *roju*, or senior statesmen, of the shogunate. The daimyo, or feudal lords, got access to these reports after persistent request in view of the social changes taking place with the coming of the Black Ships.

Meanwhile, the Dutchmen offered to present to the shogunate the *Javasch Courant*, the weekly organ of the Dutch government of Batavia, instead of the Dutch Reports. Scholars at the Bansho Shirabedokoro, or Foreign Book Inquiry Institute, translated parts of the *Javasch Courant* and published it under the title *Kampan Batavia Shimbun*, or the Official Batavian News, in January, 1862; this was published in twenty-three volumes in February of the same year. They also published nine volumes of the *Kanpan Kaigai Shimbun*, or Official Overseas News. These were the first publications that carried the world *shimbun*, or newspaper.

English newspapers published by foreigners residing in Japan also had an important role to play in opening the eyes of the Japanese to the rest of the world. The first English newspaper in Japan was the *Nagasaki Shipping List and Advertiser*, published by an Englishman, A. W. Hansard. It was launched on June 22, 1866, and was published in four pages twice a week, on Wednesdays and Saturdays. It carried the information about current events exchange rates, ships' arrivals and departures as well as advertisements. It lasted until October 1 of the same year.

Moving from Nagasaki to Yokohama, Hansard published another English newspaper, the *Japan Herald*, beginning November 23, 1861. The *Japan Herald*, like the *Nagasaki Shipping List and Advertiser*, carried news of foreign countries that had appeared in newspapers published in other lands. It lasted until the break-out of World War II as an important source of information from abroad. It started a two-page daily devoted to advertising as a supplement to the weekly beginning October 26, 1863.

To compete with the *Japan Herald*, a Portuguese residing in Yokohama, F. da Rosa, launched in 1863 the *Japan Commercial News*, which lasted until 1865. The manager of the First National Bank in Yokohama, Charles Richerby, who bought the defunct *Japan Commerical News*, published the *Japan Times*. Just a year prior to this, an American by the name of Shoyer started the *Japan Express*, which lasted only for a short while. A correspondent of the *Illustrated London News*, Charles Wirgman, published a comic paper, *Japan Punch*.

Meanwhile, scholars at the Bansho Shirabedokoro began translating news that seemed to be of interest to Japanese readers and published it in the *Yokokama Shimbun*, the *Kanagawa Koeki Shimbun*, and the *Nihon Shimbun*. An interpreter for the American Consulate in Yokohama, Joseph Hiko, or Hamada Hikozo, started the *Kaigai Shimbun* in 1865. A British missionary, Buckworth M. Bailey, published in January, 1867, the *Bankoku Shimbun*, which carried overseas information. These newspapers performed the function of furnishing informations on international developments.

The Japanese began to ask themselves whether they should open up their country or fight against foreign invaders. Japanese newspapers began to reflect the opinions of the Japanese pro and con toward the end of the shogunate and the beginning of the Meiji period. The shogunate scholar, Shunsan Yanagawa, published the *Chungai Shimbun*, which attacked the new government. The Shogunate's retainer, Genichiro Fukuchi, published the *Koko Shimbun*, which predicted the defeat of the royalists at the Toba-Fushimi battle. Against these, the new Meiji government's organ, the *Dajokan Nisshi*, advocated the restoration of the emperor's reign. These papers performed the function of a public forum stirring up public opinion as to the future directions of Japan.

It was not until Taisuke Itagaki and his followers demanded the immediate opening of the National Diet that the so-called partisan papers came on the scene. Itagaki published a petition for the opening of the National Diet in the *Nisshin Shinjishi*, a Japanese newspaper published by John Reddie Black, A. W. Hansard's partner. Kentaro Ohi and Shigeru Furusawa also wrote for the forthright opening of the Diet in their letters to the publisher of the *Nisshin Shinjishi*. Furusawa later became the editor of the *Yubinhochi Shimbun*, which was founded by Mitsu Maejima minister of communications in 1872. Furusawa invited Mokichi Fujita and Katsundo Minoura to write editorials supporting Itagaki. Tetsucho Suehiro, editor of the *Tokyo Akebono Shimbun* also published Kentaro Ohi's radical views.

Tokyo's first daily, the *Tokyo Nichi-nichi Shimbun*, launched in 1872, advocated a slow and steady policy. Genichiro Fukuchi, its editor in chief, argued for the gradual extension of people's rights, establishment of town and village councils, then prefectural councils, and finally the National Diet. Fukuchi's *Tokyo Nichi-nichi Shimbun*, which supported the government's stand, was regarded as a government organ.

With the decree for the opening of the National Diet in October, 1881, the focus of journalistic discussion shifted to the constitutional question. The emperor should invite representatives of the people to draw up the constitution, because sovereignty belongs to the people, according to the organs of the Jiyu, or Liberal Party led by Taisuke Itagaki: the *Jiyu Shimbun*, established on June 25, 1882, in Tokyo and the *Nihon Rikkenseito Shimbun*, established on February 1, 1882, in Osaka.

The sovereignty of the nation belongs to the nation. So argued the organs of the Kaishin, or Progressive, Party led by Shigenobu Okuma: the *Yubin Hochi Shimbun* under Fumio Yano and the *Tokyo Yokohama Mainichi Shimbun* under Morikazu Numa. The *Tokyo Yokohama Mainichi Shimbun* was started as the first daily in Japan on December 12, 1870. The emperor's sovereignty, they contended, is recognized by the constitution set up by the National Diet. The national right emerges from the emperor's right and the people's right. The emperor, they said, does not monopolize but represents this national right.

The constitution should be granted by the emperor, with whom sovereignty resides, argued the *Tokyo Nichi-nichi Shimbun* under Genichiro Fukuchi, the organ of the Teisei, or Imperial Party. Both liberals and progressives attacked Fukuchi's view, saying that his view opposed the spirit of constitutional monarchy. Professor Hideo Ono points out that Fukuchi's view rested on the historical fact that sovereignty belonged to the emperor. Ono says Fukuchi failed to defend his view because he attempted to do so by applying Western political theories that had been grown on different political soil. However, Fukuchi's view finally prevailed.

With the advent of the party press, political views and interests came to be articulated more clearly, However, it appeared that these party organs were too much involved with the interests of the respective parties. Need for a more independent press was beginning to be felt. Such independent newspapers as the *Jiji Shimpo*, the *Nihon* and the *Kokumin Shimbun* appeared on the scene.

Yukichi Fukuzawa appealed to the Japanese to seek national interest rather than party interests. In the *Jiji Shimpo*, launched on March 1, 1882, Katsunan Kuga spoke up for national independence against the Meiji government's westernizing policy in the *Nihon Shimbun*, which was inaugurated on February 11, 1889, the day on which the Imperial Constitution came into effect. Soho Tokutomi preached egalitarian philosophy in the *Kokumin Shimbun*, established on February 1, 1890. Independent as they were, they were opinion papers rather than newspapers.

Newspapers devoted to news reporting did not dominate the Japanese newspaper scene until the *Asahi Shimbun* and the *Mainichi Shimbun* moved to Tokyo from Osaka. Founded by Ryohei Murayama and Riichi Ueno in January, 1879, the *Asahi Shimbun* was a typical *koshimbun* devoted to news and gossip reporting. It launched the *Tokyo Asahi Shimbun* in 1888. The *Mainichi Shimbun*, which followed the pattern of the *Asahi Shimbun*, merged with the declining *Tokyo Nichi-nichi Shimbun* to make it the Tokyo edition of the *Mainichi Shimbun*. These two Osaka papers gained ground in Tokyo, giving fuller coverage to the Russo-Japanese War. Later Tokyo's leading dailies, such as the *Hochi Shimbun*, the *Jiji Shimpo*, and the *Kokumin Shimbun* declined, owing to the damages caused by the Great Kanto Earthquake (1923), which destroyed Tokyo. With financial backing from Osaka, the two Osaka papers took this opportunity to extend their circulation. Since then the *Asahi Shimbun* and the *Mainichi Shimbun*, both in Tokyo and Osaka, formed powerful cartels to maintain the nation's largest circulation.

The *Asahi Shimbun* is published today in Tokyo, Osaka, Nagoya, Northern Kyushu and Sapporo. A joint stock corporation with capital of 280 million yen, the *Asahi* maintains as of February, 1971, a daily circulation of 5,994,494 for its morning edition and 3,979,000 for its evening edition. It has an editorial staff of 9,406 persons. It also has special contracts with AP, AFP, Reuter, TASS, NANA, the *New York Times* and the *London Times*.

The *Mainichi Shimbun* is published in Tokyo, Osaka, Nagoya and Kitakyushu. A joint stock corporation with capital of 1.8 billion yen, the *Mainichi* maintains a daily circulation of 4,666,692 for its morning edition and 2,823,103 for its evening edition. It has an editorial staff of 6,000 persons and special contracts with UPI, AFP and other agencies.

Today there is another daily newspaper that circulates throughout Japan, the *Yomiuri Shinbun*. Originated as a Tokyo *Koshimbun* in November, 1874, the *Yomiuri Shimbun* was the prototype of the *Asahi Shimbun*. It had been behind the scenes while the *Ohshimbun*, devoted to editorial comments, dominated Tokyo's newspaper world. Inspired by the success of the *Asahi* and the *Mainichi*, the *Yomiuri* strove hard to make itself a third national daily under the strong leadership of Matsutaro Shoriki. It is published in Tokyo, Osaka, Kitakyushu, Sapporo and Takasaki. A joint stock corporation with capital of 153.3 million yen, it maintains a daily circulation of 5,511,600 for its morning edition and 3,029,958 for its evening edition. It has a staff of 7,267 persons and special contracts with AP, UPI, AFP, NANA and TASS.

There are two newspapers specializing in economic news, the *Nihon Keizai Shimbun* and the *Sankei Shimbun*. The *Nihon Keizai Shimbun* started as a weekly, *Chugai Shogyo Shimpo*, in December, 1896, and became a daily in June, 1885. A joint corporation with capital of 800 million yen, it maintains a staff of 2,676 with a morning circulation of 1,282,437 and an evening circulation of 892,164. It has special contracts with AP, the *Financial Times* and the *Journal of Commerce*. The *Sankei Shimbun*, started by Hisakichi Maeda in 1933, is a corporation with capital of 1 billion yen, which maintains a staff of 4,672. It has contracts with AP and the *Chicago Daily News*. Though specializing in economic news, these two newspapers circulate throughout Japan as national papers.

There are three regional papers, which are the major source of current information for the readers in the three regions: the *Hokkaido Shimbun*, the *Chunichi Shimbun*, and the *Nishi Nihon Shimbun*. The *Hokkaido Shimbun* has its head office in Sapporo and is published in Hakodate, Asahikawa, and Kushiro as well. The *Chunichi Shimbun*, with its head office in Nagoya, has subscribers in central Japan. The *Nishi Nihon Shimbun*, with its head office in Fukuoka, has subscribers all over Kyushu, as well as in Yamaguchi and Shinane prefectures. The *Tokyo Shimbun*, now owned by the *Chunichi Shimbun*, caters to the readers of the metropolitan area.

Besides these papers, each prefecture has at least one local newspaper. This distribution of local newspapers throughout Japan owes much to the wartime policy of "one newspaper for each prefecture." During World War II, the National Mobilization Act, besides restricting newsprint and limiting the items to be printed, enforced licensing on publication and reduced the number of local newspapers to one for each prefecture. Moreover, in view of the expected landing of the Allied forces, the Japanese government assigned some of the circulation of national papers to local papers. As a result of mergers that took place then, some local papers became powerful means of mass communication.

The contemporary English newspapers in Japan are the *Japan Times*, the *Mainichi Daily News*, the *Asahi Evening News* and the *Daily Yomiuri*. The *Japan Times*, founded in 1897, has the longest history. Its title was changed to the *Nippon Times* during World War II but this was changed to the *Japan Times* in 1956. The *Mainichi Daily News*, founded in 1922, is an English daily published by the *Mainichi Shimbun*, Mainly translations from the *Mainichi Shimbun*, the *Mainichi Daily News* has a circulation of 53,000. The *Asahi Shimbun*'s English edition, the *Asahi Evening News,* founded in 1953, has a circulation of 40,000. The *Daily Yomiuri*, founded in 1955 as the *Yomiuri*, is an English edition of the *Yomiuri Shimbun*. These English dailies read mainly by foreign readers are the window through which they can look into Japan.

2. Freedom and Responsibility in the Postwar Japanese Press

General MacArthur reported in March, 1946, on the performance of the postwar press in Japan.

> Improvement of news treatment and the increasing development of the characteristics of a free and democratic press are evident each month. . . Editorials are becoming more soundly based. Both sides of controversial issues are presented and reporting is showing a greater responsibility.[8]

In his survey of Japanese dailies as of April, 1947, Dr. Frank L. Mott remarked:

News is generally confined to reports of significant matters: under the tutorage of C.I.E. [they] learned to make news fairly objeetive, with little comment. Editorials still incline too much to fine writing, but are less flowery than they used to be.[9]

Professor Hideo Ono, then chairman of the Department of Journalism at Sophia University, Tokyo, also commented:

. . . under the press unit of the Civil Information and Education Section of the G.H.Q. the Japanese newspapermen have to come to appreciate the way of a democratic press in a few years after the war's end. They are endeavouring to turn out daily news sheets capable of contributing toward the building of a democratic Japan, along the lines of the newly established Canons of Journalism. It is considered therefore that it will not be in the distant future that the press in Japan regains prosperity with the development of industry in general.[10]

The Japanese press developed a sense of freedom and responsibility in their performance with the help of the Allied occupation.

The prewar Japanese press was influenced by the Japanese government, which was controlled by the military clique. The Meiji Constitution, the Constitution of the Empire of Japan, provided "Japanese subjects shall, within the limits of the law, enjoy liberty of speech, writing, publication, public meetings and associations." But the elastic phrase "within the limits of the law" invited government control over the press. Even before the war, the metropolitan police had full command over press contents, either directing changes or suppressing news.

So as to control public information, the Japanese government established the Bureau of Information, Jōhō Kyoku, in September, 1937, when the Manchurian Incident grew into the Sino-Japanese War. Prior to the formation of the Bureau of Information, the Japanese government attempted to excercise influence through the Domei News Agency over the situation at the League of Nations. It attempted to control public opinion, by merging local newspapers according to the principle of "one newspaper in one prefecture." It also began the allocation of newsprint, as well as the cooperative distribution of newspapers through another governmental agency, the Japan Corporation of Newspapers, or Nihon Shimbun Kosha.

The Supreme Commander of the Allied Power, or SCAP, issued in September, 1945, a memorandum and directives, forbidding the Japanese government to censor, suppress or control news or public discussions.[11] As a result, legal provisions restraining the mass media ceased to exist, except for cases of libel and obscenity. The Jōhō Kyoku lost controling power over the press and ceased to exist in February, 1946. The Domei News Agency was disbanded to make way for the Kyodo and the Jiji news agencies. The allocation of newsprint was divorced from the Nippon Shimbun Kōsha and entrusted to a newly selected committee. SCAP also attempted to ensure the decentralization of newspapers, encouraging the growth of newspapers. According to Dr. Mott's survey as of April, 1947, 139 dailies, nearly triple the wartime number, existed, with more than twenty million circulation, more than double the previous total circulation.

The Constitution of Japan guaranteed on November 3, 1946, the freedom of the Japanese press, declaring "Freedom of assembly and association as well as speech, press and all other forms of expression are guaranteed." "No censorship," it provided, "shall be maintained nor shall the security of any means of communication be violated."

From October, 1945, the Japanese press was under the supervision of the press and publication division of the Civil Information and Education Section, or C.I.E., in the G.H.Q. of the Allied Forces. The C.I.E.'s prepublication censorship covering news and editorials of sixteen dailies and three news agencies began on October 9, 1945. The dailies were: the *Asahi Dai Ichi Shimbun, China International, Hokkaido Shimbun, Jiji Shimpo, Kokusa Times,* the *Mainichi, Nihon Keizai Shimbun, Osaka Nichinichi, San Shashin Shimbun, Sangyo Keizai, Shin Osaka Shimbun, Tokyo Shimbun, Tokyo Times,* the *Yomiuri,* and *Yukan Mainichi.* The news agencies were: Jiji, Kyodo and Radio Press. Radio stations, minor newspapers and magazines were subject to postpublication censorship. SCAP's censorship was concerned with misrepresentation, improper news or adverse comments on the military, as well as civil activities of the Allied occupation. Though it stirred up criticism among the Japanese, it helped the Japanese press to develop the practice of objective reporting and fair comment. All G.H.Q. censorship eased on July 15, 1948.

Meanwhile, the SCAP urged Japanese newspapers to adopt a code of ethics, which ran as follows:

1. News must adhere strictly to the truth.

2. Nothing shall be printed which might directly or by interference disturb the public tranquility.

3. There shall be no false or destructive criticism of the Allied powers.

4. There shall be no destructive criticism of the Allied forces of occupation and nothing which might invite mistrust or resentment of those troops.

5. There shall be no mention or discussion of Allied troop movements unless such movements have been officially released.

6. News stories must be factually written and completely devoid of editorial opinion.

7. News stories shall not be covered to conform with any propaganda line.

8. Minor details of a news story must not be overemphasized to stress or develop any propaganda line.

9. No news story shall be distorted by omission of the pertinent facts or details.

10. In the makeup of the newspaper no news story shall be given undue prominence for the purpose of establishing or developing any propaganda line.[12]

The SCAP later urged Japanese newspapermen to formulate their own code of ethics. Masanori Ito, then chairman of the board of directors, Kyodo News Agency, drew up a new professional code of ethics, which was adopted by the *Nihon Shimbun Kyokai,* the Japan Newspaper Association, at its inaugural assembly on July 23, 1946. The preface of the code states:

> The role to be played by newspapers in rebuilding Japan as a democratic and peace-loving nation is decidedly of great importance. In order to realize this mission in the most speedy and effective manner possible, it is necessary for every newspaper in the nation to adhere to a high ethical standard, elevate the prestige of its profession and fully execute its functions.
>
> Fully aware of the significance of their mission, democratic Japanese daily newspapers, big and small, have met in the most cordial spirit, have organized the Nihon Shimbun Kyokai, have formulated as its moral charter the Canons of Journalism, and have pledged to endeavor with the utmost sincerity to realize these principles.
>
> The Canons of Journalism, which stresses the spirit of freedom, responsi-

bility, fairness and decency, constitute a standard which should govern not only news and editorial writers but to an equal extent all persons connected with newspaper work.[13]

The Canons of Journalism states that the press should enjoy complete freedom in reporting news and in making editorial comment. This freedom of the press, it urges, should be defended as a vital right of mankind. Exceptions should be made only when such activities interfere with public interests or are explicitly forbidden by law. It adds, however, that the press should be free to criticize the restrictive statutes themselves.

The canons enumerate the voluntary restraints to which the freedom of news reporting and editorial writing should be subject:

1. The fundamental rule of news reporting is to convey facts accurately and faithfully.

2. In reporting news, the personal opinion of the reporter should never be inserted.

3. In treating news, one should always remember and be strictly on guard against the possibility of such news being utilized for propaganda purposes.

4. Criticism of persons should be limited to that which can be made direct to the persons involved.

5. Partisanship in editorial comment, which knowingly departs from the truth, does violence to the best spirit of journalism.[14]

The newspapers, unlike other commercial enterprises, exercise great influence over the minds of the public. The public, the canons point out, depends chiefly on newspapers as its source of information and the basis of its judgment on public events and issues. Such responsibilities of the mass media confer public character on journalistic enterprise and special social status upon journalists.

In writing editorials, a journalist should bravely express his own convictions. He should also speak for those who otherwise have no means of voicing their opinions. If he criticizes others, he should give those who are criticized the opportunity to defend themselves. If he makes any mistake, he should correct it as soon as possible. In all, the canons assert, the tolerance for individual assertions and counterassertions should be respected.

The canons urge Japanese newspapers to have a high sense of public decency, saying

A high sense of public decency is naturally required of newspapers because of their share in influencing public opinion. Such a standard of decency can be achieved by abiding by the above-mentioned principles. Newspapers and journalists when they fail to observe those principles will invite public condemnation and disapproval by other papers and journalists and in the end will be unable to operate or work. Therefore, all members of the Nihon Shimbun Kyokai should make efforts to cooperate and maintain a higher ethical standard by promoting their moral unity, guaranteeing free access to news material and assisting each other in newspaper production. Thus, the association of newspapers which strictly observes the Canons of Journalism shall be able to accelerate and ensure the democratization of Japan and simultaneously elevate Japanese newspapers to world standards.[15]

The Nihon Shimbun Kyokai has been responsible for setting up a new standard for journalism in postwar Japan. In addition to setting up the Canons of Journalism, it sponsored in various cities a series of lectures on journalism by professional Japanese experts as well as foreign experts with assistance from the C.I.E. It also encouraged journalism education, granting subsidies to universities and colleges.

3. A Content Analysis of Japanese Dailies

To analyze trends in the contents of Japanese dailies, I chose the three national dailies: the *Asahi Shimbun,* the *Mainichi Shimbun,* and the *Yomiuri Shimbun.*[16] Each of these papers maintains from four to six million circulation. Together, they account for more than half of the total circulation of more than one hundred newspapers that belong to the Nihon Shimbun Kyokai. Consequently, we hoped that the analysis of these three dailies would throw some light upon the role of the Japanese press.

As a starting point, I singled out April 28, 1952, the day Japan became an independent nation when the peace treaty became effective. As elsewhere, Japanese newspapers have a cycle on the basis of one week. So I picked out one week including three days before and after April 28, namely, April 25–May 1, 1952. To see later developments, I picked out another week of the same dates in 1960 and 1969. 1960 was the year the Japan-U.S. Security

Treaty was revised. April 28, 1969, marked the return of Okinawa to Japan, for whose reversion violent students demonstrations had been organized. These are the three sample weeks chosen to represent the postwar trends of Japanese dailies.

I classified the contents of these sample papers according to four categories, journalism, education, entertainment and advertisements, and ascertained the space devoted to each of these.

Journalism includes all the communications in words or pictures on events or situations of the day. This category is further broken down into three: simple news reporting, interpretative reporting and editorials. A report that a certain event occurred or will take place may be considered to be a simple news reporting. An article that gives background information about the news or its causes may be considered interpretative reporting. I classified as interpretative reporting both the articles labelled as such and any reading matter designed to give background. Editorials include all articles giving comments and judgments on news, including such short columns as "Tensei Jingo," "Henshu Techo," or "Yoroku" (Vox populi vox dei; Editor's Notebook; or Miscellany, respectively), as well as formal editorials. Letters from readers are also included.

Education contains all information that is designed to enlighten readers. It contains scholarly articles, advice columns, medical advice, as well as school entrance examination guides. But it excludes articles dealing with education, unless they perform an educational function.

Entertainment includes material whose function is to entertain readers, such as fiction or comic strips. Articles about entertainers or movie stars are normally excluded from entertainment, unless they are giving entertainment.

Advertising contains every notification about commodities or services published at the expense of advertisers. For readers, it performs a persuasive function, moving them to buy such commodities or services. For publishers, it is a source of income to support the operation of neswpapers. For the purpose of our analysis, announcements of staged events by newspapers as well as name plates are included.

Nevertheless, it should be noted that the above normative

classification often contradicts the objective functions for readers. For example, a news report may be read as a piece of entertaining material as well as journalistic information. Or, an advertising copy may be used as the source of information on commodities or services. Such are the objective functions of mass media that occur regardless of the intention of communicators.

Going through the files of sample papers, we first note that the number of pages in postwar Japanese newspapers has been increasing.[17]

During the one-week period from April 25 through May 1, 1952, the *Asahi* morning edition, for example, normally contained 4 pages, and the evening edition 2 pages. The only exception was April 28, the day the peace treaty became effective, when the morning edition consisted of 8 pages and the evening edition of 4 pages. Both the *Mainichi* and the *Yomiuri* contained almost the same number of pages. The *Mainichi* had a 4-page evening issue on April 29, and the *Yomiuri*, on April 29 and 30. Consequently, the daily average for both editions in those days consisted of 6 pages.

During the one-week period from April 25 through May 1, 1960, the *Asahi* morning edition consisted of 12 pages, and the evening edition of 8 pages, except on Sunday, May 1, when the morning edition consisted of 20 pages, and the evening edition of 6 pages. Besides this, the Tuesday evening edition contained only 6 pages. During this period, the *Asahi* daily paper consisted of 20 pages. The *Mainichi* daily paper also consisted of 20 pages, of which the morning edition had 12 pages, and the evening edition 8 pages. The only exception was the Sunday edition, which consisted of 16 pages in the morning, and 4 pages in the evening. The *Yomiuri* daily paper consisted of 20 pages, of which the morning edition had 12 pages, and the evening edition 8 pages. Its Friday morning edition consisted of 16 pages, but its Sunday morning paper consisted of 12 pages, and its evening paper, only 4 pages. In all, the *Asahi* contained 144 pages, while both the *Mainichi* and the *Yomiuri* contained 140 pages, three times as much as they did in 1952.

During the one-week period from April 25 through May 1, 1969, the *Asahi* contained a total of 220 pages, the *Mainichi*, 218 pages, the *Yomiuri*, 204 pages, four times as much as they did in

1952 and nearly twice as much as they did in 1960. The morning editions varied from 16 pages to 28 pages. The evening editions normally contained 12 pages. The number of pages for the whole week is as follows.

The *Asahi*, April 25-May 1, 1969:

			Morning Edition	Evening Edition
April 25, 1969	(Friday)	28 pages	12 pages
26	(Saturday)	16	12
27	(Sunday)	28	–
28	(Monday)	24	12
29	(Tuesday)	16	12
30	(Wednesday)	16	12
May 1	(Thursday)	16	12

The *Mainichi*, April 25–May 1, 1969

			Morning Edition	Evening Edition
April 25, 1969	(Friday)	20 pages	12 pages
26	(Saturday)	20	12
27	(Sunday)	28	–
28	(Monday)	16	12
29	(Tuesday)	20	12
30	(Wednesday)	20	12
May 1	(Thursday)	20	10

The *Yomiuri*, April 25–May 1, 1969

			Morning Edition	Evening Edition
April 25, 1969	(Friday)	16 pages	12 pages
26	(Saturday)	16	12
27	(Sunday)	24	–
28	(Monday)	16	12
29	(Tuesday)	24	12
30	(Wednesday)	16	12
May 1	(Thursday)	16	12

The Sunday morning edition contains more pages, but the Sunday evening edition no longer exists. For all three papers, the days that carry more pages have speical sections, a new trend in this period.

The overall trends of Japanese dailies are summed up in the following tables.

In spite of an overall increase in total space, the proportion of space devoted to journalistic communication is not increasing. The *Asahi*'s journalism accounted for 57.3 percent of the total space in 1952; 51.4 percent in 1960; and 42.5 percent in 1969. The

Table 1. Contents of Three National Dailies

1952

Type of Communication	Newspaper	*Asahi*	*Mainichi*	*Yomiuri*
Journalism	News Reporting	71.6%	70.6%	70.5%
	Interpretative Reporting	14.5%	15.1%	11.0%
	Editorial	13.9%	14.3%	18.5%
	Sub-total	100.0%	100.0%	100.0%
	Journalism Total	57.4%	53.9%	53.4%
Education		0.4%	0.7%	2.4%
Entertainment		3.7%	3.7%	4.2%
Advertising		38.5%	41.7%	40.0%
Total		100.0%	100.0%	100.0%

1960

Type of Communication	Newspaper	*Asahi*	*Mainichi*	*Yomiuri*
Journalism	News Reporting	64.4%	64.4%	66.1%
	Interpretative Reporting	22.4%	25.0%	21.2%
	Editorial	13.2%	10.6%	12.7%
	Sub-total	100.0%	100.0%	100.0%
	Journalism Total	51.0%	51.9%	48.9%
Education		3.8%	5.3%	4.4%
Entertainment		2.3%	2.8%	3.9%
Advertising		42.9%	40.0%	42.8%
Total		100.0%	100.0%	100.0%

1969

Type of Communication	Newspaper	Asahi	Mainichi	Yomiuri
Journalism	News Reporting	63.2%	64.3%	59.5%
	Interpretative Reporting	23.8%	22.9%	30.6%
	Editorial	13.0%	12.8%	9.9%
	Sub-total	100.0%	100.0%	100.0%
	Journalism Total	42.5%	44.9%	44.0%
Education		3.9%	3.5%	4.1%
Entertainment		1.7%	1.8%	1.3%
Advertising		52.0%	49.8%	50.6%
Total		100.0%	100.0%	100.0%

Mainichi's journalism accounted for 53.9 percent of the total space in 1952; 51.9 percent 1960; and 44.9 percent in 1969. The *Yomirui*'s journalism accounted for 53.4 percent of the total space in 1952; 48.9 percent in 1960; and 44.0 percent in 1969. The role of newspapers as a news medium does not seem to have gained after the advent of television.

On the other hand, advertising has been increasing both in space and percentage. The *Asahi*'s advertising accounted for 38.5 percent of the total space in 1952; 42.9 percent in 1960; and 52.0 percent in 1969. The *Mainichi*'s accounted for 41.7 percent of the total space in 1952; 40 percent in 1960; and 49.8 percent in 1969. The *Yomiuri*'s advertising accounted for 40 percent of the total space in 1952; 42.8 percent in 1960; and 50.6 percent in 1969. Postwar Japanese newspapers seemed to have attained a more healthy balance as business enterprises deriving more income from advertising rather than depending solely on subscription.

Japanese newspapers have been assuming more and more the characteristics of magazines. They have been stressing interpretative reporting rather than spot reporting. The *Asahi*'s interpretative reporting accounted for 14.5 percent of the total journalistic communication in 1952; 22.4 percent in 1960; and 23.8 percent in 1969. The *Mainichi*'s interpretative reporting accounted for 15.1 percent in 1952; 25.0 percent in 1960; and 22.9 percent in

1969. The *Yomiuri*'s interpretative reporting accounted for 11 percent of the total journalism in 1952; 21.2 percent in 1960; and 30.5 percent in 1969. The increase in interpretative reporting seems to have been due to the advent of television. Japanese newspapers, finding it impossible to compete with television on spot news reporting, turned to interpretative reporting, which provides more news background.

The educational content definitely increased in total space, in spite of light ups and downs in percentage. The *Asahi*'s educational content accounted for 0.4 percent of the total space in 1952; 3.8 percent in 1960; and 3.9 percent in 1969. The *Mainichi*'s educational content accounted for 0.7 percent of the total space in 1952; 5.2 percent in 1960; and 3.5 percent in 1969. The *Yomiuri*'s educational content accounted for 2.4 percent of the total space in 1952; 4.4 percent in 1960; and 4.1 percent in 1969. The overall gain in educational articles is another indication that Japanese newspapers have assumed the characteristics of a magazine.

Nevertheless, entertainment is decreasing in percentage although the total space devoted to it is not necessarily decreasing. The *Asahi*'s entertainment accounted for 3.7 percent of the total space in 1952; 2.3 percent in 1960; and 1.7 percent in 1969. The *Mainichi*'s entertainment accounted for 3.7 percent in 1952; 2.8 percent in 1960; and 1.8 percent in 1969. The *Yomiuri*'s entertainment accounted for 4.2 percent in 1952; 3.9 percent in 1960; and 1.3 percent in 1969. This trend shows that Japanese newspapers are entrusting the entertaining function to other media particularly weekly magazines and television, in spite of the increased magazine characteristics.

More recently Japanese newspapers have been criticized for their sensationalism. The oil crisis, the Watergate incident, and highjacks have been much played up in Japanese newspapers. Though not apparent from figures, the Japanese press seems to have been infected by sensationalism, which was phenomenal in American journalism at the turn of the century.

Newspapers with a large circulation tend to become sensational, so as to maintain their circulation. During my trip to Europe last fall, I had an opportunity to read various newspapers in Europe. I was impressed while reading these papers that newspapers in free countries tend to become sensational to attract the attention of readers. Like popular papers in free countries, Japanese newspapers have become sensational.

The defects of the press might not be as apparent in a society where a free flow of information is guaranteed as in a society where such is restricted. In a controlled society, newspapers carry only such news as the government or party leaders consider appropriate for the public to know. With limited information the people are given only limited freedom to form their own judgments. The press subsidized by government or a political party does not worry about how to finance itself. It does not have to cater to the popular taste of readers to maintain its circulation. In such a situation, however, it is rather difficult for healthy public opinion to grow spontaneously.

Owing to the recent shortage of newsprint, the sensational press is likely to invite distrust against itself. If the free press goes astray, it might be threatened with being entrusted to the hands of a responsible third party. Such a social opinion easily accepts censorship of the mass media. Then, tolerance for the press, which exists today, will be lost. A society without a free press cannot be considered to be a free society any longer. Consequently, the Japanese press, if it is to remain free, should be on guard against criticism of the press that tends to deny the conditions necessary for a free press.

As the Japanese Canons of Journalism points out, the press should report "accurately and faithfully" because the general public comes to know the facts through newspapers and forms its judgments. The basis of the public character of journalistic enterprise and the special social status of journalists lie here. Japanese newspapers should reflect on the spirit of their own codes, which they formulated nearly thirty years ago, and try to live up to them.

1. Nihon Shimbun Kyokai, "The Canons of Journalism," in Ejiri, Susumu, *Characteristics of the Japanese Press* (Tokyo: Nihon Shimbun Kyokai, 1972), p. 156.
2. Royal Commission on the Press, 1947–1949, *Report* (London: Her Majesty's Stationery Office, 1949), pp. 100–106.
3. The Commission on Freedom of the Press, *A Free and Responsible Press* (Chicago: University of Chicago Press, 1947), pp. 20–29.
4. Peterson, Theodore, "The Social Responsibility of the Press," in *Four Theories of the Press* (Urbana: University of Illinois Press, 1956), pp. 73–103.

5. Schramm, Wilbur, *Responsibility in Mass Communication* (New York: Harper and Brothers, 1957).

6. Kawanaka, Yasuhiro, *Shimbun no Jiyu to Sekinin* (Freedom and Responsibility of the Press), (Tokyo: Nansosha, 1972).

7. For the growth of the Japanese press, see Kawanaka, *ibid.*, pp. 141–150. C. Ono, Hideo, *Shimbun no Rekishi* (Tokyo: Tokyodo, 1961). Also, *Sandai Genronjin Shu* (Three Generations of Opinion-Makers), (Tokyo: Jiji Press, 1962), 6 volumes.

8. Allen, Lafe F., "Effect of Allied Occupation on the Press of Japan," *Journalism Quarterly*, 24, no. 4 (December, 1947): 329.

9. Mott, Frank L., "A Survey of the Japanese Daily Press as of April 1947," *Journalism Quarterly*, 24, no. 4 (December, 1947): 337.

10. Ono, Hideo, "The Postwar Press in Japan," in Nihon Shimbun Kyokai, *The Japanese Press, Past and Present* (Tokyo, Nihon Shimbun Kyokai, 1949), p. 23.

11. Cf. Supreme Commander for the Allied Powers, *Political Reorientation of Japan, September 1945 to September 1948: Report* (Washington, D.C.: U.S. Government Printing Office, 1949, 2 volumes). For the policy of the Allied occupation regarding freedom of the press, see Martin, Robert P., "The Japanese Press, Problem of Freedom," *Nieman Reports*, 6, no. 2 (April, 1952): 3–5.

12. Supreme Commander for the Allied Powers, *Press Code for Japan*, September 19, 1945.

13. Ejiri, *op. cit.*, p. 154.

14. *Ibiid.*, p. 155.

15. *Ibd.*, pp. 156–157.

16. For my earlier study, see Kawanaka, Yasuhiro, "An Analysis of the Japanese Dailies," *Gazette*, 6, no. 1 (1960): 1–8.

17. For a fuller report of my analysis, see Kawanaka, Yasuhiro, "Shimbun Shimen no Keiko ni Kansuru Kenkyu" (A Study in the Trends of Newspaper Content), *Masukomi Bunka* (Mass Communication Culture), 1 (January, 1971): 32–37.